Children in the New England Mind

Children
in the
New England
Mind

WITHDRAWN

*in death
and in life*

BY PETER GREGG SLATER

ARCHON BOOKS
1977

Library of Congress Cataloging in Publication Data

Slater, Peter Gregg, 1940-
Children in the New England mind.

Bibliography: p.
Includes index.
1. Children—Death and future state. 2. Children—
(Christian theology)—History of doctrines. 3. Children
—Management. 4. Puritans—New England. I. Title.
BV4907.S58   261.8'34'314   77-7352
ISBN 0-208-01652-X

For Vicki

Contents

It should be understood and remembered, that the question is one that involves, in one way or another, all the most abstruse points in theology; one, moreover, that concerns a child, a very peculiar being, whose internal history is the darker, that it does not lie within the scope of adult consciousness and experience. Therefore my readers will have to have some patience with themselves and it will not be wrong if they extend some degree of patience to me.

HORACE BUSHNELL
Views of Christian Nurture
[1847]

Preface

THE SUBJECT OF THIS BOOK is ideas about children between the seventeenth century and the mid-nineteenth century in New England. Its leading characters are grownups, and the approach is that of intellectual history. My concern is with adult minds rather than with what children themselves thought and felt, a topic that requires a different kind of investigation. Adult perceptions of children are significant both for their inherent interest and for their influence on behavior within the family. I have attempted to indicate some of these linkages between ideas and behavior, without feeling obligated to do so at every possible point.[1] The subject also lends itself to the exploration of such larger patterns of beliefs and emotions as bereavement responses, theological doctrines, and psychological theories. Even when ideas about children reveal little about what families were actually like, they can indicate much about those who produced the ideas. As John Demos has stated, the child can be studied "as a kind of mirror which focuses and reflects back cultural themes of central importance."[2]

In this type of approach children appear as constants while adults are variables. Arnold Geseli and his associates, writing in the 1974 revision of their 1943 classic, *Infant and Child in the Culture of Today*, declare: "All in all, children today do seem to be the same children we have always known. Their behavior develops and unfolds in the same predictable, patterned pathways it has always followed. Only the grownups seem to change."[3] The statement is exaggerated—children develop through interaction with adults rather than through a completely autonomous process—but it is nevertheless insightful. Certainly, the range of adult behavior is far broader than the range of child behavior, as is the range of adult thought. During the course of the two hundred years of New England history discussed in this book, children were variously viewed as twisted toward evil, as totally plastic, and as inclined to the good. Even granting the unlikely possibility of changes in the congenital nature of children during that time span, it could hardly account for such divergent opinions, especially when opposing views were being upheld during the same generation. The causes of the disparity must be sought in the adult mind and the factors which influenced it.

The choice of New England as the site of this study needs little explanation. Its inhabitants articulated their thoughts about children at considerable length in both public and private, as they did with so many other subjects. To understand their thinking requires an understanding of the Calvinist faith which long dominated the region. Calvinism does not explain everything—recent scholarship has shown that New England was never a simple Calvinist monolith—but from Puritan times up to the late eighteenth century it was the dominant influence on the region's more systematic beliefs about life in general, and about children in particular. During a long twilight which extended well into the nineteenth century Calvinism continued to play an important role. And conscious or unconscious opposition to the old faith did much to shape alternative perspectives on children in the years of its slow decline.

I have selected for examination a few segments of this complex story where the surviving material is sufficiently rich to allow analysis in depth. After writing and discarding many outlines and draft pages, I reached the conclusion that what I was trying to do would be better accomplished in four semi-independent essays than in a conventional monograph. Each of the essays can stand on its own, but each has a greater value when read in the context of the others. All four essays have as their main theme the Calvinist outlook on children as it was affected by the faith's inner tensions, by other points of view, or by changing cultural patterns.

The first half of the book discusses adult ideas about dead children; the second half discusses ideas about living children. The proportion would be a strange one for a work on the modern family, but is fitting for a time of comparatively high mortality rates. In the not too distant American past, the death of a child was a common event. The reactions of parents to this loss were complicated in Puritan culture by the notion of infant damnation. The first essay examines the resulting patterns of Puritan bereavement, relying in part on the techniques of psychohistory. By the mid-nineteenth century infant damnation had ceased to be a disturbing issue. The second essay attempts to explain why it faded away. Much of this history involves events that had no direct tie to the family, such as the strife between Calvinists and Unitarians during the early nineteenth century. It is a good example of how the factors which affect adult perceptions of children can come from many different places in the larger society.

When children lived, they had to be reared. By the early nineteenth century a fair amount of literature on upbringing was in circulation. Although this literature can readily be separated into different types on the basis of its most theoretical elements, it is less easily classified on the basis of its specific methods for child management. Experts who disagreed about abstract issues often gave similar advice about everyday matters. To avoid repetition, I decided to concentrate in essay three on one expert's suggestion for how parents should deal with the problems of obedience, socialization, discipline, and the like. I selected the child psychology of the Calvinist leader Timothy Dwight for this purpose because of its mixture of traditional beliefs with newer ideas.

The more abstract levels of child-rearing literature are presented through the writings of a variety of authorities. Until well into the eighteenth century, the systematic theories of upbringing set forth by New Englanders were of the Calvinist type. The situation became more complex during the early national period when two other theories appeared. Native versions of Enlightenment child-rearing ideas could be found from the 1780s. A Romantic alternative to both the Calvinist and the Enlightenment systems began to be heard around 1830. The fourth essay examines the structure of these theories on a comparative basis, and then considers Horace Bushnell's epochal *Views of Christian Nurture* which drew on all three.

My own conscious view of children is an eclectic one. I accept various aspects of modern theories about them—Freudian, post-

Freudian, Eriksonian, etc.—as being more correct than the older views I consider, but not necessarily as the final word on the subject. The modern theories are brought into the discussion from time to time when they help explain what people in the past were thinking, or not thinking, about children. However, I have tried to avoid seeing the history of ideas about children as simply a nightmarish journey through darkness to the light of today, an attitude which characterizes one recent approach to the study of the family.[4] The past was not as obtuse about children as we of the present sometimes seem to think, nor are we nearly as knowing as we would like to believe.

In the course of completing this study I have been helped in many ways, both large and small. At Dartmouth College, a Faculty Fellowship provided released time as well as ample research support. Patricia Carter of the school's inter-library loan staff was most resourceful in tracking down obscure works. The psychohistorical parts of my study were discussed in a Dartmouth Department of History Honors Seminar, attended by psychiatrists Raymond Sobel and Peter Whybrow. I also learned much from the Columbia University Faculty Seminar in American Civilization, to which I presented a paper on the child psychology of Timothy Dwight. Several historians have taken time from their busy schedules to review parts or all of the manuscript: Robert Middlekauff, Winthrop Jordan, Philip Greven, Daniel Howe, Charles Rosenberg, Jere Daniell, and Michael Ermarth. I am especially indebted in this regard to Henry May who has long given me encouragement and advice, and to Donald H. Meyer who better than anyone else knows how this book came to be. My most outstanding obligations are to my parents and siblings, and to my wife Vicki and son Randy, who have taught me far more about the richness of family life than even the wisest of the many books I read.

PART ONE

The Dead Child

I. "From the *Cradle* to the *Coffin*"

Parental Bereavement and the Shadow
of Infant Damnation in Puritan Society

Death in Infancy

IN CONTEMPORARY AMERICA children seldom die in infancy.
Parents are a bit apprehensive about the possibility anyway. A
child psychologist notes: "A new mother may be so unsure of
herself that every little thing tends to worry her. She has not had
enough experience with young babies to know how to interpret
different things that may happen. If the baby is sound asleep, he
may not seem to be breathing. She rushes over to see if he's still
alive!"[1] And, of course he is, as she knew he would be. Parents
worry about many things—kidnappings, accidents, animal attacks—without truly expecting them to happen to their children.

In the Puritan era (defined as New England's first century, the
1620s to the 1720s), parental apprehensiveness about death had a
different quality. Mothers and fathers genuinely expected to lose
some of their babies. The Puritans saw infants as passing away at a
disheartening rate, fragile, death-prone beings.[2] Describing her
late grandchild, Anne Bradstreet used similes evoking transciency:
"Like as a bubble, or the brittle glass,/ Or like a shadow turning as
it was." After losing several youngsters, Samuel Sewall was so
disturbed by his awareness of a child's tenuous hold on life that he
dreamt that all his surviving offspring but one had died. Cotton
Mather, who suffered in waking hours the torments the less
anxiety-ridden confined to nightmares, lived "in a continual
Apprehension" that his son Samuel "(tho' a lusty and hearty
Infant) will dy in its Infancy," which, alas, was what eventually
happened.[3]

Recent historical research has demonstrated that the actual rate of infant mortality was not as high as the Puritans thought, and as scholars had long believed to be the case.[4] The objective figures are high enough, however, to indicate that the death of a young child was a frequent occurrence. In the healthiest communities, such as Andover and Ipswich in the mid-seventeenth century, one of every ten infants died, as contrasted with one of every sixty in present-day America. In less favored places during the seventeenth century, like the towns of Salem and Boston, as many as three infants of every ten expired.[5] The probability that parents would lose at least one child was increased by the high birth rate. With seven or more children per family,[6] even repeated bereavements were not unusual, especially during epidemics of such diseases as measles, dysentery, diphtheria, and smallpox. In the first marriage of the poet Edward Taylor, five out of the eight offspring died in infancy. Of his fourteen children, Samuel Sewall buried seven who were under two years old. Cotton Mather saw eight of his fifteen children die before reaching that age, and one soon thereafter. Three of these Mather children perished from the measles in a period of five days.[7] Death seemed to sit on the doorsteps of unfortunate families, waiting to devour their young.

Having expected one or more of his children, as well as those of his close kinsmen, to die in their earliest years, even a Puritan who was fortunate enough to escape this form of bereavement was likely to be concerned about what happened to infants in the afterlife. The average layman may not have been aware of all the theological complexities of the future state, but from both formal statements and casual talk he had undoubtedly picked up enough information to realize that life on earth was only a preface to an eternal existence in heaven or in hell. The devout were said to be particularly "anxious and sollicitious about the everlasting estate of their friends and relations [for] they know a great deal more than others do concerning the terrors of God and affairs of another world."[8] They realized that the torments of the damned or the comforts of the saved did not await Christ's Second Coming, but were proceeding even as they mourned. A departed soul instantly ascended to God or descended to the devil. At the Day of Judgment, it would reunite with the body, newly emerged from the grave, and receive a sentence returning it to heaven or hell to remain for all eternity.[9]

Where did children under the age of four fit in? [10] The clergy was positive that some would go to heaven. They were less certain about the rest, but generally upheld the doctrine of infant damnation: those dying during the first years of life who were not recipients of saving grace would spend eternity in the fires of hell. Yet, unlike their continental predecessors, the ministers of Puritan New England were reluctant to discuss infant damnation at length. Michael Wigglesworth's well-known poem of 1662, *The Day of Doom*, which graphically portrayed condemned infants, is often taken to be representative of their approach, but the piece appears to be unique. The researcher who scans Puritan materials for other detailed depictions of hell-bound infants comes away empty handed. Even nineteenth-century Unitarian scholars, who hunted for such passages in order to embarrass Calvinist rivals, could not find them, despite having the advantage of vestiges of cultural memory which are lost to us.[11]

A belief that is little talked about is not necessarily without psychological effects. The clergy might have been brief when considering infant damnation, but as long as they made people aware of what the doctrine meant, anyone pondering the fate of deceased infants would have to reckon with it. The doctrine especially had to be taken into account by grieving parents and those seeking to comfort them. Like an insane relative pacing the attic in a nineteenth-century novel, hardly mentioned by the characters yet throwing a pall over their lives, infant damnation cast its shadow over Puritan households in mourning for deceased babies. Some of the ramifications can be observed in surviving documents, others can only be inferred. As a result, parts of the following discussion lack the support of evidence that satisfies traditional canons. Yet, the subject itself, the psychological meaning of infant death in a past society, is of major importance and warrants explorative treatments where definitive ones are not possible.[12]

Love for Infants

When someone dies, people's feelings about the loss are to a large extent determined by the relationships they had with him while he was alive. Those in the immediate family are expected to experience grief and undertake mourning, the normal characteristics of the state of bereavement. If an individual is little touched by the death of a family member, either he is suffering from an abnormal emotional condition or he has not been involved in an affective relationship with the deceased. The application of this pattern to the Puritan past raises important questions. Were parents emotionally attached to their children, or were they indifferent to them? Did they grieve when infants died, or were they uncaring?

Evidence shows that in many cases Puritan parents had sufficient affective investment in their offspring to make a death deeply felt. "A most lovly and pleasant child," wrote Deacon John Paine about his deceased Benjamin, "my precious Babe." Similar phrases appear in other diaries.[13] Thomas Shepard described his young son who had sickened and died shortly after a stymied departure from England as "very precious to my soule & dearly beloved of me." As a practicing Calvinist who was required to wean his affections from the world, Shepard felt it necessary to reproach himself for such an "immoderate love of creatures, & of my child especially," a theme that would continue to crop up in private journals into the eighteenth century.[14] The emotional attachment of parents to their offspring was one of the subjects that Cotton Mather reflected upon to a greater extent than most. He advised himself, "These are *my Children*, I am therefore from Nature and from Duty to *love* them. . . . I see *my Image* on my Children. Does this *endear* them to me?" It must have, for his devotion was strong. He eulogized a late daughter as "The dearest thing on earth I have."[15]

The particular children so warmly spoken of in the above citations were all less than four years old when they died. This point is important because some scholars have made a sharp distinction between parental feelings for little children and for older ones, claiming that in the past the very young were seen as somewhat less than human, "unconsciously regarded like the embryos of marsupials."[16] This assertion is hard to sustain for New England. Even still-borns or babies dying after a few days of life could be described as "my poor litell infant," or "a child of a most *comely* and *hearty* Look." Samuel Sewall, away from home during his wife's labor, "was grievously stung" upon his return soon after to "find a sweet desirable Son dead, who had none of my help to succour him and save his Life. . . . These Tears I weep over my abortive Son."[17] Such statements were not expressions of love, which took time to develop, but did represent recognitions of the fundamental humanity of the newborn. On that basis, a genuine love for infants who survived could be established during the first months of their existence.

Several historians have attempted to make a case for parental indifference to children while they lived, and unconcern when they died, on the grounds that the high mortality rates of the past necessitated emotional detachment, an argument that does not hold up for the Puritans.[18] Other historians have reversed the causal sequence: children died in large numbers *because* their guardians were deficient in parental love.[19] If the latter argument is accepted, there is added significance to the discovery that the death rates for children in New England towns, although high in comparison with modern levels, were often lower than contemporary European ones.[20] The divergence can perhaps be partly accounted for by the greater amount of love in Puritan families than in those of the old world. The Puritans had abandoned the indifference to the young which marked the traditional family of Europe, without becoming child centered, a trait of the modern family.[21] Measured against the lack of parental affection which characterized the stolid peasants of their own epoch, the Puritans were warmly loving of their children and took better care of them; measured against the lavish outpourings of affection that became common among the middle classes in the nineteenth century, they maintained a limited love and took worse care.[22] The Puritan family, along with Puritan economic and political relationships, was part of the passage from medievalism to modernity. It was not "born modern,"[23] but half modern.

The meaning of children to Puritan parents was complicated by the Calvinist doctrines of original sin and native depravity. According to the "Augustino-federal" version of original sin, which held sway in New England until the reformulations of Jonathan Edwards, infants entered the world carrying the crush-

ing burden of a multiple sinfulness. Their initial guilt stemmed
from Adam's transgression in the Garden of Eden. This first man
had covenanted with God to serve as the representative of the
human race for all time to come. His crime was therefore
humanity's crime, the resultant guilt charged ("imputed") to each
and every one of Adam's descendants down through the ages.
What gave this rather legalistic conception its full force were
elements that St. Augustine had contributed to Christian theology. His belief that all mankind was literally rather than
symbolically present with Adam in Paradise had by the seventeenth century dropped from sight (the ministry was astonished
when Edwards attempted to revitalize it), but his argument that
the primal crime had corrupted the very soul of the father of the
human race was of great importance. It meant that all future men
inherited depraved natures. Their corrupted souls were both
intrinsically sinful, veritable sinks of pollution, and the cause of
the many sins that each individual personally committed during
his life ("actual sin"), beginning in childhood.[24] (Precisely *when*
in childhood would in a later period turn out to be a nettlesome
problem.) Through the notion of native depravity, the other
aspects of infant sinfulness joined with the legal one in a blanket
condemnation of the young soul as spiritually loathsome. Ministers told parents: "Your *Children* are born with deadly *wounds* of
Sin upon their souls"; "There is a *Corrupt Nature* in Every Child,
in its Infancy: Yea from the *very Birth, they* Go *Astray Speaking
Lyes.*"[25]

Nineteenth-century opponents of Calvinism doubted that parents who held such doctrines could genuinely love their children.
The Transcendentalist Bronson Alcott suspected that an avowal
of original sin and native depravity must lead to child neglect or
abuse.[26] Alternatively, parents who did behave decently towards
their children could not truly believe such ideas. A Unitarian
boldly claimed in 1819, "Let a parent's speculative views be what
they may, and his professions of them sincere as they ought, we are
persuaded that he never will, that he never can, look upon his
infant child as a being totally depraved. . . . This dogma might
enter into his theological creed, and darken his views of mankind
in general; but the common sensibilities of his nature would be
perpetually opposing its influence within the circle of his
family."[27] The Unitarian critic may have been perceptive about

the inner feelings of the Calvinists of 1819 for the old faith was by then nearly on its last legs, its sturdier adherents voicing their own complaints about the waning of parental belief in juvenile depravity.[28] The applicability of his views to the still robust Calvinism of earlier New England is more doubtful. Our post-Freudian understanding of the psychodynamics of the family allows for the compatibility of these doctrines with love relationships.

Most likely, Puritan mothers and fathers did not see vessels of sin and depravity every time they glanced at one of their infants. The images parents maintained of their various children during the bustle of daily family life were not hard and constant, but varied among positive and negative shadings. Puritan infants could, on occasion, be as attractive as those of any other era, capable of charming all but the most austere of Calvinists with their "pretty features, pretty speeches, pretty actions."[29] As the Unitarian critic implied, during such moments of affection the fundamental iniquity of the child would not be uppermost in a parent's mind. "WE have seen *Lovely Qualities* in our *Children,* by which they have been mightily Endeared unto us," noted Cotton Mather.[30] Yet, if the sleeping baby, the smiling little one, or the prattling tot did not evoke unfavorable theological depictions, the inevitable fits of crying and of pique readily brought to mind condemnatory doctrines. When Samuel Sewall found his four year old son attempting to hide after misbehaving, the scene summoned forth "the sorrowfull remembrance of Adam's carriage." Such thoughts could occur even without specific provocation. Cotton Mather's daughter Katherine appeared in the recesses of his diary as the very symbol of innocence, "a *Lamb* that was indeed unto me *as a Daughter,*" but he dutifully made occasion to speak to the girl of her depravity and of how she must pray for grace.[31]

If sufficiently internalized, the doctrine of juvenile depravity could be projected onto the parent's own early life in his version of personal history. Joseph Green reflected, "In my Infancy I can remember as soon as I came to use my reason ye corruptions of my own heart began to break forth into sinfull transgressions and my Enmity to God did plainly discover itself. . . . I remember my perverse frowardness when I was (I beleive [sic]) about 3 years old."[32] Since, as Cotton Mather pointed out, parents tended to see

themselves in their children, a self-conception of this sort would
foster images that suggested juvenile sinfulness.[33] Reinforcement
came from the parent's awareness of his child's physical origin in a
sex act, an experience which was too carnal for a Puritan to feel
completely comfortable with it, as joyous and as necessary as he
might find it.[34] In one of the most intriguing passages in his diary,
Cotton Mather considered his children and declared: "I ought to
bewayl some inexpressible Circumstances of Meanness, relating to
their Original, their Production and Conception. I ought to
obtain a Pardon thro' the Blood of that Holy Thing, which was
Born of the Virgin. That so no Vileness of that Nature may have
any Influence, to render them abominable to Heaven."[35]

The doctrine of juvenile depravity may have even played a
stabilizing role in parent-child relationships. If the Puritan
nuclear family had but a small part of the charged emotional
atmosphere of contemporary nuclear families, feelings of intense
jealousy and of acute annoyance must have at times arced between
parent and child, even an infant in a cradle, as well as between
siblings and between husband and wife. Such feelings might not
have been explicitly verbalized by parents as the society disap-
proved of their expression.[36] But by talking about a child as
iniquitous in the eyes of God, the parent's own sporadic dislike of
his offspring could be vented in a socially approved way. The
doctrine of original sin thus served as a lightning rod for what Dr.
Benjamin Spock calls "the inevitability of parental impatience
and resentment," forestalling that anxiety that many twentieth-
century parents experience because "when they detect such
emotions stirring in themselves, they either feel unbearably guilty
or try strenuously to deny them."[37]

Although images of child loveliness and of child sinfulness
could not simultaneously occupy center place in parental consciousness, ultimately there was no contradiction between them.
The Puritans viewed the child as a paradox—an innocent facade
behind which lurked all sorts of wicked desires—a perspective not
unlike the one Freud later employed to shatter the nineteenth-
century idealization of the very young. The child in an Anne
Bradstreet poem is characterized by "A perverse will, a love to
what's forbid,/ A serpent's sting in pleasing face lay hid." Samuel
Willard made the same point in describing infants as "*innocent
vipers.*"[38] In the nineteenth century the paradox would be

dissolved by those who accepted the Romantic notion that the physical qualities of a person were symbols of his inner state. William Ellery Channing would exclaim, "What! in the beauty of childhood and youth, in that open brow, that cheerful smile, do you see the brand of total corruption?"[39] That is just what the Puritans had visualized, without relinquishing their love for their children. Indeed, in a way depravity humanized children and made it easier to relate emotionally to them as beings who were as morally flawed as adults (or more so if the adults had received grace), despite their superior beauty. The Romantics were the ones who lost sight of the humanity of the infant when they endowed him with such ineffable goodness that mere mortals, having little in common with this superior being, were not so much to love as to worship him. "Infancy is the perpetual Messiah," sang Emerson, "which comes into the arms of fallen men, and pleads with them to return to paradise." No wonder that Bronson Alcott, committed to a view of childhood as "above Nature—yea, above men," found his less than perfect infant daughters to be in some respects puzzling and disappointing.[40] The rehumanization of the image of the child had to await the advent of Freudian theory.

The Theological Quandary

In the routine of everyday family life, a precise determination of the spiritual worth of children was not a paramount problem even for so intellectual a group as the Puritans. A parent could wash, dress, feed, and supervise a little one without consciously thinking of him or her in moral terms, imaging neither depraved serpent nor sinless lamb. The situation reversed itself in the event of the child's death. The body had ceased to be, but the soul endured, its spiritual qualities now central in any consideration of that child. No longer could these qualities be taken for granted during his daily activities, or apprehended with a shifting mental and emotional orientation that responded to the ambiguous rhythms of family life. No longer could people say that a definitive reckoning of the state of the soul was not possible because the child might change considerably for better or for worse in the future. With a dead child the future had suddenly arrived. Whatever the condition of his soul at the moment of departure, it would remain so for all time, sealing his eternal fate. In this context, the fact of juvenile depravity and the possibility of its removal by divine grace were matters of intense concern. Parents and close relatives longed to know what became of deceased infants on the other side of the grave.

Puritan mourners realized that of children above the age of infancy some would wind up amongst the damned. Youngsters who lied and stole were likely to be thrown "down to HELL" and sent into the *"Everlasting Fire."*[41] Could children too young to do these things also go to hell? If so, were they treated no differently from the flagrant sinners and the wanton hypocrites who anguished in the tortures of Satan's realm? And what proportion of those deceased in infancy ended up with the saved in heaven? If a Puritan turned to theology for the answers, he would soon have discovered that they were not readily forthcoming. A subject that gave heartaches to parents and close relatives gave headaches to the clergy.

In the labyrinths of theology the fate of children dying in infancy constituted a particularly perplexing stretch. That infants, "even . . . of a Span long," would be tried and judged in the afterlife, like all the rest of humanity, was beyond doubt.[42] What made the matter so troublesome was that infants while on earth gave little evidence of the state of their souls, lacking the actions, and presumably the thoughts, which in older children and adults offered clues. Samuel Willard could say of those beyond the age of infancy, "There are greater hopes concerning some than others, of some there are such probabilities as give us a great deal of settled satisfaction concerning them: their lives are so holy, their Testimonies are so clear, their conversations so shining, that we may hope without any doubt concerning them."[43] Infants could not be expected to offer this sort of evidence of regeneration. "They doe not put forth acts of Reason," explained Increase Mather.[44] They represented a special case, one that was close to the emotional core of Puritan culture.

Faced with a complex issue which could cause deep anxiety, but which had little value for homiletic purposes, the clergy were not inclined to dwell upon it. There were numerous Puritan sermons and treatises, bearing titles like *The Doctrine of the Last Judg-*

ment; *A Plain Discourse, Shewing Who Shall & Who Shall not Enter into the Kingdom of Heaven*; and *Practical Discourses on Death, Judgment, Heaven, & Hell,* which explored their subjects in great detail but provided no treatment of the problem of infants.[45] Even when willing to say something about the issue, Puritan ministers often pleaded ignorance of many of its aspects. Cotton Mather, who considered himself to have a greater understanding of the Lord's ways than his fellow mortals, knew so much about the Day of Judgment that he was able to calculate the spatial requirements for the assembled multitude. (An area equivalent to the Southern part of England would suffice.) Yet, his expertise on the fate of the very young at the final reckoning was far more limited: "The Children who are such *Infants,* that ... they *cannot Speak,* it is but little that *We* can Speak about their State in the *Day of Judgment.*" With similar candidness, his father termed the problem of the precise nature of faith in redeemed infants "another Question, which I meddle not with."[46]

Such reticence had not always characterized theological considerations of this topic. Augustine had discussed it at length, arguing that unbaptized infants were damned (except for martyrs), suffering, however, the mildest of the degrees of misery.[47] Although he is commonly regarded as the advocate of a severe position, other theologians made more forbidding representations of the doctrine.[48] In the middle ages, scholastics like Aquinas modified the traditional version by eliminating physical pain for unbaptized infants, consigning them to a "children's limbo."[49] Some Roman Catholics continued to insist on the patristic position, but by the time of the Reformation the mainstream followed the scholastic view that unbaptized infants did not suffer bodily torment, but a negative loss only, the deprivation of heaven and its beatific vision.[50]

Reformation Protestantism radically transformed the categories of discussion. The Lutheran wing was close to the Catholic position in its insistence on the necessity of baptism for salvation, but the Reformed wing made the central issue one of election through God's free and arbitrary grace rather than the fulfillment of an external rite.[51] Many of the Reformed theologians were certain that numerous infants were excluded from the elect and were therefore destined for hell.[52] Calvin, whose justification for burning the heretic Servetus was partially based on his having suggested the universal salvation of infants, believed that "God . . . hurls innocent new-born babies, torn from their mothers' breasts, into eternal death."[53] In the seventeenth century, English contemporaries of the American Puritans made less dramatic presentations of the doctrine of infant damnation. The Reverend William Twiss, who had served as Prolocutor of the Westminster Assembly of Divines of 1643, declared that "Every man that is damned, is damned for original as well as actual sins, and many thousand infants only for original." The Puritan Richard Baxter stated in far more guarded language that "*All Infants baptized without title or right* by mis-application, and so *dying,* are not *undoubtedly saved.*" As for the unbaptized, "there can no promise or proof be produced that all . . . are saved."[54]

In the light of this long and involved theological history (Baxter lists thirteen different positions upheld by divines),[55] the discussion of infant damnation in New England was remarkably terse and undeveloped, suggesting a definite unease with the subject. The greater emotional attachment to children in the Puritan family than in the traditional family of the continent made the New England public more apprehensive about the possibility of doomed infants and the New England ministry warier of dwelling upon it.[56] Instead of directly affirming the presence of infants in hell, ministers denied that all of them went to heaven. It was infant damnation by default, often merely by implication: "God forbid, that we should imagine a *Believer* to have no better ground of *Hope* for his Departed Offspring, than an *Infidel.*"[57]

When confronted by a critic in the middle colonies, the ministry did more definitely avow the doctrine. In a tract of 1689, the Quaker George Keith attacked New England's Presbyterians and Congregationalists for believing that infants could be sent to hell for original sin alone, a notion "expressly contrary to Scripture."[58] The next year saw the publication of a rebuttal, *The Principles of the Protestant Religion Maintained,* by five ministers of Boston. Their willingness to take on Keith's challenge to prove the existence of *"Reprobate Infants"* attested to their belief in the doctrine, although their language remained cautious. "God hath nowhere revealed to us," observed the ministers, "that He hath accepted of the satisfaction of Christ for all that dy in their infancy; and where there is no Revelation, there is no ground for Faith. . . . There is merit enough for *Damnation* in them."[59]

The one member of the clergy willing to abandon the cautious approach to the doctrine was Michael Wigglesworth, a man unusually morbid, even by Puritan standards.[60] His poem about the Last Judgment, *The Day of Doom,* presented infant damnation in detail. The early verses depicted the ranks of the elect, drawn up at the right hand side of Christ the Judge, the position reserved for the heirs of heaven. At the front of this line were the storied martyrs and at its rear those of small but genuine faith, including "an Infant throng/ of Babes, for whom Christ dy'd."[61] For families concerned about the fate of their deceased offspring, the scene became even more heartening when none of these smallest of children were enumerated among the gathered ranks of the Reprobate (although older children were). Standing on Christ's left, this line extended from the hypocrites through the heathen.[62] How disturbing then to find out many stanzas later that infants were, after all, among the ranks of the condemned! Wigglesworth had overlooked them in the initial panorama, inadvertently causing a false security. It was suddenly dashed when he remembered to have non-elect infants make their pleas before the bar, the very last group to do so.[63]

Having gone in a short space of time "from the womb unto the tomb," these unfortunates complained that they were to be punished not for anything they had personally done, dying before they had a chance to sin, but for the transgression of Adam.[64] In response, Christ showed himself to be well-versed in the federal theology of the Puritans. He explained to the Reprobate infants that Adam was the representative of all mankind and so the fall "both his and yours it was." Christ charitably acknowledged that:

> '. . . to compare your sin with their,
>   who liv'd a longer time,
> I do confess yours is much less,
>   though every sin's a crime.'

> 'A crime it is, therefore in bliss
>   you may not hope to dwell;
> But unto you I shall allow
>   the easiest room in Hell.'[65]

This lame attempt by Wigglesworth to be lenient with the condemned infants only made the horror of their fate all the more

patent. Anxious relatives could gain little solace from imagining
their little ones in the devil's mildest chamber for they soon read
that in hell,

> The least degree of miserie
>   there felt is incomparable
> The lightest pain . . .
>   more than intolerable.[66]

The genuine alleviations of the children's limbo of Catholicism
were lacking in Wigglesworth's "easiest room." Mercy had never
been one of the Calvinist strong points.[67]

Even so, in this instance Wigglesworth had ventured into an
area where his colleagues were not eager to follow. Harsh as the
Puritans were in real life to Quakers and witches, many of them
drew back from the hypothetical burning of departed infants. The
orthodoxy of Wigglesworth's "versified theology"[68] was not in
question: he had said nothing that the rest of the ministry did not
state in more veiled language. It was his elaboration that was
unusual. As a rule, his fellow ministers stopped short of explicitly
placing infants in hell. In its insistent detailing of the process of
infant damnation, *The Day of Doom*, on the whole the most
representative of Puritan poems, was unrepresentative.

But everyone read it. Hawked about the region in broadsides,
recited by adults who as children had memorized sections of it with
their catechisms, *The Day of Doom* had a dissemination second
only to that of the Bible itself.[69] The poem became so familiar to
the Puritans that it must have contributed to their mental pictures
of situations for which they had no experience to draw upon—
Judgment Day, heaven, hell—as in the twentieth century mass
media like the movies shape widely shared images of strange
monsters, remote planets, and so on. One such Puritan was Mrs.
Elizabeth Fitch Taylor: "The Doomsday Verses much perfum'de
her Breath,/Much in her thoughts."[70] This poem alone guaranteed that the Puritans understood what infant damnation was all
about.

The general ministerial reticence about infant damnation was
replaced by effusiveness when the converse was considered: infant

salvation. Like most Puritan preaching, the message was mainly directed towards the faithful, the visible saints and their families.[71] Samuel Willard was mildly encouraging about infants: "God . . . hath given Godly parents good reason to hope well concerning them, (but this dispensation is a secret)." He thought it a good sign that there were probably a greater number of infants in heaven than individuals of any other age.[72] More confident promises came from Cotton Mather: "The children of *Godly Parents,* we are bound in a *Judgment* of *Charity* to reckon, as much belonging unto the Lord, as *Themselves.* . . . You may inscribe upon their Grave-stone, that *Epitaph,* OF SUCH IS THE KINGDOM OF HEAVEN . . . or that *Epitaph,* GONE, BUT NOT LOST."[73] On one occasion, Mather dutifully preached the Thursday lecture while his infant son lay at home in convulsions, at "every Minute looking for the Death of the Child." He deliberately took for his text, *"I know, that my Redeemer lives;* . . . a matter of Satisfaction to us, at the Sight of our *dying* Friends." The epitaph read, "NOT AS THEY THAT HAVE NO HOPE."[74]

Still, even the most fervent hope about the prospects of a deceased infant could not give the bereaved the assurance that knowledge of a certainty brings. The clergy could carry their optimism only so far before being checked by basic elements of Protestantism in general and Calvinism in particular. The Reformation had eliminated the guarantees provided by the sacraments so that the individual soul, whether juvenile or adult, was completely at Gods's mercy. And, in Perry Miller's phrase, the Puritan's God was ultimately "hidden . . . unknowable . . . unpredictable."[75] Who could say with surety what fate He had determined for any particular infant? "No man can infallibly know anothers good estate without divine revelation," wrote Samuel Willard, ". . . . It is Gods alone prerogative to judge the heart."[76]

The Roman Catholics had the advantage here for they could be more definitive about infant destinies. Believing that a vital regeneration in Christ occurred through the administering of baptism, the Catholics unconditionally promised salvation to a baptized child dying in infancy. Alternatively, they said with certainty that babies who died without the sacrament must go to hell.[77] Baptism thus provided a touchstone which even the simplest laymen could use to distinguish saved infants from

damned ones. That situation may have created guilt for those
families who had delayed having their child baptized. In the
middle ages the souls of unbaptized infants were said to roam
howling in the night, "hell-hounds" searching for water.[78] But the
existence of a touchstone prevented the gnawing anxiety of not
knowing for sure about the fate of an infant.[79]

The main line of Puritan theology was opposed to interpreting
the rite of baptism in the Catholic manner. According to the
Westminster Confession, "Altho' it be a great sin to contemn or
neglect this ordinance, yet grace and salvation are not so inseparably annexed unto it, as that no person can be regenerated or saved
without it, or that all that are baptized are undoubtedly regenerated."[80] Cotton Mather acted correctly when he buried his
unbaptized four day old son under the epitaph, "RESERVED FOR A
GLORIOUS RESURRECTION."[81] Nevertheless, a few English Puritan
theologians made an elaborate case for the baptismal regeneration
of infants, while some of the New England public held a less
sophisticated belief that through baptism or its absence all was
won or lost.[82] Clear-cut pronouncements on the infant question
had a definite attraction.

Within the main line Puritan tradition, the only way to even
partially satisfy the needs met by the Catholic version of baptism
was to link that sacrament to the doctrine of the covenant, which
was done increasingly in New England. According to Puritan
theologians, God had covenanted with the Jewish patriarch
Abraham to provide eternal salvation for both him and his
posterity in return for their faith. When the Jews failed to
acknowledge the divinity of Christ, the covenant was transferred
to patristic Christianity. Many centuries later, in the post-
Reformation period, it bound God to His newest band of chosen
people, the Puritans. A New England infant with a true-believing
parent came under the terms of the promise to Abraham and was
included with the mother or father in the covenant of grace.[83] The
correct meaning of Puritan baptism, allowed at first only to
children with such a parent, was but to symbolize publicly
guarantees which had already been made: "Baptisme is not that
which gives being to the Church, nor to the Covenant, but is for
confirmation thereof. . . . Children that are borne when their
Parents are Church Members are in Covenant with God even from
their birth, Gen.17.7.12 and their Baptisme did seale it to them."[84]

This interpretation of the doctrine of the covenant underlay the numerous ministerial assurances to the pious that their deceased infants were heaven-bound. "I do *Hope*," exclaimed Cotton Mather, "(and God forbid that I should easily *Cast away* the *Confidence!*) That when my *Children* are *Gone* they are not *Lost*; but carried unto the *Heavenly Feast* with *Abraham*, whose *Blessing* is come upon them through Jesus Christ."[85]

The seemingly safe ground of the covenant contained, however, treacherous patches. Puritanism would not have been Puritanism if it had not set at certain points little traps for the complacent (although over the years more and more learned to elude them). One could never be absolutely sure that the dead baby of a visible saint was truly in the covenant of grace and therefore certain to be saved. The parent might have deceived himself and others about his own conversion and not actually be numbered among God's elect, his child not really the heir of grace.[86] Furthermore, the baptized offspring of New England's first generation by-and-large failed to display the recognized signs of regeneration as they matured. They did not become, as had been expected, visible saints like their parents. In response, the hard-pressed Puritans developed an old distinction between the internal and external parts of the covenant. New England's apparent declension indicated that many children had been accepted only into the external portion rather than into the internal one which guaranteed salvation.[87] Of course, only a malicious enemy would imply that the perished infant of a believer was linked merely to the inferior part of the covenant and public presentations invariably suggested the opposite. Nevertheless, the possibility remained, eroding somewhat the Matherian assurances and giving during the bereaved's bad moments some credence to the Wigglesworthian vision.

Yet another problem with the doctrine of the covenant was its failure to explain what would happen to the dead babies of those who were not included within its terms, these unregenerated parents being much more numerous than converted ones. Their children's chances for heaven were obviously not as good as the offspring of pious lineage, but the clergy was reluctant to cast any little ones into the pit. Increase Mather granted, "There are, it is true, Elect Children who are not born of Elect Parents."[88] In Europe as well as America, this cautious view tended to become

the general Calvinist one.[89] In contrast to the Catholics who paid
for the advantage of proclaiming the sure redemption of baptized
infants by having to portray unbaptized ones as in the realm of the
devil, Calvinists could avoid being pinned down on the negative
side of the infant issue, their compensation for lesser certainty on
the positive side. The destiny of uncovenanted infants was left
undecided, but the prospects were not highly encouraging:
"Though God can as well save the Child of an unbeliever, as of the
most eminent Saint in the world, yet the unbeliever cannot so well
hope for it."[90]

Puritan Mourning: The General Pattern

Since theology provided, at best, only partial answers to
pressing questions about the fate of deceased infants, further
answers were free to arise out of the complex emotions of the
bereaved. To discover these responses, the mourning process of
early New England must be reconstructed, which is a difficult
task. The lack of substantial psychohistorical materials from the
Puritans, as well as the incompleteness of our present knowledge
of the process of mourning, or of the role played in it by religious
beliefs, necessitate that much of the discussion be hypothetical.[91]
Probably the major obstacle to a more definitive presentation is
the scantiness of direct information on the response of Puritan
women to bereavement. Most of the material which we do have
comes from fathers and male relatives. Yet, the mother-child
relationship is considered to be more "reciprocally intense" than
the father-child one,[92] and women in general are regarded as
responding to death somewhat differently than men.[93] The
inability to make sexual distinctions when discussing Puritan
bereavement is a serious deficiency.

An advantage is gained from the recent demonstrations that
early New Englanders lived in nuclear families,[94] and placed a
relatively high value on children. If we can assume that some of
the emotional ties and ambivalences that characterize modern
child-centered nuclear families were also present to a degree in the
half-modern Puritan household, then the findings of psychosocial
research on the contemporary effects of parental bereavement
become applicable. Of course, these data must be used with great

selectivity. For example, a study among mothers of children dying from leukemia speaks of "so massive a threat . . . so profound a defeat" to the parent, her "inner devastation, rage, and turmoil," and her conviction of "unendurable tragedy."[95] Such language would appear to be overstated if applied unchanged to the Puritan case where the loss of a child was likely to be less central in a mother's life because of the smaller emotional investment in him, the greater number of siblings, and the commonness of this form of bereavement. The matter is one of degree. The "suffering and anguish" of contemporary parents facing the loss of a child[96] could also be felt by Puritan mothers and fathers, but probably without all of the intense reverberations that constitute the present-day reaction.

Another difficulty in reconstructing Puritan mourning involves the drawbacks of generalizing about a process where the range of emotional possibilities was immense.[97] We are compelled to focus on a broadly defined "average" or "normal" parent, omitting from discussion such extremes as full-fledged sadists who might enjoy visions of their children burning in hell, or, alternatively, masochists who might derive a vicarious pleasure from that vision. The spotty nature of the evidence also does not allow for the investigation of many other variables that influence the individual response to bereavement: additional dimensions of basic personality structure (oral or anal, aggressive or defensive, etc.); life history, especially whether the loss of a parent had been experienced while a child; socio-economic class; and so on.[98] Nevertheless, the Puritans had enough in common, especially because of their religion, "a kind of underlying presence, part of the very atmosphere which surrounded and suffused all aspects of experience,"[99] to allow some generalizations to be made.

"We have our CHILDREN taken from us; the *Desire of our Eyes taken away with a stroke.*" This outcry of Cotton Mather suggests both the emotional investment of the Puritans in their children, and their well-warranted fear of sudden death for these loved ones. The seemingly healthy infant could expire in but a few days time.[100] Without the opposition of antibotics and similar devices of modern medicine, viruses and other infections once they had overcome the body's natural defenses could be quickly lethal.

There were also many deaths that in a physiological sense were not sudden at all, but nevertheless appeared that way to Puritan parents who had not the questionable advantage of a physician's previous diagnosis of a disease or congenital condition as fatal. In one of her verses on children, Anne Bradstreet declared, "I knew she was but as a withering flower,/ That's here today, perhaps gone in an hour."[101] Continually on the lookout for the swift killing stroke, the Puritans multiplied the situations in which death seemed to be looming, keeping many last watches that turned out to be, happily enough, unnecessary. Diaries are filled with stories of vigils over groaning, feverish, fading children who, despite all expectations, managed to survive: "Our son Edwd has been so bad with a cough that we thought several times he had been quite dead.... Our son Benja was very sick of a fever, and near unto death"; "Samuel was . . . so bad yt he was given over as a dying child"; "My Little Dauter Molly was extremely ill. So that we thought between 9 and 10, She would have expir'd."[102]

Because Puritan parents were involved in many more scenes that suggested death as the outcome than what the actual infant mortality statistics required, they must have often been in a state of anticipatory mourning. There is something of a paradox in this reaction, for the sudden deaths that were common in early New England by their very nature usually preclude anticipatory mourning. However, the conviction that "the *King of Terrors*"[103] often came quickly made the Puritans anxious not to be caught unready. Part of this orientation would have been established even if dying was always prolonged—the relatively high mortality rate was obviously itself a major causal factor entirely apart from the tempo of death—but the number of rapid expirations spurred the vigils at a moment's notice. When the death watches where the youngster actually did succumb[104] are added to those which proved unfounded, the likelihood is that a Puritan family during its child-rearing years experienced successive expectations of the demise of various offspring. In these vigils, whatever their eventual outcome, parents prepared themselves emotionally to cope with the anticipated loss.

As a result, the responses to juvenile deaths were often subdued in comparison with modern reactions which, moreover, tend to be most extreme when triggered by the type of sudden demise the Puritans so often witnessed.[105] This fact has fostered the suggestions that the Puritans did not have deep attachments to their children.[106] The truth is that where some of the mourning process is worked through before the actual death there is that much less left to do afterwards.[107] Thus, the ready weeping of modern mothers when informed of the terminal illnesses of their children changed during vigils of several months into "calm acceptance of the fatal outcome. There was almost no tendency to weep."[108] In a similar fashion, one can imagine a Puritan mother crying copiously at the first death-threatening illness of her first child. By the time of the third such illness of her fifth child, she was likely to be more restrained, the periodic intervals of anticipated mourning having the same cumulative effect as the one prolonged vigil of the modern mother. In both cases there might even be some degree of relief at the actual death, particularly when the physical suffering of the child had been long endured or severe.[109] The Puritan was the more directly exposed to terrifying symptoms in that his children died at home rather than in the semi-isolation of a hospital ward. No medical team shielded the parents from the sight of hemorrhages, convulsions, or swellings:

> But oh! the tortures, Vomit, screechings, groans,
> And six weeks Fever would pierce hearts like stones.[110]

Although anticipatory mourning and relief at the termination of a child's suffering moderated the Puritan reaction to death, grief (which is "the response of emotional pain . . . to the deprivation") was still present when there had been an affective investment in the child.[111] At the death of Samuel Sewall's two year old daughter, the family gave way to "general Sorrow and Tears." Mary Hinckley was reported to be "deeply dejected" over the death of a young grandchild. "I lost my hope," wrote Wait Winthrop after the expiration of an infant son, "and the greatest part of my comfort."[112] Grief was real when the Puritans lost children.

The rules on mourning approved its expression. Intuitively recognizing the abnormal nature of lack of grief when a loved one died,[113] Puritan ministers advised the bereaved not to suppress their emotions. Instead, healthy relief should be obtained by venting pain and sorrow in the ritualized gestures and actions of the mourning process.[114] As with the other areas of life, a good Puritan was required to keep such behavior well under control.

The ministers were more alarmed by manifestations of what today would be termed acute grief than by signs of the absence of grief: "We must not be Stocks and Stones: But yet, we may *do much Amiss in* our *Lamentations.*" They criticized those who lost all composure, who fell into excessive weeping and wailing while rejecting every solace, or who continued to mourn for years without abatement.[115] When such behavior occurred—that the ministers felt compelled to criticize it suggests its existence—the occasion was more likely to be the death of an adult than of a child as anticipatory mourning would play less of a role.[116] Nevertheless, moderation was expected for deaths both great and small: "Not to mourn at all, is unnatural; and to mourn beyond the stinted bounds is unChristian."[117]

A proper moderation in mourning required an attitude of resignation. Clergymen worked hard at impressing their congregations with the importance of accepting the divine decision that had brought about the loss of the loved one: "We are to Mourn without Murmuring, and Weep without Repining; not entertaining any hard thoughts of God, nor allowing any swellings of spirit against His disposals."[118] Fatalistic acceptance of the inevitable was merely the minimum expected. The grief stricken were advised to make a virtue out of a necessity by cheerfully approving what God had willed, demonstrating that they valued Him above their dearest relations: "We are to Bless God even when He takes away."[119] The private writings of bereaved individuals indicate that these attitudes were more than just formal norms. Self-counsels called for ready emotional compliance with the Lord's dictates, no matter how painful they were: "God's will is don, and he is just in all his dealings with us"; "Griefe o're doth flow: and nature fault would finde/Were not thy Will, my Spell Charm, Joy, and Gem."[120]

An attitude of resignation was supposed to prevail before the loved one expired as well as afterwards, but that was a more difficult requirement to fulfill. When Thomas Shepard's second son "began to grow weake," instead of resigning himself Shepard raised in prayer "many arguments to presse the Lord for his life." Some of them were frank special pleadings: "I thought if the Lord should not heare me now, my soule would be discouraged from seeking to him because I sought for the first [child] & could not prevayle for his life, and this was sore if the Lord should not heare me for this."[121] Even when in a state of anticipatory mourning, a parent could retain considerable hope for a child's life. Unlike modern parents, Puritan fathers and mothers did not receive a physician's report showing their child's illness to be terminal. If the lack of reliable prognoses meant on the one hand that the Puritans expected death in many situations where they need not have, it meant on the other hand that they would not go as far in anticipatory mourning as modern parents who may come to regard the still living child as in essence dead.[122] Furthermore, in periods of crisis psychological states tend to be shifting and not fully integrated. A parent can be resigned one moment and hopeful the next, or even contradictorily hold both attitudes at once—consistency is not a major concern in a time of mental and emotional upset. A study of modern mothers with children suffering from leukemia found that the parents's eventual "Rejection of hope on an intellectual level . . . was not accompanied by an acceptance of the prognosis in terms of feelings as well. Not a single mother in the study completely gave up all hope of thwarting the loss of her child through treatment until the exhaustion of treatment resources and the child's obvious moribund state."[123]

Cotton Mather represents an elaborate example of the Puritan whose outlook during vigils fluctuated between resignation to whatever God had chosen and schemes to influence His choice. This counterpoint paralleled the larger cultural interplay, brilliantly depicted in the writings of Perry Miller, between a Puritan fatalism expressed in the doctrine of predestination and a Puritan activism expressed in the notion of preparation for grace. The form this activism took when death threatened could not be that of the modern parent's frenzied search for the best treatment, hospital facilities, and physicians,[124] but would be a last ditch attempt to convince God, that omnipotent doctor, to spare the child. Time after time, Cotton Mather looked heavenward and "begg'd for the Life of the Child in the World," ignoring his own public and private counsels about the necessity of contented resignation. He supplemented these pleas with fasts and abundant tears. When in desperate straits, Mather even "wrestled with the *God of Jacob* for my threatened family."[125] While life remained in a child, the attitudes that death was likely and that it should be readily accepted warred with various paternal or maternal affections, hopes, and expectations, including economic and dynastic calculations.[126] After death, when these were irrevocably dashed, full resignation was easier to attain.

Puritan Mourning: Visions of Heaven and of Hell

Unfortunately for Puritan mourners, the maintenance of an attitude of resignation did not eliminate all of the difficulties of bereavement. This attitude contained fundamental ambiguities that gave very different shadings to prospects in the afterlife depending upon the parent's mood. Was he resigning his infant to joy in heaven or to agony in hell? Since even the experts on religious matters could not provide definitive information, the answers would have to arise from out of the complex, fluctuating attitudes of the parent before and after his child's death.

The truest resignation was ready acquiescence in whatever God had decreed for one's child in the afterlife, be it heavenly glory or hellish torment. Michael Wigglesworth sounded this note in his private diary, an indication that the remarkable visions of *The Day of Doom* were genuine and not contrived for effect: "I have given up my daughter to him with all my heart desiring she may be his, rejoycing he hath given me a child to give up to him. And shall he not do with his own as he will, either to afflict it or take it to himself." Other parents were less explicit, but something of an attitude of ungrudging compliance with whatever God planned for deceased infants is suggested in statements that the child was a sacrifice, an offering: "I resigned the Child unto the Lord; my Will was extinguished. I could say, *My Father, Kill my Child, if it be thy Pleasure to do so!*"[127]

A completely open resignation was not, however, the predominant attitude of Puritan parents. Just as they asked God to extend the life of a dying child, so they bombarded the deity with requests that in the event of death the little one be taken into heaven. Such pleas were the last things that a parent could do for a child, the final gestures of Puritan activism. "In Pray're to Christ perfum'de it did ascend," remarked one parent. Another noted, "My little Judith languishes and moans, ready to die. . . . Told Mr. Walter of her condition . . . desiring him to give her a lift toward heaven."[128]

No theme was more common in private writings about departed children, indicating that bereaved Puritans had to assume that their perished offspring were going to glory in order to make resignation a viable attitude. Only a definite determination could give satisfying meaning to the course of events; to have left the outcome unknown and the ultimate meaning of the death inscrutable would have meant intensification of the pain of loss.[129] Parental love required that the outcome not only be definite (damnation is definite), but positive in meaning—salvation. These psychodynamics behind the assumption of infant salvation were sensed by contemporaries: *"Certainly it cannot but be some relief to a Sorrowful Christian, when his infant dies, to think with himself, the child of mine was in Covenant with God."*[130]

The psychological processes of *idealization* and *rationalization*, which are commonly found in mourning, furthered the assumption of infant salvation and the emotional relief it provided. In idealization the dead child becomes endowed in the memory with superior characteristics, often in invidious contrast to still living siblings.[131] For Puritan mourners, the images of departed offspring would no longer be scored with reminders of depravity, but would evoke rare goodness: "a most lovly and pleasant child," "sweet Flowers," "innocent children," heightening the credibility of the assumption that the deceased were heaven bound.[132] In rationalization, the loss of the child is justified on the basis that it is best for all concerned. The death of a child before its parents, although not unusual, was still felt to be a departure from the natural ordering of things. Whereas the demise of mature adults was inevitable, "By nature trees do rot when they are grown,/ . . . And corn and grass are in their season mown," the death of the young was not: "But plants new set to be eradicate,/ And buds new blown to have so short a date,/ Is by His hand alone that guides nature and fate."[133] According to the voice of rationalization, this break in the course of nature was advantageous because the little ones had passed from the world of trial and temptation to the security and bliss of the divine kingdom. As Cotton Mather put it, "'tis better for our Children to be safely Lodg'd among the Angels of God in *Heaven*, than for them to be sinning against Him like *Devils* on *Earth*."[134]

Those parents and close relatives who believed themselves to be regenerated could look forward to one day being reunited with their young in heaven. The bereaved had become aware, consciously or subconsciously, of their own mortality, for in the death of the infant a part of their own beings had died. Beloved children were both extensions of the self, now severed—"The dying of a child is like the tearing of a limb from us"—and internalized elements in the self, now ripped out.[135] The massive wounds in the ego raised in the mind doubts about the continuation of its own existence.[136] Both the threat to the survival of the mourner's self, and the pain of its raw incompleteness, could be partially overcome by positing an eternal future amidst the restored love objects. The vision of a heavenly reunion made for a powerful rationalization theme: "I say, take, Lord, they're thine./ I piecemeal pass to Glory bright in them"; "The death of our children is not the loss of our children. They are not lost, but given back; they are not lost, but sent before."[137]

Reinforcement of the assumption that individual infants were bound for salvation came from friends, relatives, ministers, and the community in general. When the Winthrop's little son died, Samuel Sewall penned a reassuring poem which concluded, "JESUS will call John from the Grave,/ From Sin eternally to save." John Cotton sent a similar message to a grieving grandmother.[138] Although Puritan clergymen like Cotton allowed in their theology for the possibility, even the likelihood, that some infants were damned, when they discussed specific children the presumption was almost always made that heaven was the destination.

Explicit suggestions that a particular child might be bound for hell were put forth only in exceptional circumstances. In one case, a young mother had murdered her illegitimate infant. If any baby was likely to arrive in hell, this was the one. The product of an illicit union, almost certainly not covenant seed, it had passed from the world without benefit of even initial subjection to the means of grace. In a harangue directed at the nineteen-year-old mother, condemned as both a fornicator and a killer, Increase Mather intoned, "Methinks you should sometimes hear the blood of your woful Infant, Crying *Vengeance! Vengeance! Lord,* upon my unnatural Mother, who murdered me as soon as I came into the World. And what if you murdered its Soul as well as Body?" A similar accusation was made against a mother who had slain two illegitimate children. The evening before the execution, "One of the Company asked her, what she thought of the poor murdered Infants, whom she was instrumental to bring into the world, and then perhaps of sending them to Hell."[139]

A more terrible charge could not be levied against a parent in Puritan society. Only cases of extreme iniquity allowed it to be presented openly, and only the worst enemy of an ordinary mother or father would whisper it. Yet, if sympathy for the bereaved, hardened into a convention, dictated that friends and acquaintances speak of the afterlife of the dead child solely in terms of heaven, this ritual did not prevent the parents themselves from entertaining, perhaps only fleetingly or subconsciously, the possibility of hell. What others would not charge against a parent—the responsibility for the eternal damnation of an infant—he would charge against himself in some inner portion of the psyche. Of course, we have no direct evidence that this was actually the case, nor can we expect to find any. There is at hand considerable circumstantial evidence which, when put together with modern knowledge about the mental processes of adjustment to death, makes it quite probable.

Puritan mourning occurred in a milieu in which hell fire was real. The bereaved had heard about it all their lives and had been highly aware of the threat it posed to their children, not to mention their own souls.[140] When Cotton Mather's little daughter Nibby fell into a fire, he could not help but see the event symbolically. He wrote that she was "pull'd out without the least scorch upon Hands or Face, to damnify her." After two other of his children suffered injuries from gunpowder he decided to "improve this Occasion to inculcate Instructions of Piety on them and the rest; especially with relation to their Danger of Eternal Burnings."[141]

The menace of hell acquired a special immediacy when a death occurred. A bereaved parent had almost certainly read in *The Day of Doom* about infants condemned to the nether world. If these sections of the poem disturbed him he may have repressed them, but a time of grief is a time when repressions can become unsealed. Fragments of the Wigglesworthian vision of babes in hell could readily flit across a mind subjected to the upheavals of bereavement.[142]

They were all the more likely to do so because in the Puritan outlook the act of dying itself suggested depravity. The curse of death had originally come upon the human race as a punishment for the transgression of Adam. Forever after, man's mortality signified his iniquity: "*Sin* is the cause of *Death*."; "All have *sinned*, and therefore all die. . . . Original Sin carries Infants into the Grave."[143] Death meant sin, and sin meant hell, an unavoidable association. Idealization of the deceased child with related assumptions about the availability of purifying grace somewhat obscured the death-sin-hell triad, but it remained a palpable part of the mental environment in which the mourning process was encompassed and could cast an occasional pall over the bereaved's spirits.

It was also a part of the physical environment of mourning. The Puritans did not isolate remains in funeral parlors or subject them to cosmetic arts.[144] A corpse's facial grimace or bodily contortions could be taken as symbols both of that individual's inner sinfulness and of the anguish of his soul in hell. A parent who was not a visible saint, so that his own prospects in the afterlife were less than hopeful (as the ministry had reminded him again and again), was probably especially likely to be receptive to such gloomy associations.

During the mourner's mood of optimistic resignation, when he was imagining his infant approaching heaven with an angel escort, grimmer pictures of the afterlife did not intrude, just as in moments of familial affection the notion of juvenile depravity was shut out. Comforters did their best to sustain the buoyant mood and the pleasing image. Nevertheless, during mourning mental states tend to fluctuate and the bereaved often has periods of depression.[145] A depressed individual is inclined to think in ways that heighten grief and increase pain. Like a probing tongue intensifying the pressure of an aching tooth, he obsessively tortures himself with frightening images and unpleasing interpretations. Samuel Willard told of many mourners "who seem to take a kind of a sullen contentment in nourishing and giving way to sinking reflections on their spirits, whereby they may aggravate instead of mitigating their Grief."[146] How better to heighten grief than by entertaining, even for a moment, the prospect of one's infant suffering in hell? The Reverend Jonathan Mitchel was in this frame of mind when he anguished over the death of his infant without baptism, although he did not believe that this sacrament was necessary for salvation: *"Yet, as it is appointed to be a Confirming Sign, and as it is an Ordinance of Grace, so to be deprived of it, is a great Frown, and a sad Intimation of the Lord's Anger: And though it may be well with the child notwithstanding (that it becomes me to leave unto the Lord!) yet it is to us a Token of Displeasure."*[147]

In the case of infants who lived long enough for a love relationship to develop, the bereaved's periods of depression were deepened by the feelings that in losing the child he had lost a part of himself. If in optimistic moods he obtained some relief by rationalizing an eventual reunion in heaven, in pessimistic periods he confronted the possibility of permanent loss. Wigglesworth played upon this form of separation anxiety[148] in *The Day of Doom*, providing a very different type of rationalization:

> The tender Mother will own no other
> of all her numerous brood,
> But such as stand at Christ's right hand,
> acquitted through his Blood.
> The pious Father had now much rather
> his graceless Son should ly
> In Hell with Devils, for all his evils
> burning eternally,
> Than God most high should injury,
> by sparing him sustain;
> And doth rejoyce to hear Christ's voice,
> adjudging him to pain.[149]

If the mourning parents who pondered such images were engaging in a form of self-torture, simultaneously they were obtaining a kind of self-gratification. Insofar as the bereaved were in a deepening depression, subjected to a need to intensify their suffering, they fell under the masochist's paradox: pain is satisfaction. When not in depression, bereaved parents could gain gratification from the image of the damned infant by having it serve as the consummation of their hostility towards the child, who was all the more resented because his death had caused pain.[150] This expression of strong dislike, even hatred, for one's own offspring was not pathological, but existed to a degree in every parent.[151] Even the best of young children had often been an annoyance and a burden, especially for the mother who had risked her life in labor. Those women who had murdered their infants were exceptional, yet probably other mothers had at times felt similarly inclined.[152] The death wish the parent harbored for a child was in normal cases consistent with love and affection for him. Human feelings are incredibly convoluted, especially in relationships where there are both great demands and great joys, such as characterize the nuclear family. Freud wrote in regard to a mourner:

> There was something in her, a wish of which she herself was unaware, which was not displeased with the fact that death came, and which would have brought it about sooner had it been strong enough. . . . Such hostility, hidden in the unconscious behind tender love, exists in almost all cases of intensive emotional allegiance to a particular person, indeed it represents the classic case, the prototype of the ambivalence of human emotions.[153]

The part of the parent that was gratified by the death of the child could also be gratified by the image of damnation, particularly if, as some have conjectured, the devil himself was a projection fantasy.

To a great extent, the "opposition between the conscious grief and the unconscious satisfaction at death"[154] unfolded in subsurface levels of the mind, only occasionally sending fleeting images and thoughts into the mourner's everyday awareness. However, other types of bereavement reactions entered more directly into conscious experience, being somewhat easier to face openly. Many of them involved guilt. The Puritan parent's web of guilt embodied so many complex twists that it could lead to both expectations of infant damnation, some of which have been seen, and to expectations of infant salvation, furthering those engendered by optimistic resignation, by idealization, and by rationalization.

One line of guilt arose from the belief of the bereaved that he had caused, or contributed to, his child's demise by failing to provide proper care. This form of self-reproach has been commonly found among present-day parents of fatally ill children, although there is usually no medical evidence indicating that negligence brought on the sickness.[155] Such self-reproaches must have been all the stronger among the Puritans with their hazy ideas about disease. Soon after the death of a child, Samuel Sewall sadly thought: "I had not been so thorowly tender of my daughter; nor so effectually carefull of her Defence and preservation as I should have been."[156] A related consideration was whether the parent had paid sufficient attention to the spiritual welfare of the child: "It will be a great damp to our minds, to have such a reflection upon them as this, I do not so much as pray earnestly to God for the Soul of this Child, and now it is gone past all prayers."[157] The fires of hell loomed out of the bereaved's guilt over negligence, as forbidding when the negligence was merely a projection as when it had been real.

A further source of self-blame was the parent's own religious and moral qualities. God took children to punish adults for hearts set too much on worldly affairs and too little on spiritual ones, for lack of sufficient gratitude when He bestowed mercies, and for overt sins of thought or deed.[158] These ideas were so common a refrain among the Puritans that they can be considered a standard element in the mourning process. Its function was to turn the anger at God that would arise if He was held culpable for the child's death back upon the parent himself.

A search for someone or something on which to lay the responsibility for the death of a loved one is a part of the bereaved's effort to imbue the event with significant meaning. Blame can be directed both against the self, and against others. Modern parents who believe that they have somehow caused disease in their offspring often also bear accusatory attitudes towards the attending physicians for not achieving a cure.[159] In the Puritan case the equivalent figure would be God, except that He was supposed to be beyond criticism and blame. Even so, the need to find fault was so strong that some muted resentment came His way, expressed through a covert language that depicted God as the abductor of children: "It pleased God to send ye Messenger of Death to sease and Carry away my little Babe"; "The Lord Jesus Christ . . . has Ordered the *Death* of my Children, and it is *the Lord that hath taken them away."* The same perception of God as a voracious agent of death revealed itself in a dream of Samuel Sewall's in which his little daughter vanished from a closet while in prayer.[160] Some mourners made explicit what remained latent in most and openly muttered against God for the harshness of His providences.[161] The conspicuous presence of the young children of other families at the funeral of their own little one[162] may have added to their bitterness.

Since good Puritans could not give way to outbreaks against God, they had to turn the anger back onto themselves, adding that much more to the burden of guilt. "I desire to acknowledge ye hand of God in all," wrote Joseph Green, "& quietly to submit unto him, and I think yt I never did once murmur agt God for ys stroke: but have cause to say yt God has punished me far less yn I deserve."[163] An individual who craved still more severe chastisement, perhaps out of guilt over his ambivalence towards God, could find it in imagining a child not only dead, but damned because of parental transgressions. Cotton Mather's emotional reaction to a household accident in which a daughter was seriously burned, vividly symbolizing the threat of hell, suggests this pattern of response: "Alas, for *my Sin* the just God throwes *my Child* into the *Fire!*"[164]

Entwined with the negative side of the bereaved's ambivalence towards God the web of guilt led towards damnation; entwined with the positive side it led towards salvation, forming the last element in the intricate cycle of mourning. In wrath against parents, God had seized their beloved babies, but this aggressive act could be balanced by the awareness that the little ones had been His bestowals to begin with, and that out of mercy He had many times intervened when children had lain at death's door: "The Lord gives, & ye Lord takes; blessed be ye name of ye Lord."[165] Whereas God's punitive actions were less than parents had due, His kindnesses were more than they merited.[166] During bereavement, such divine goodness could be most convincingly demonstrated by viewing God as gathering to His side departed infants, undeserving though the parents might be of such a glorious outcome. Cotton Mather declared, "This is, by far the best of all to have children this day in heaven. Truly this is an honour which neither you nor I are worthy of. But so it is; the King of kings has sent for our children to confer a kingdom on them."[167] While emphasizing the guiltiness of man before God, this feeling alleviated some of the guilt stemming from the bereaved's belief that as a parent he had contributed to the death of his child by faulty care. If the little one attained heaven, things had turned out for the best after all: *"A Glorious CHRIST fetches away these Children to a World, where they are treated with Comforts, which this mean and vain World could never yield unto them."*[168] What more could a bereaved parent want?

The End of Mourning

The normal mourning process requires the bereaved to turn over and over in his mind memories and images of the perished loved one in the way that we have seen. By doing so, he gradually comes to terms with the full significance of the loss and begins to accept it.[169] The process does not take place in isolation, but is influenced by the death-related roles, rituals, and beliefs of a particular society. Such "death systems" can serve to lower the stresses of mourning or to raise them.[170] In the case of the Puritans the death system did both. With heaven and hell as facts, deeply embedded in Puritan culture, the pressing questions were who would go where, rather than as later became the issue, whether these realms actually existed. By providing no sure answers about the fate of specific children, the Puritans left the way open for the fluctuating emotions of the bereaved to flow successively, or even simultaneously, into channels that diminished stress and channels that heightened it.

In normal situations the mental crisis which constitutes bereavement eventually subsides, the rapid oscillations of thought, feeling, and behavior giving way to a state of equilibrium.[171] Often, the transference of emotional investment from the lost object to a substitute eases this change.[172] According to the official Puritan death system, God was to be the recipient of the love detached from the deceased. After the loss of his three young children in a span of two years, John Hull exclaimed, "The good Lord, by all these various changes, make me more his own, and wean me more from myself and all fading comforts, that he alone may be my portion!"[173] Hull soon had two other children who undoubtedly competed with God as sites for emotional transference. The high birth rate of Puritan society provided a steady succession of infants who in capturing the attentions and affections of parents and grandparents helped to alleviate their grief for the perished siblings, if somewhat at God's expense. Naming a new baby for a dead one, as was common, emphasized its role as a substitute.[174]

With or without transference, a successful termination of mourning requires a resolution of the conflicting thoughts, images, and feelings that have poured through the mind of the bereaved.[175] The Puritan death system made this achievement a difficult one by raising anxieties about the afterlife that it could not completely allay. Samuel Willard observed: *"We are apt to say, oh! if we were but sure of their well-being, we could then be quiet and contented; but, this is to fight against God: it is his pleasure to keep these things secret for the present."*[176] The mourner was cast upon the twisting stream of bereavement emotions in which guilt could raise expectations of heaven or of hell for perished infants; rationalization could make a case for their comfort or for their torment; and God could appear as an agency of salvation or of damnation. The Puritan death system, which is sometimes touted as exemplary in contrast to the much criticized present American way of death, did not function that smoothly at all.[177]

In the long run, most Puritans seemed to have achieved an equilibrium which allowed them to be convinced that their infant children had indeed reached salvation, although perhaps exposing them to tinges of the old bereavement doubts whenever they reread *The Day of Doom* or heard it recited, or saw a tombstone adorned with bats of hell.[178] This resolution was the easiest to achieve because throughout the mourning process the possibility of heaven had appeared large, detailed, and persistently in the foreground of the conscious mind. The alternative possibility of hell had been a smaller, less definite presence flickering on the periphery of awareness. When the mental conditions of the bereaved reached the final stage of equilibrium, the shadow of infant damnation faded away, leaving in the historical record almost as little trace as the shadows cast by material objects.

II.   "Unsullied Back to Heaven"

The Disappearance
of Infant Damnation

The Doctrine in a New Age

AROUND THE TURN of the nineteenth century, the Reverend
William Patten visited a home in Newport, Rhode Island, which
happened to be near the Congregationalist church of the notable
Calvinist theologian, Samuel Hopkins. Struck by the location,
Patten inquired of the householder, who was not a Congregationalist, whether she had ever availed herself of the opportunity
to see the famous clergyman at work. The woman responded
heatedly, "No, I hope not; a man of such doctrine I never wish to
hear." "What doctrine?" asked Patten. "Why, that *there are
infants in hell not a span long.*"[1] In back of the indignant answer
lay the stereotype which by the late eighteenth century had been
fastened upon New England Calvinism: a sadistic creed designed
to stifle tenderness and warmth. Its portrayal of helpless infants
writhing in the clutches of Satan was one of the most striking
proofs of this terrible cruelty.

That Samuel Hopkins, as well as most of the other Calvinist
ministers of his day, did not speak of infants in hell, much less
describe the torments they underwent there, was somewhat beside
the point. The particular nature of a stereotype often takes its form
more from the projections of the disseminator than from the
actualities of the subject. Hopkins's accuser had not only never
heard him preach, but had "never read any of his writings, nor
would allow one of his books to be in my house."[2] She had formed
her opinions about Calvinist doctrine from hearsay and from what
she had wanted to believe.

This vignette of 1800 would not have been likely in New England in 1700. In Puritan times, rejections of infant damnation, if they existed, had not been conspicuous. Despite the private anxieties the doctrine caused, it was generally accepted and did not raise much public controversy. Following the Great Awakening of the 1740's, however, it became a center of debate as the newly emerged and emboldened enemies of Calvinism pushed it out of the theological wings into the spotlight. The shadow of 1700 materialized as the grotesquerie of 1800, which New Englanders increasingly felt free to ignore. A generation later, the doctrine no longer had an emotional or intellectual base among the general populace, although a rump group of unwaveringly orthodox did continue for a time to be troubled by it, and a handful of ministers to defend it.

More than theological warfare was involved in the disappearance of infant damnation. By the early nineteenth century major changes had taken place in the views of hell, of God, and of children, which had the effect of making the doctrine untenable. The least alterations were in regard to hell. In the early nineteenth century, its existence was beginning to be widely questioned and even many of the Orthodox undoubtedly had a less tangible sense of the Satanic kingdom than had their grandparents. The diminished salience of hell to some extent undermined infant damnation. But belief in an underworld had not ceased; a place of torment remained available.

The change in the view of God was a more important cause of the doctrine's decline. Increasingly looked upon as a being devoted to love and mercy, rather than to wrath and punishment, He retained arbitrary sovereignty only in name. In practice God was required to act in ways acceptable to men. The idea that this benign deity might give tender infants over to the devil became preposterous, an impossible contradiction in the divine character, even if He ordered them sent to the easiest room in the nether region.

The most fundamental cause of the extinction of the doctrine was the shifting view of infants themselves. The depraved vipers of the Puritans were rivaled by the neutral *tabula rasas* of the Enlightenment and then supplanted by the sweet angels of the Romantic era. Not only had God become too good in heart to damn infants, but infants had become too good in nature to warrant damnation. The possibility of hell for beings of such exalted status, once a real threat to bereaved parents, was now out of the question. Deprived of its main supports, the doctrine of infant damnation disappeared from the New England mind well before the Civil War.

In the present century infants have lost their halos and acquired Freudian impulses. Some of these propensities tend to be as displeasing to adults as the sinfulness of the Calvinist child had been to God.[3] But most people no longer believe in a literal hell and the doctrine of infant damnation has not been revived.

Liberal Challenge and Calvinist Response

The years following the mass revivals which swept New England from 1740 to 1742 were a new age for Protestantism in New England. The Great Awakening had transformed the faith, even if the intense piety which characterized the movement could not be generally sustained, but it had also instigated heated factionalism. Lines of cleavage that in Puritan times had been latent, or at least not polarizing, had under the stress of the Awakening widened so as to create definite groupings. The Old Calvinists, who believed that they upheld the Puritan version of theology, contended with the Strict (or New Divinity) Calvinists, who had been influenced by Jonathan Edwards. Both were opposed by the Liberals (or Arminians), who were no longer Calvinists at all, although they remained for generations within its institutional shell of Congregationalism. There were even schismatics who found no alternative but to leave the denomination to form their own churches. Over time these Separate churches died out or were absorbed, along with many individual defectors, by the expanding Baptists.[4]

Among these various groups polemics flew back and forth as each sought to define and defend its theological convictions and to overthrow those held by the others. Children came into the controversies at several points, as in arguments over who was a proper subject for baptism or over who was included in the covenant. Lengthy and involved as these areas of discussion were, they shed little light on changing views about children in New England, tending to be narrowly focused on questions of scriptural and historical interpretation. A sector of the theological battles that is more revealing was the long-lasting dispute over original sin and total depravity. Because discussions of this subject usually included a review of man's native characteristics as manifested in early childhood, they reflected, and influenced, shifts in New England's sentiments towards the very young. Some of these changes were already occurring before the Great Awakening, but only in its aftermath did they become highly visible.

The Calvinist view, which had prevailed in New England from its founding, held that children were thoroughly stained by the Adamic sin. In the years following the Great Awakening, this view was openly challenged by the Liberals, the precursors of nineteenth-century Unitarianism. Although this faction within Congregationalism was rooted in domestic social forces, its members drew heavily on the religious thinkers of England for the particulars of their dispute with the Calvinists.[5] John Taylor of Norwich was especially influential. In his manifesto of 1740, *The Scripture-Doctrine of Original Sin Proposed to Free and Candid Examination,* Taylor forcefully attacked both the federal and the Augustinian parts of the belief. He maintained that guilt was personal and so could not be transferred from Adam to others: "Imputed Guilt is imaginary Guilt." Taking issue with the Augustinian element, Taylor denied that a depraved soul was conveyed by reproduction from one generation to the next. Children therefore entered the world unstained. As John Locke had earlier suggested in his *tabula rasa* psychology, they possessed a neutral moral status. Taylor proclaimed: "We are born neither righteous nor sinful; but capable of being either."[6] In New England, theological dissent from Calvinism's view of human nature would draw on Taylor for almost a century, adding Lockeanism after 1760.

A major example of Taylor's influence was the Reverend Samuel Webster's tract of 1757, published anonymously, which disputed the Augustino-federal version of original sin by reiterating the arguments of the Englishman. Scripture did not show that Adam served as the representative of the human race. Furthermore, sin and guilt were individual matters and could not be imputed from Adam to newly born children, nor transmitted by natural generation. Infants were, therefore, innocent creatures, "God knows as innocent can be."[7] Anticipating the type of argument that would be much favored by the foes of Calvinism in the nineteenth century, Webster contended that parents who really believed in original sin "must take their tender infants into their arms with reluctancy, and look upon them with hatred every time they attend those services their necessities call for."[8] This dubious charge probably had less effect in Webster's time than later; the Puritan culture which had managed to synthesize a love of children with an awareness of their sinfulness was not very far in the past. Such arguments did help to give the Liberals the initiative in the discussion of infants and the considerable advantage of appearing as the party most concerned for their well-being.

The Calvinists were thrown even more on the defensive by Webster's extravagant depiction of the doctrine of infant damnation, a subject that John Taylor had not raised. *A Winter Evening's Conversation* spoke luridly of "myriads of infants . . . *tormented with fire and brimstone,*" weltering in a lake of flame, suffering a black doom and so on, and asked how the supreme being could be good if responsible for such barbarities.[9] Webster also used theological exposition, although vituperation and emotional appeals were the more effective parts of his attack. He held that since infants had no share in Adam's sin, but were "perfectly *innocent* and *blameless,*" a just God would not consign any of them to hell.[10] As a class, they were exempt from damnation.

To get them into heaven was another matter because the mediation of the Saviour was necessary. This requirement presented something of a problem for Webster and numerous succeeding theologians: if infants were truly innocent, on what basis could Christ intervene to bring about their salvation? Webster's explanation, given in a following pamphlet, was that infants did suffer from the consequences of Adam's transgression insofar as they were mortal. A mediator was needed, not to rescue them from a hell to which they were not liable, but to free them from a state of perpetual death. Christ bestowed eternal life. For all infants, He "purchas'd and prepar'd a Heavenly Zion."[11] Salvation was no longer confined to elect babies; it now included the entire group, completely negating the doctrine of infant damnation.

At this early point in New England's rejection of the venerable doctrine, the operative force was less a fundamental reassessment of the nature of infants than of the nature of God and of legal process. In an age increasingly emphasizing individual rights as Enlightenment political and social theory took hold, the notion that a child was guilty of a crime committed several millennia before his birth, by a representative he had no part in selecting, lost its credibility. Webster spoke for the times when he said, "*Sin* and *Guilt* . . . are *personal* things."[12] Men were only now coming to a realization of this truth, but, of course, God had always proceeded by it.

Relieved of complicity in the Adamic sin, infants were in a legal sense innocent, but viewed in moral terms they were not good or even wholly neutral. Webster was writing before the full absorption of Lockean psychology wiped out the last vestiges of original sin in the Liberals' presentation of infant nature. He conceded in his second pamphlet that the native human endowment was faulty, corrupt, susceptible to temptation and sin, but in opposition to the Augustinian view, he held that this weakness was not sinful in and of itself and did not warrant damnation.[13]

To concentrate too heavily on the complexities of Webster's pamphlets is to miss their true thrust. Taken as a whole, they were superb as propaganda. Charles Chauncy, the most prominent of the Liberals, noted with approval that Webster's initial tract was "in its manner . . . the most fitted, of any piece I have seen, to lead the common people into other sentiments concerning the doctrine of *original sin*, than *those* they had been taught in our *Catechism*, and the *Confession of faith*."[14] Peter Clark, an Old Calvinist, complained that Webster was conducting this battle to turn the public against the theory of original sin in the form of a smear campaign.[15] To be sure, the Liberal's lurid descriptions of the tortures of infants in hell had little counterpart in Orthodox writings in New England. While upholding the doctrine of infant damnation, they had usually avoided specific details. Webster, however, was making visible the implications of the doctrine, showing how if pressed, it led to nightmarish images. Knowingly or not, he had caught the spirit of the fleeting visions which had disturbed parents grieving for deceased infants. Since the usual resolution of the bereaved's emotional fluctuations between hope and doubt favored a heavenly destiny for the lost, parents were open to an argument which made the salvation of their child more certain than Orthodoxy ever could, and which told them that their upsetting doubts had been unnecessary. Webster played this advantage for all it was worth: "Any thing is better than to suppose the tender Infants sent to hell: I cannot bare that thought."[16]

By such means, the Liberals, who had mostly opposed the Great Awakening, and were in many respects elitists, demonstrated that they knew how to offer some popular appeal. The rhetorical assault on original sin and its corollary of infant damnation was part of their answer to the revival. This counterattack was only begun in the 1750's and did not reach full force until the development of nineteenth-century Unitarianism. Illustrations, often exaggerated, of the treatment of children in Orthodox theology played an important role by inducing emotional as well as intellectual alienation from Calvinism.

The Old Calvinists were bewildered by this type of campaign. All they could offer in opposition was an inept defense of the Augustino-federal version of original sin that had been handed down to them, diluting it by a few concessions to those worried about infants, a defense sadly lacking in intellectual or emotional force. Charles Chauncy accurately described the Reverend Peter Clark's attempted rebuttal of the writings of Samuel Webster as a compound of "ambiguity, darkness, and perplexity."[17]

Clark was hardly the ideal apologist for Orthodoxy, but Webster had placed him in a situation that would have posed difficulties for any theologian. A defender of Calvinism had to affirm the sinfulness of every infant, yet deny that it necessarily led to the damnation of any particular infant, without coming to the conclusion that all infants were saved. This position was actually the standard New England one upon which most divines had long relied, the difference being that its effectiveness was now questionable. In a way that had not been previously done within New England, Webster had exposed the theological and psychological weaknesses. Nevertheless, in *The Scripture-Doctrine of Original Sin, Stated and Defended. In a Summer Morning's Conversation,* Clark sometimes used the traditional explanations. As an act of mercy, an autonomous deity might redeem for heaven some of the

infants born outside of the covenant, or even all of them, along
with the ones born with a genuine title to its guarantees. Since no
man could know the extent of divine mercy, the issue should be left
undecided, a secret of God.[18]

More often, Clark employed a new and dangerous argument
which released the uncovenanted babies from Satan's grasp, not by
extending saving grace, but by denying that they had ever deserved
hell. In direct violation of the *Westminster Confession* and
authoritative American Calvinist writings, Clark suggested that
even though infants possessed the guilt of original sin, it was not
sufficient to damn them without the commission of personal sins,
of which they were incapable: "And tho we don't . . . hold Infants
to be *perfectly innocent*, but the contrary; yet neither do we hold
Infants liable, eventually, to the Punishment of *Hell* hereafter."[19]
By making this concession, Clark showed that he understood the
appeal of Webster's arguments and the corresponding danger of
the Calvinists being stereotyped as the enemies of infants.
However, Clark did not know how to match the Liberal's appeal,
or how to refute his lurid exaggerations, while remaining true to
Calvinism's tenets. This would-be defender of original sin,
sponsored by ministers who advised congregations to reject any
one for pastoral office that did not strongly support it,[20] had
himself seriously compromised that keystone of the Calvinist
system.

Charles Chauncy, an acute polemicist, one more fairly pitted
against a Jonathan Edwards than against a lightweight like Clark,
exploited the latter's vulnerability. If infants do not deserve to be
damned, then Clark cannot continue to pretend that he cham-
pions the traditional doctrine of original sin which makes *every*
human fully accountable for Adam's transgression. If infants
really do deserve to be damned for original sin alone, then in all
probability some end up in hell and Calvinism therefore main-
tains the damnation of infants. To prove that this view had been
held by prominent Calvinists and their forerunners, Chauncy
cited Augustine, Calvin, and, of course, Wigglesworth.[21]

Clark was panic-stricken. Out of his depth and foundering,
borne down by his own confusion, he grasped in subsequent tracts
at falsehood and equivocation. He made the preposterous assertion that his first effort had "wholly set aside" the matter of infant
damnation as an unnecessary question.[22] Clark then fell back on

the standard Calvinist obfuscation, stating that although there were no reasons to believe that any babies went to hell, this fact did not mean that there were reasons for believing that they all avoided hell; he denounced those who had reached a conclusion one way or the other. His previous suggestion that infants did not deserve eternal punishment was now treated as a claim "which I do not here either affirm, or deny."[23] Clark did make a definite stand on the degrees of pain babies would suffer in Satan's realm, should any of them perhaps turn up there: "I am persuaded, no considerate Man can think them liable to those extream Torments expressed by suffering the Pains of Hell-Fire, by weltring in the burning Lake, and the like; much less that they actually suffer them." These afflictions were reserved for the most hardened sinners: the unbelievers and the wickedly impenitent.[24] In the end, the most that one could do was to be hopeful for infants in general, relying upon the mediation of Christ, and not be "ever-busily inquisitive into the future State of Infants, in which we have no Matter of Concern"; "Whether all, or how many or few are saved? Who they are? And what their State is? Which are all Questions, that it can be of no Use or Profit to us to have resolv'd."[25] The uncertainty which had plagued the bereaved as a result of Calvinism's past handling of the infant issue was to be continued without abatement.

If all that the Calvinists had to offer in their defense were the tracts of Peter Clark, they would have quickly lost the battle over original sin and infant damnation on both the theological and the popular levels. Fortunately for their cause, the followers of Jonathan Edwards joined with Old Calvinists like Clark to dispute with the Liberals. Edwards' disciple, Joseph Bellamy, wrote a brief tract pointing out that Samuel Webster was inconsistent in maintaining that infants did not share in the guilt of the primal sin, and yet holding that their mortality was a part of the punishment for that crime: "It cannot be just, that God should put Infants to Death for *Adam's* Sin, unless *Adam's* Sin is imputed to them.—If *Adam's* Sin is imputed to them, God may justly cast them off for ever."[26] Infants were thus liable to damnation, a more forthright statement than Clark ever made, although Bellamy continued the customary evasion of not indicating what proportion of them went to hell.[27] As a polemical exercise in defense of

traditional doctrines, Bellamy's book was more effective than
Clark's puzzling tracts, but its small size and narrow focus did not
allow it to come to grips with the full range of the Liberal attack.
In order to do so, the Liberals would either have to be met on their
own ground of popularized rhetoric, which was not attempted in a
major way until the coming of Timothy Dwight and Lyman
Beecher, or else be out-thought on the most fundamental levels.
Jonathan Edwards undertook this latter task, the metaphysical
vindication of Calvinism, to the relief of his hard-pressed
brethren.[28]

The specific issue of infant damnation did not especially
interest Edwards. Aware of the "great disputes and many controversies" that surrounded the question, he believed that to do it
justice required a full-scale treatise. For such an undertaking he
had neither the time nor the inclination. He did not want to
become entangled in a question that in large part was unanswera-
ble: "The revelation of God's word is much plainer and more
express concerning adult persons, that act for themselves in
religious matters, than concerning infants."[29] Insofar as Edwards's casual opinions on the infant issue can be gauged from
remarks scattered throughout his works, he seems to have shared
the traditional belief of New England Calvinism that not all of
those dying in early life would be saved. In opposing the English
divine Isaac Watts, who had presented the unusual argument that
non-elect infants endured a permanent death rather than an
afterlife in hell, Edwards remorselessly stated: "To think of poor
little *infants* bearing such torments for Adam's sin, as they
sometimes do in this world, and these torments ending in death
and annihilation, may sit easier on the imagination, than to
conceive of their suffering eternal misery for it. But it does not at
all relieve one's *reason*."[30] Unlike Peter Clark, Edwards had no
desire to temper the Calvinist system to meet the new solicitude for
infants. He continued to perceive them in the Puritan way,
convinced that an infant possessed the characteristics of "a young
viper [which] has a malignant *nature*, though incapable of doing
a malignant action."[31]

Of greater interest to Edwards than the destiny in the other
world of these malignant creatures was the explanation of how
they became that way. Edwards's magnum opus on the subject,
The Great Christian Doctrine of Original Sin Defended, was

published in 1758, shortly after his untimely death. In discussing the makeup of human nature he was more willing to take into account the Enlightened spirit than in treating infant damnation, but he did so in his distinctive way, using elements of the new thought to support his opposition to its main thrusts. Any resulting modifications in the doctrine of original sin were bound to have important repercussions for the closely related issue of infant damnation, Edwards's lack of interest in it notwithstanding.

He had a far better comprehension than most of his fellow Calvinists of the serious difficulties which in the mid-eighteenth century beset the traditional interpretation of original sin. The Augustinian belief that all men had directly participated in the primal crime had long been abandoned, and now the theories that Adam was a federal representative of the human race and that an evil nature was transmitted by physical reproduction were becoming less credible. A conviction that mankind in general was depraved remained strong—even the early Liberals held to the notion[32]—but the connection between this condition and the apostasy of Adam had become tenuous. In reconstructing the doctrine of original sin, Edwards did not attempt to restore the imputation of Adam's sin to his posterity as the main explanation of the connection. He noted in one or two places that God had dealt with Adam as a federal head, but he did not discuss it at length.[33] Instead, he chose to revive the forgotten Augustinian theory of direct participation. The daring of this attempt can be measured by a statement Peter Clark made in the same year that Edwards's treatise appeared: "No man in his right Wits ever held, that the actual sin of *Adam* was the *personal* sin of all."[34]

Drawing on Locke's theory of identity, Edwards made the sin of the first human the sin of everyone by claiming that in the most fundamental sense Adam and his entire posterity were but a single entity—*mankind*—so that metaphysically the whole race had been coexistent with Adam in the Garden of Eden. Just as people regard a large oak as the same tree as the small sapling of sixty years before, although physically it is different, an omnipotent God saw Adam and his diverse descendants as "one complex person, or one moral whole: . . . by the law of union, there should have been a communion and coexistence in acts and affections; all jointly participating, and all concurring, as one whole, in the

disposition and action of the head."[35] This startling conclusion
made everyone as immediately guilty of the primal sin as Adam
himself. The guilt of the apostasy belonged to men "not . . . merely
because God *imputes* it to them; but it is *truly* and *properly* theirs,
and on that *ground*, God imputes it to them."[36] Against the
Liberals who would absolve infants of all culpability in the
Adamic sin, Edwards argued for a more total complicity than even
the Puritans had urged.

The final step in the reconstruction of original sin was to
suppress the other element of the Augustino-federal version, the
gob of depravity passed down from Adam through the generations. Edwards rejected the old idea that there was some sort of
taint, pollution, fountain of evil or the like in the soul at birth,
deserving of punishment in itself. Native depravity could instead
be explained by God's withdrawal of the divine principles that
had been present in human nature before the race's joint apostasy.
With their controlling influence removed, the remaining principles, which were merely natural and by comparison infinitely
inferior, impelled men into sin. Evil was not intrinsic to human
nature, but was the invariable result of it: "These inferior
principles are like *fire* in an house; which, we say, is a good
servant, but a bad master; very useful while kept in its place, but if
left to take possession of the whole house, soon brings all to
destruction."[37]

The Liberal Samuel Webster made a similar distinction between the sinfulness of a thing itself and the sinfulness of its
effects, an indication of how the spirit of an age can bring about a
convergence of assumptions even among those with opposing
positions. Edwards's repudiation of the belief that human nature
was sinful in its very essence represented a real break with the past,
from Calvin as well as from Augustine.[38] However, the Liberals
and Edwards used the new view very differently. For the former, it
was a way of removing the onus Calvinism had attached to human
nature. The Liberals' sinless child was led into corruption
through the faults of upbringing and the temptations of the
world, which exploited what they conceded to be native weaknesses. On balance, the environment was more at fault than
human nature. Before the Revolution, Charles Chauncy would
claim that in the rare cases of flawless child rearing, corruption
could be mostly avoided; human nature did not make it a

certainty.[39] Unitarians of the nineteenth century would counter Calvinist examples of man's wickedness with instances of the goodness of human nature.

In contrast, Edwards thought that sinfulness was inescapable, unless divine grace intervened, and that the cause was the individual himself rather than the environment. That human nature was not intrinsically evil made a person all the more vile: he could not explain away his sinfulness as a part of his inheritance, an excuse which under the new ideas of justice would have relieved him of guilt. Human nature was indeed the problem, but that nature entirely by itself, with nothing sinful added to it: "In order to account for . . . a total native depravity . . . there is not the least need of supposing any evil quality, *infused*, *implanted*, or *wrought* into the nature of man."[40] The correct explanation was that human nature's constituent principles of self-love, passion, and appetite, although not evil as such, always coerced the will by improper motives, except when combined with the divine elements that the regenerate obtained through grace. The sinner was left with no one but himself to blame for his sins. Those who attempted to use the imperfection of their native endowment as an excuse deserved the remark made by a later follower of Edwards, "As though their nature and heart were not *they themselves*."[41] Edwards had accepted the Enlightenment challenge and sought the indictment of the individual on the basis of his own qualities and actions, but these were characteristic of his species just as venom marked the viper. No wonder that Edwards regarded children as anything but little victims, for they came into the world with the human's "infallible disposition to be wicked."[42]

The Calvinist defense of original sin drew on Edwards for generations to come, paralleling the Liberal attack which drew on John Taylor. Edwards, however, had left his heirs a mixed legacy. To their advantage he had made the doctrine more modern and consequently less vulnerable to critiques based on Enlightenment ideas of justice. (Although opponents asked whether an irresistible tendency to be wicked was compatible with moral accountability, an issue society is still trying to decide.) To his heirs' disadvantage, Edwards had replaced the relatively simple and easy to understand categories of the Augustino-federal version of original sin—Adam the representative of mankind, depravity an inherited pollution—with far more difficult ones that must have

gone over the heads of much of the public. His notion of every
person being with Adam in Paradise eluded the grasp of even
learned clergymen. Perry Miller termed this theory, Edwards's
"most original and brilliant conception," but insofar as it puzzled
both laymen and ministry, the difficulties of upholding original
sin were only increased by Edwards's efforts to strengthen the
doctrine.[43]

The corollary of infant damnation was in even greater straits.
Not only had Edwards unintentionally weakened it through his
undermining of original sin, but he had chopped away part of its
foundation. Traditionally, infants had been liable to damnation
both for their share of the guilt of the Adamic sin, and for their
inherited depravity. Edwards had transformed the latter element
into an inevitable tendency towards evil which was not punishable for itself, but for its results. Freed from intrinsic sin, and
apparently as yet incapable of committing punishable actual sins,
infants under the Edwardean scheme could be sent to hell only for
a complicity in Adam's transgression which required sophisticated metaphysics to explain. Edwards himself seemed to be
willing to go down the line with infants damned on this basis, but
few, if any others, were brave enough—or reckless enough—to
follow.

Impasse in Theology

The debates between Liberals and Calvinists in the 1750s
represented the emergence of infant damnation as a controversial
subject in New England. Another round of debates in the 1820s
would signal the beginning of its end as an issue of public interest.
For the years between these divides definite trends are hard to
detect, especially in the realm of formal theology, as distinct from
popular religious thought (a reversal of the historian's usual
problem). This situation can be partly explained by the turmoil of
the colonial conflict, the American Revolution, and the search for
national stability. The onrush of events sometimes disrupted
theological speculation, or reoriented it towards political issues.
Nevertheless, the ministry was too disciplined to be long distracted
from intellectual labors by the happenings of the day, and too
concerned about the questions of damnation and salvation to be

persistently neglectful of them. The real problem was the state of the venerable questions themselves, at least those aspects involving original sin and infant damnation. The debates of the 1750s had left the Calvinist side, the clear majority in New England, perplexed. The clumsy obtuseness of Peter Clark and the surpassing brilliance of Jonathan Edwards had each in its own way confused or undermined the conventional explanations of the doctrines so that following generations were in doubt about how to anchor them. The result was a long period of drift.

Some of the Calvinist ministry did have sufficient confidence in the traditional accounts to make a case for them. In treating original sin, which was always more extensively discussed from the pulpit than was infant damnation, explanations like imputation continued to be presented.[44] However, those Orthodox clergymen who had been influenced by the work of Edwards, and to a lesser extent by the Enlightenment, could not simply repeat the old litanies. Nor, alternatively, could they present adequate substitutes. This plight can be seen in the thought of three of the most important ministers of the late eighteenth and early nineteenth centuries: Samuel Hopkins, Timothy Dwight, and Nathaniel Emmons. Hopkins was the most prominent of Edwards's disciples, taking upon himself the task of further elaborating the master's system. (The post-Edwardean vein of theological speculation was sometimes termed "Hopkinsianism.") Dwight generally adhered to the main lines of Edwardean theology, but without subjecting them to the metaphysical refinements of the Hopkinsians.[45] Emmons was also under the Edwardean influence, yet could be unusually independent in his thinking.

This trio generally followed Edwards in abandoning the Augustino-federal version of original sin and native depravity. Imputation, which Edwards had deemphasized, was now rejected altogether, especially by Dwight and Emmons who insisted as strongly as did the Liberals that guilt and punishment could not be transferred from one individual to another.[46] The trio also went along with Edwards by dismissing inherited sinfulness. "We cannot suppose," stated Emmons, "that infants derive their moral corruption from Adam."[47] Difficulty began at this point. As a substitute for what he had dismantled, Edwards had forged a new

linkage between the episode in the Garden of Eden and the
depravity of mankind, the metaphysical identity of the human
race and Adam. His successors found it unreliable.

Hopkins, true to his discipleship, attempted to retain the
theory, but could not present it in a convincing manner.[48]
Emmons thought it absurd: "Since [Adam] committed that
transgression before we were born, it is a plain dictate of common
sense that we had no concern in it."[49] To account for depravity,
Emmons claimed that God, acting on the basis of arbitrary
sovereignty, had organized creation in a pattern which required
that any lapse by Adam would result in the corruption of all his
posterity. In accord with this arrangement, God turned the souls
of infants towards evil: "He works in them . . . produces those
moral exercises in their hearts, in which moral depravity properly
and essentially consists."[50] The daring Emmons had made God
himself the immediate cause of infant sinfulness, a conclusion
with even less general credibility than Edwards's explanation. It
also played into the hands of the Liberals who were telling the
public that odious beliefs of this sort were indeed the real stuff of
Calvinism.

As for Dwight, whose talents and interests lay more in the
institutional and proselytizing aspects of religion than in speculative theology, the attempt to account for depravity was simply
given up. That it existed he was sure; the evidence was overwhelm-
ing: "I have been employed in the education of children and youth
more than thirty years. . . . I cannot say with truth, that I have seen
one, whose native character I had any reason to believe to be
virtuous; or whom I could conscientiously pronounce to be free
from evil attributes."[51] Dwight was convinced that such juvenile
traits as selfishness, anger, vengefulness, cruelty, etc., were the
consequences of Adam's act. What he could not say was exactly
how that first transgression caused all children to become sinners:
"Many attempts have been made to explain it; but I freely confess
myself to have seen none, which was satisfactory to me; or which
did not leave the difficulties as great, and, for aught I know, as
numerous, as they were before. I shall not add to these difficulties
by any imperfect explanations of my own. At the same time, I
repeat, that the fact in question is not at all affected by these
difficulties."[52] Depravity was still certain, but it floated in the air,
its *modus operandi* unknown. With the collapse of the Edwardean

explanation, even some of those who considered themselves to be his intellectual descendants were forced in the early nineteenth century to return to the traditional grounds of imputation and the inherited evil taint.[53]

The failure to offer a case for original sin that was compatible with Enlightenment rationalism compounded the already formidable difficulties of the infant damnation issue. Those ministers who had accepted the Enlightenment view that an individual was punishable only for his own transgressions were compelled, like Dwight, to insist that children personally commit sins. At the same time, however, the Enlightenment raised questions about the limits of accountability. The capacity of being answerable for one's thoughts and actions was called "moral agency," a distinct status that animals, for example, did not possess. According to the new ideas, only those were moral agents who had sufficiently developed faculties to make them directly responsible for their own character and conduct. Using this assumption, the argument could be made that the very young were not liable to charges of personal sinning, not qualifying as moral agents, and were therefore guiltless and undamnable. Charles Chauncy had employed this reasoning in behalf of juvenile innocence, contending that years elapsed before a child became morally accountable.[54]

The problem had not existed in Puritan times when the traditional explanations of original sin were fully credible, making infants damnable at birth without the necessity of proving their personal commission of evils. Wigglesworth had represented the non-elect babies of *The Day of Doom* as hell-bound solely for Adam's crime, while allowing that they themselves had not transgressed. Nor had Edwards encountered trouble on this point. He was able to accept the basic Enlightenment line on moral agency[55] and still, without inconsistency, retain infant damnation because, according to his theory, the newly born had already personally sinned through their metaphysical coexistence with Adam. Ministers who gave up the old charges of imputation and inherited depravity, but could not uphold Edwards's theory, discovered that unless they had moral agency begin at birth, their theologies suggested the existence of a period of time in which children were completely free of sin.[56] During this interim, the damnableness of infants was open to question.

Wrestling with the problem, Nathaniel Emmons once again

came to an extreme conclusion, an indication of the strain on post-Edwardean theology as it attempted to explain the nature and fate of children. Emmons admitted that, "It is certainly supposable that children may exist in this world some space of time, before they become moral agents; but how long that space may be, whether an hour, a day, a month, or a year, or several years, as many suppose, we do not presume to determine."[57] In any event, a period might transpire during which infants were not properly subject to praise or to blame. If they died during that time, they could not fairly be punished with hell, nor, on the other hand, be rewarded with heaven. Emmons solved the problem by deciding that such beings were annihilated.[58] This conclusion could please few, if for no other reason than that it seemed to deny the immortality of the soul. When Emmons's collected works were prepared for publication, the discreet editor took pains to have the aged clergyman repudiate it.[59]

Unlike Emmons, many ministers were unaware of the complexities of the infant damnation issue, or chose to ignore them. Calvinists could be exceptionally resolute in defending the received doctrines of the past without heeding disturbing questions that had been raised about their legacy. On the matter of departed infants, as well as on certain other theological issues, sermons of the late eighteenth and early nineteenth centuries frequently sounded the same sort of notes as had come from the Puritan pulpit. Ministers assured those parents who appeared to have a genuine claim to the covenant that in all probability their infants were resting with God.[60] Other parents were left with the usual implication that a real possibility of damnation existed for their offspring: "The Children of God's People, being thus taken into covenant with God, gives that Hope . . . of their Salvation, if they die in Infancy: which we cannot have for those without, or in a State of Heathenism."[61]

In light of the assertion by some nineteenth-century Calvinists that infant damnation was not preached in New England after the time of Edwards, the rather strong affirmations of it that occasionally came forth in the late eighteenth century should be mentioned. The Reverend Jonathan Parsons wrote that "It is as evident as any conclusion can follow from its premises, that infants dying without any interest in the covenant of grace, do perish forever."[62] The Reverend John Murray, a Presbyterian, hoped for a somewhat milder hell for infants than for others, in the manner of Wigglesworth's "easiest room": "Having proved the infant to be born a child of wrath, this doctrine cannot concede that GOD was bound to give him grace and salvation. . . . It concludes, however, that if that grace should not be given, if that penalty be inflicted, in fact, the state of such infant must be vastly preferable to that of the adult, who perishes too."[63]

Such frank talk was, to be sure, somewhat atypical. The standard Calvinist response continued to be evasiveness. The average minister did not clearly place any infants in hell, but, also, refused to state that they all went to heaven.[64] The concerned public wanted something more definite, but was informed that it was all a great mystery beyond man's ken.[65] On one occasion, the Reverend Joseph Bellamy was visited in his study by a "plain, but inquisitive" parishioner, who asked, "I wish, sir, that you would tell me whether any infants are lost?" True to form, Bellamy parried the question by instructing the man to leave their fate to God and return to his work.[66] Answers of this sort could hardly satisfy legitimate and natural inquiries, which had been made all the more pressing by the lurid caricatures of infant damnation that the Liberals kept putting out.[67] In the absence of clear-cut pronouncements by the Calvinists, with the exception of a bold few like the Edwardean Nathaniel Emmons and the traditionalist John Murray, the general public was largely left to its own resources in reaching definite decisions about the fate of departed infants, just as it had been in Puritan times.

Trends in Lay Belief

The private feelings of laymen in the late eighteenth century and the early nineteenth were shaped by some of the same conditions that had affected the Puritans. Children, especially infants, continued to be regarded as fragile, death-prone beings, reflecting the mortality rates that remained quite high as compared with later American figures.[68] Tombstone inscriptions of the era sometimes set forth records of juvenile fatalities that are in certain ways as frightful as the casualty lists on war memorials. A long New Haven epitaph reads, in part:

IN memory of 6 children of
Henry & Elizabeth Daggett,
inter'd in the public square

Viz ELIZABETH I. died
Nov. 19, 1772. AE. 36 days

REBECCA
Dec. 16, 1773. AE. 47 d's.

ELIHU
May 17, 1775. AE. 16 d's.

HENRY, I.
Jan. 21, 1777. AE. 93 d's.

ELIZABETH, 2.
June 1, 1778. AE. 72 d's.

HENRY, 2.
Feb. 3, 1784. AE. 22 d's.[69]

The briefer inscription on a Grafton, Vermont family stone of 1803 also suggests the type of ordeal that unlucky families had to undergo:

IN Memory of
Thomas K. Park Junr
and thirteen Infants,
Children of Mr.
Thomas K. Park and
Rebecca his wife.[70]

A portion of the public incorporated much of the Puritan pattern in their response to the loss of infants. While the sinking child was still alive, parental emotions were torn between resignation and hope; and after the demise, between contentedness with God's will and covert resentment of His abduction.[71] The common interpretation that the loss of a child was a divine rebuke for the faults of the guardians prevented anger at God from becoming too open by turning most of it back upon the mourner's self. The theme of death as a punishment for the survivor also reflected the guilt feelings of grief-stricken mothers and fathers who believed that they had somehow failed in the care they had taken of the perished loved one.[72] To further the attitude of acquiesence in God's ordering of events, and to rationalize death more effectively, the assumption was usually made that departed infants were saved. "The fond and cherished babe left me, at a moment's warning," wrote a mother, "It fell upon me like a thunderbolt.— But my mind is comforted now. My child, my lamb, is in heaven. He has gone to the Savior."[73]

For orthodox Calvinists who were genuinely devout, retaining a strong conviction of original sin and native depravity, the mourning process was complicated by the persisting shadow of infant damnation. A Baptist poem of 1817, which pondered the possible death of a new born infant, captured their anxiety: "Then, babe! shall thy immortal mind,/ . . . With seraphs soar to realms of light,/ Or sink in everlasting night."[74] When Susan Huntington wrote that, in regard to her sickly year-and-a-half old daughter, "I feel a strong assurance that, whether she lives or dies, she is the Lord's," the mother implicitly acknowledged the possibility that it could be otherwise with infants; they were not guaranteed salvation. Also indicative is the passage in the journal of Sarah Connell Ayer in which the deaths of four infants were mentioned, but of only one was it said, "He was a lovely flower, and I trust he is now transplanted in the garden of Heaven."[75]

At the same time that a Puritan-like response to the infant issue continued among one part of the public, other sectors developed a new approach. These people were surer than devout Calvinists could ever be that the young were saved; the peripheral awareness of the possibility of damnation had disappeared. The change in attitudes can be seen in poetry. Before the late eighteenth century, poets usually viewed deceased infants as having reached heaven only through the mercy of Christ. Occasionally, they touched upon the infant's guilt for original sin which the mediation of the Saviour removed: "JESUS will call John from the Grave,/ From Sin eternally to save."[76] These themes continued into the nineteenth century,[77] but were less frequently employed than a new interpretation in which infants were guiltless innocents and for that reason won acceptance into heaven. As early as 1784 it was defiantly proclaimed in a poem entitled, "An Epitaph on an Infant, found dead in a Field, supposed to be left by Vagrants, and which was denied Christian burial":

> . . . Hear this, ye mighty proud!
> A Spotless life my coffin is,
> And Innocence my shroud. . . .
> And tho' deny'd God's House on
>   Earth,
> I tread his Courts in Heaven.[78]

In the 1820s the Romantic note began, the endearing physical qualities of the dead infant becoming the symbol of his inner purity and consequent happy fate: "Death found strange beauty on that cherub brow,/ And dash'd it out. . . . / But there beam'd a smile/ So fix'd and holy . . . / Death gazed and left it there;—he dared not steal/ The signet-ring of heaven."[79] An interpretation which made infant salvation a certainty made infant damnation impossible.

Death itself took on an altered significance. The Puritans had discovered in the frequent loss of the very young a sign of the sinfulness of mankind: the death of babies not yet out of the cradle showed that the entire human race was subject to the punishment of the apostasy, and therefore must share in the guilt. This association of sin with death had helped to remind mourners of the possibility of infant damnation. The early nineteenth century was even more fascinated by death than the seventeenth century, but in the popular view it no longer represented a just punishment of infants for the Adamic sin. Instead, death signified that infants were too pure for an evil world: "Weep, O, mother!/ But not that from this cup of bitterness/ A cherub of the sky has turn'd away."[80] If the very act of dying became a sign of salvation, then the threat of infant damnation could fade from people's minds during a period in which there was more interest in death watches, final moments, funerals, and graveyards than ever before. Grief was ceasing to be a form of self-discipline and was becoming an act of "therapeutic self-indulgence."[81]

The shifts in the public's view of the infant issue were closely related to the changing opinions on the doctrine of original sin. People might still apply the doctrine to infants, but because of its erosion in theology they did not necessarily consider the degree of guilt as sufficient to warrant damnation.[82] A more far-reaching development was that many no longer applied the doctrine to infants at all. The growing feeling in New England was that the very young were not guilty or depraved in any way, nor even merely neutral in the *tabula rasa* sense, but were unequivocally good, far too good to be threatened with damnation. Infants represented the great exception to the sinfulness that marked the rest of mankind, including children beyond the first years of life. Resolute Calvinists who realized what was happening were scandalized by the new kind of mothers and fathers whose parental love, in contrast to the Puritan type, barred a sense of their offspring's depravity:

> The parent cannot, or will not, believe, that *his* child, *his* offspring, *his* darling, is naturally dead in trespasses and sins; that *his* [sic] nature is corrupt. . . .
>
> We often hear parents calling their children 'harmless creatures,' 'pretty innocents,' and other fond and endearing names which *figuratively* denote the same thing, such as 'little doves,' 'harmless birds,' with a thousand other equivalent appellations; and, I confess, I never hear them without trembling.[83]

Popular poetry gave vibrant expression to the new attitudes. Verses describing the baby as "A smiling cherub" and a "Dear innocent" were being turned out by the first decade of the nineteenth century, became common in the 1820s, and appeared as almost the only word on this subject at the height of the Romantic era in the 1830s and 1840s.[84] Although such rhetoric was being used more effusively than it had ever been before, it was not without precedent. Seventeenth-century Puritan poets had sometimes played with similar phrases in characterizing infants, as in Anne Bradstreet's "fair flower," or "sweet babe." Unlike the later writers, however, the Puritan ones did not intend to imply a genuine inner purity for they had not forgotten that "a serpent's tongue in pleasing face lay hid," the newly born child "a bloody *Cain*."[85] The "white and innocent heart"[86] did not appear in Puritan poetry.

The change in the status of infants that took place between the Puritan seventeenth century and the Romantic nineteenth century is easier to demonstrate than to fully explain. The story is larger than the decline of original sin, although that development is certainly a major part of the plot. Henry Adams offers a clue to other causes in his statement that "the popular reaction against Calvinism" was "felt rather than avowed," hinting at a transformation of basic elements of the New England mind.[87] A modern historian makes a similar point in concluding that on the question of infant damnation "the ultimate decision was left neither to logic nor to science but to the drift of social experience."[88] These suggestions are helpful, they widen the context, but they are not very revealing as to why fundamental socio-cultural patterns shifted. Those old standbys of historical explanation, urbanization and industrialization, will not suffice because the change was well under way before they became major developments in New England.

Philippe Ariès's thesis, that since the middle ages the Western family has become increasingly child-centered, provides a broad-level explanation for the alteration of New England's perception of infants. Ariès writes that once the "old indifference" was breached and a greater amount of care devoted to children, there arose "new feelings, a new emotional attitude" towards them. The new affection eventually evolved into an "obsessive love" of the child which "was to dominate society from the eighteenth century on," a transformation marked by the "invasion of the public's sensibility by childhood."[89] With some qualifications, these phrases accurately describe what was happening in New England. An intense public awareness of childhood came later there than in Europe, as did other major ideological trends of Western civilization, not really blossoming before the turn of the nineteenth century. On the other hand, the "old indifference" had never characterized the region's attitudes toward her young because New England missed the medieval phase of family evolution. The Puritans' greater degree of emotional involvement with their children helps to explain why they were more disturbed than Christians on the continent by the possibility of infants suffering in hell and less eager to discuss it.

As the modern family began to emerge fully in New England, the Puritan love for offspring, which was relatively restrained and at least in theory secondary to the love of God, became Ariès's obsessive love. The evolution of parental love of this type was probably related to the birth rate which began to decline in New England in the late eighteenth century.[90] Fewer children per family meant that a greater amount of attention could be extended to each one, with a corresponding intensification of the parent (especially mother) -child relationship. Parents in such families were likely to be more devoted to their children as individuals than the mother of 1739 whose large brood was wiped out by diphtheria and "afterwards was unable to decide whether she had twelve or thirteen children."[91] In the three most populous New England states, Massachusetts, Connecticut, and Maine, the decline in the birth rate during the period 1800 to 1860 was greatest in the years from 1810 to 1830.[92] It was in these years that the new sensibility towards children first became highly visible.

With the development of obsessive parental love, hostility to infant damnation increased because obsessive love put children before all things. Even God's sovereignty would have to be abridged if it stood in the way of guaranteeing their safety. The deity was now required to keep infants out of hell; He ceased to have a choice. Thus, a spectator at a baptism complained to the presiding clergyman, "'If that had been my child I would not, after your prayer, have allowed you to baptize it.' 'Why, sir?' 'Because you prayed if it died in infancy, it might be taken to heaven; as though God might not save it.'"[93] By the early nineteenth century, infants meant so much to most people that intellectually and emotionally they could no longer afford to entertain the possibility of damnation for them. Only an unusual burden of guilt could sustain that threat, one probable reason that the doctrine persisted among the dwindling number of devout Calvinists.

The guarantees of safety in the afterlife which infants had obtained could not be given to the other children in a family, although parents undoubtedly wished that they could, without overturning the traditional Christian scheme entirely. The child of eight, of ten, of twelve, had invariably stained his original purity as he discovered some of the temptations and evils of the world, making him, unlike his sibling in the cradle, liable to damnation. Infants alone were ensured salvation. In the realm of religion, they had benefited the most from the rise of obsessive love and the penetration of the public sensibility by childhood.

The Great Debates

The 1820s were the bicentennial decade of New England Calvinism, but from the point of view of the strictly Orthodox it had declined rather than progressed since Puritan days. Thrown onto the defensive, some of the ministry tried to revive the waning belief in original sin and native depravity by making minor concessions to the popular point of view. Unfortunately for their cause, they ran into the same problems that had beset previous clergymen who had made the attempt. Such was the dilemma of the Calvinist, Leonard Woods of Andover Seminary, in his pamphlet battle with the Liberal, Henry Ware of Harvard, one of the last feuds between theologians in which the New England public took an interest. That Liberalism had finally assumed a separate institutional form as the Unitarian denomination made the debate all the more noteworthy.

The Unitarian position, as upheld by Henry Ware, was not without its own difficulties, although they were by no means as severe as those of the Calvinists. The *tabula rasa* imagery of the Enlightenment, on which the Liberals had long depended, was falling out of step with the popular view as it advanced to the position that the very young were natively good rather than either depraved, or neutral. For the Liberals to get too far behind the changes in public sentiment towards children would jeopardize a major advantage they had enjoyed over the Orthodox. Ware showed that he sensed the problem by using varying images of infants. Sometimes, he spoke of them as having "no moral character," and as being "by nature no more inclined or disposed to vice than to virtue," which was the Enlightenment frame of reference.[94] On other occasions, he described the very young as "innocent and pure," the possessors of a native "gentleness and good disposition," phrases which would not have been used by eighteenth-century forerunners like Charles Chauncy.[95] Although Ware was inconsistent, the overall direction of Liberal thought was clear. William Ellery Channing would soon be telling the public that "I do and I must reverence human nature"; "You must have faith in the child. . . . Believe in the greatness of its nature."[96]

Leonard Woods won a few points by indicating Henry Ware's inconsistency,[97] but was bedeviled by an even more damaging inconsistency of his own. To oppose Ware's imagery, whether it was the infant as neutral or as paragon, he presented the Calvinist picture of the infant as sinful. Little children "have the understanding, the bodily strength, the features, and all the attributes of a man, though in miniature. And who that watches the character of children, with the eye of a Christian or a philosopher, can have the least doubt, that they possess in a correspondent degree, all the moral attributes, and especially all the moral corruptions, which appear among men?"[98] Here was the Puritan idea, for which Jonathan Edwards had so valiantly struggled, of infants as part and parcel of humanity. Nevertheless, Woods was sufficiently aware of the growing feeling that babies were really not little men, but a special class of beings, to make a few gestures towards it. He admitted that young children possessed qualities which were "amiable," "useful," and "charming." However, he would not grant these characteristics any moral status, offering the curious argument that they were merely natural and could not serve as evidence of infant goodness.[99] Since Woods had bestowed moral status upon the negative characteristics of infants, viewing them as indicators of corruption, his refusal to do the same for the positive ones seemed most arbitrary. Unfavorable natural qualities demonstrated the existence of complete native depravity, but favorable natural ones did not demonstrate the existence of any native goodness.

Like Peter Clark of sixty years before, Woods had placed himself in a strained position by trying to uphold traditional Calvinism while also giving some recognition to the changing popular feelings of the day. Outmaneuvered in the debate by Ware, who exploited his inconsistencies, just as Samuel Webster and Charles Chauncy had profited from Clark's clumsier gaffes, Woods had to fall back upon received authority as the means of sustaining his version of infant nature: "Whether I succeed or not in my attempt to show, by another mode of reasoning, that the doctrine of depravity is reconcileable with the moral perfection of God and the moral agency of man, I shall consider the doctrine as worthy of unhesitating belief, if it has no support but this, which is indeed the best support of all,—that it is taught in the holy Scriptures."[100]

As long as Calvinists like Woods clung to the doctrine of infant sinfulness with no more than minor concessions to the popular view, the Unitarians could continue to use the issue for polemical advantage, especially if they were willing to place greater emphasis on infant goodness than a strict *tabula rasa* theory allowed.

Even before Ware took this route, it was being followed on less formal levels. An 1814 letter in the *Christian Disciple*, a Unitarian periodical, asked: "If children were demons, fit for hell, would God have given them that attractive sweetness, that mild beauty which renders them the most interesting objects on earth, and which compels us to shrink with horror from the thought of their everlasting ruin? . . . Is this winning child, whom God has adorned with charms the most suited to engage the heart, abhorred by God, and fit only for the flames of hell?"[101] During the 1820s, Unitarian journals were able, as Calvinist journals were not, to print poems on infant salvation that embodied the emergent Romantic approach. Verses told of the smiles of dying babies, revelations "sweetly given/ Of all that man can learn of heaven," and of young souls ascending to their maker, "unstained with sin,/ in robes of innocence arrayed."[102]

In a period when strife between Unitarians and Calvinists occasionally reached such extremes that people were on their guard for sabotage and assassination,[103] casual poetry was not the most fearsome weapon. But more than in any other section of the country, the written word counted in New England; the couplet could strike a real blow for the Unitarian cause. The denomination did remain a minority one, with its main strength confined to the seaboard, but the effectiveness of its propaganda cannot be measured only by how many were converted to Unitarian ranks. If caricatures of infant damnation[104] and poems on infant innocence did not bring the general population rushing into the fold, they did contribute to the breaking down of its hard core Calvinism. Old Nathaniel Emmons complained of the trend in 1824: "How many are halting between two opinions, in respect to the doctrine of total depravity; the doctrine of divine agency; the doctrine of divine decrees; the doctrine of divine sovereignty. . . . Is not moderate Calvinism . . . creeping in and spreading?"[105]

Despite the damage that a belief in the sinfulness of infants did to the general popularity of Orthodoxy, it stayed a part of the theological system of conservative Calvinists, a conviction from which they would not be shaken. In contrast, Calvinists who felt less beholden to tradition were willing in the 1820s to alter substantially received doctrines so as to bring them more into line with the thought patterns of the nineteenth century. In a choice between maintaining total fidelity to the Calvinism of the past with its diminishing popular appeal, and undertaking modifications to produce a brand of Calvinism less than strictly orthodox, but more attractive to the public, they tended to favor the path of innovation. Lyman Beecher was the strategist of this group, Nathaniel W. Taylor served as the leading theoretician for its "New Haven theology," and Chauncey Goodrich and Eleazar Fitch were important associates.[106]

Goodrich was the first to break openly with the Calvinist heritage and confidently declare the nonsinfulness of children before they assumed the status of moral agents. Taylor, his friend and colleague at Yale, concurred.[107] A point that earlier theologians had found perplexing, they initially saw as an advantage. Furthermore, the logic of their theory of original sin required the nonsinfulness of infants. In the manner of Emmons and Dwight of the previous generation, these New Haven ministers followed Edwards in rejecting imputation and inherited depravity, while dismissing his theory that all men had directly participated in the apostasy as absurd.[108] According to the New Haven school, Adam's crime did not make anyone else guilty, but did establish the certainty that every individual, by acts of his own will, would commit personal sins. A more precise account of the operation of this divine arrangement could not be given.[109]

All that survived of the hoary doctrine of original sin and total depravity was a native human endowment which was constituted in a way that inevitably led to sinning, although it was not intrinsically evil. This remnant became the pivot of New Haven thought. As Taylor painstakingly explained it in his most important sermon, *Concio ad Clerum*, "When therefore I say that mankind are entirely depraved *by nature,* I do not mean that their nature is *itself* sinful, nor that their nature is the *physical* or *efficient* cause of their sinning; but I mean that their nature is the occasion, or reason of their sinning;—that *such is* their *nature,* that in all *the appropriate circumstances of their being, they will sin and only sin.*"[110] In apparent agreement with modern ideas of justice, men were condemnable not for their native inheritance, but for what it produced (a distinction the Unitarians regarded as tenuous). In young infants, however, human nature was probably not yet spawning actual evils, certainly not in their conduct, and perhaps not in their characters either—no one was very sure about the innermost aspects of infant life. In any event, their mental capacity was obviously too undeveloped for them to understand that particular thoughts, feelings, and actions were wrong. Thus, as Emmons had believed, between birth and the commencement of moral agency a period existed during which infants, alone among the legions of unconverted mankind, were sinless. Attempting to convince Lyman Beecher of the validity of this view, Goodrich explained, "Previous to the *first* act of moral agency, there is nothing in the mind which can *strictly* and *properly* be called sin—nothing for which the being is accountable to God. . . . There is no sin previous to moral agency."[111]

Beecher, however, was disturbed by the revisionary position on infants. He suspected that any benefits it provided in the effort to make Calvinism more presentable to the public would be outweighed by the troubles it would bring with conservative Calvinists, who were unlikely to accept the abandonment of infant sinfulness. Instead of having a united force fighting the Unitarians, the Orthodox would again be rent by internal strife, as in the decades after the Great Awakening. Years later, Beecher reminisced about the situation:

> We had got through with the slang of Old Side and New Side. The opposition to Hopkinsianism was all still, asleep, gone by. . . . Goodrich, in one of his lectures to the students, came out in a form that seemed to imply the denial of original sin—nothing sinful in infants. The minute I heard of that I saw the end. I never felt so bad. I wrote a long letter to him and Taylor, telling them they must take that back, or they would have the old fight over under new names.[112]

Prodded by the urgings of Beecher, made more persuasive by signs of the anticipated conservative discontent,[113] the New Haven school staged a tactical retreat. The infant question threatened to become an embarrassment and they desired to downplay it. Goodrich, who had started the fuss in the early 1820s, decided by the end of the decade that the real issue "is not, then, what is the character of infants, but what is the nature of sin."[114] Yet, the New Haven school could not surrender on the main point—the innocence of infants before moral agency—without pulling down its central tenet that each individual was absolutely responsible for the evils he committed, having the knowledge and the power to act otherwise. To make Calvinism compatible with the logic of the nineteenth century, the interval of nonsinfulness at the start of life had to be retained. Even Beecher saw that: "Neither a holy nor a depraved nature are *possible* without understanding, conscience, and choice."[115]

The danger, sensed by the conservatives, was that if the interval appeared to be of significant duration it jeopardized the elemental Orthodox principle that graceless beings were sinners, the dogma which all Calvinists upheld against the Unitarians. As a Calvinist pointed out to a comrade-in-arms, "We meet the enemy on very disadvantageous ground when we attempt to determine *when* man becomes a moral agent."[116] Caught between conflicting pressures, the ministers of the New Haven school took the path of least resistance. They insisted that upon the assumption of moral agency sinning immediately began, and then suppressed discussion about the exact time that infants attained this status, while endeavoring to leave the impression that it was near the start of their existence. By treating the innocence of infants as a minor matter rather than as a major exception, the New Haven ministers hoped that the conservatives could be appeased, and the Unitarians denied a significant concession. The dogma of the universal sinfulness of natural men would be kept afloat, if with a bit of a list. Taylor advised:

> Instead then of attempting to assign the precise instant in which men begin to sin, we choose to say they sin as soon as they become moral agents—they sin *as soon as they can*; and who will affirm that this is not soon enough? If it be asked how soon, can they sin? I answer very early . . . *so early* that the literal interval, if there be such an interval, between birth and the commencement of sin is either so short or unimportant, that the Spirit of inspiration [Scripture] has not thought it worthy of notice.[117]

The conservatives were not satisfied. Beecher's fears came true as the New Haven school was drawn into public controversy not only with the Unitarians, but with those among the followers of Edwards and Hopkins who disliked these modifications of

Calvinism, as well as with the tribe of Old Calvinists who still clung to Puritan formulations. The battle over revisionism spread outside of New England to include clergymen in New York, Pennsylvania, and New Jersey. And it involved other thorny areas besides the infant question, such as the nature of regeneration and the dialectics of free will and necessity.[118]

Amidst disputations that tended to be very abstract, the infant issue offered a refreshing concreteness. The conservatives asserted that a native endowment which inevitably led to wickedness was intrinsically evil: "The causes of sinful choices, which exist in the disposition, or temper of the soul itself, are sinful."[119] To justify being born already guilty, some of the conservatives attempted to refurbish the much battered idea of Adam as a federal representative, his guilt imputed to the infant.[120] They dismissed the problem of accountability for personal sins by contending that since infants possessed rational souls, and were capable of exercises of pleasure and displeasure, they must be moral agents from birth.[121] At Presbyterian Princeton, the securest bastion of the Old Calvinists, the Puritans' Augustino-federal version of original sin would be maintained for the rest of the century, [122] the theology of Cotton Mather in the age of Charles Darwin.

The question of infant nature had turned into a technical problem for the New Haven school, an aspect of the interminable theological debates in which it engaged, rather than a device which could be used to make Calvinism more acceptable to the general public. The practicality of a man like Taylor only went so far.[123] He very much wanted to increase the attractiveness of Calvinism and, unlike the conservatives, he was not bound by tradition. Yet, in the final balance, Taylor was more concerned about the internal logic of his position, and about how to shape his arguments so as to minimize disharmony among the Orthodox, than about popular effects. His basic stance was that of the theologian rather than of the preacher, as in this rebuttal of a conservative's attack: "Should Mr. Harvey consent simply to say, that there *may be* at least *one indivisible moment* between the event of birth and the event of sin, and that the language of the Scriptures in its true import does not *deny* this; then the parties may come together on the point."[124] The notion of an instant of existence free from sin was not going to make the slightest change in the public's unfavorable impression of the Calvinist version of infant nature; only on the battlefields of logic did it have value. A conservative aptly designated the discussion of the moral agency gap, "a mere metaphysical quibble."[125]

The New Haven school was more successful in dealing with the allegation that Calvinism consigned numerous infants to hell. Coming to terms with it was risky. "In respect to the entire doctrine of original sin," wrote Lyman Beecher in 1825, "... I have long been of the opinion that the policy is unwise of making that doctrine the hinge of controversy between the orthodox and Arminians, because, as it respects the character and destiny of infants, it gives to the enemy the advantage of the popular side; [and] because the discussion carries us unavoidably into darkness and depths where the enemy have as good a chance as ourselves."[126] Lyman Beecher, however, was not a man who liked to back down from a fight. Within three years, he was ignoring his own advice and attempting to use the destiny of infants to bolster Calvinism's appeal. The premier issue of his magazine, *Spirit of the Pilgrims,* contained a Beecher article which in its very title made the daring announcement: "Future Punishment of Infants not a Doctrine of Calvinism." Lyman Beecher thus became the first major American Calvinist to disavow infant damnation publicly and explicitly, as bold a stroke in its way as Jonathan Edwards's theological reformulations. His action reversed the traditional Calvinist policy, which had been to separate the question of infant character from that of infant destiny in order to be definite about the existence of depravity, while being evasive about the possibility of damnation. Beecher continued the separation, but was evasive about the innocent stage of infant character, along with the rest of the New Haven school, and definite about the impossibility of damnation. By implication, he upheld the certainty of infant entry into heaven, just as past Calvinists had by implication suggested the likelihood of an infant presence in hell.[127]

The moment was ripe for Beecher to make his stand. By the 1820s, hints from the Calvinist pulpit of infant damnation had become few and far between as the clergy either absorbed the public's intensified hostility toward the doctrine, or prudently chose not to stir up such feelings. However, the specific timing was dictated by the Unitarians. The rumors and misinformation they spread about Calvinist positions had long bothered the Orthodox. Beecher was convinced that many knew of Calvinism only "as caricatured *in terrorem*."[128] An accusation that a particular theological position dictated the damnation of infants was believed to be so effective a polemical device that on occasion the Congregationalists themselves lobbed a few stones of this sort at Baptists and Episcopalians, ignoring for the moment their own glass dwelling.[129] In the 1820s the Unitarians added an important new element to such campaigns by employing formal scholarship. Luminaries like Andrews Norton of the Harvard Divinity School supplemented the work of the rumor mongers with historical commentary designed to demonstrate that Calvinism had always upheld the doctrine of infant damnation.[130] If these scholarly indictments were to go unanswered, New England's Calvinists would be more yoked to the repellent doctrine than ever before, at the very time when the New Haven school's emphasis on voluntarism and the use of the related techniques of revivalism offered the chance to increase Orthodoxy's popular appeal.

Beecher, who in 1826 had moved from a pastorate in Litchfield, Connecticut to one in Boston, carrying the counterattack into the very heartland of the foe, assumed the responsibility of replying to the formal Unitarian charges, although he was far from being the most able scholar among the Orthodox.[131] The ensuing debate differed from previous Calvinist-Unitarian encounters on the infant question in being a rather tedious dispute about the history of theology, with comparatively slight use of lurid rhetoric (but with considerable personal abusiveness), and in having the crafty Lyman Beecher rather than the maladroit Peter Clark or the leaden Leonard Woods as the champion of Calvinism.

At the start of the encounter Beecher acted with less than his usual shrewdness. He exposed himself to the barrage of Unitarian scholarship by making an extraordinary remark that his own son later conceded to have been rash:

> I am aware that Calvinists are represented as believing, and teaching, the monstrous doctrine that infants are damned, and that hell is doubtless paved with their bones. But having passed the age of fifty, and been conversant for thirty years with the most approved Calvinistic writers, and personally

acquainted with many of the most distinguished Calvinistic divines in New-England, and in the middle and southern and western States, I must say, that I have never seen or heard of any book which contained such a sentiment, nor a man, minister or layman, who believed or taught it.[132]

To refute Beecher was easy. The Unitarians used explicit declarations of infant damnation by European Calvinists, usually of the sixteenth and seventeenth centuries—Calvin himself, Turretin, Beza, Twiss, etc.—men who had been singlemindedly concerned with upholding the absolute sovereignty of God. A second line of attack consisted of citations from various Calvinists on native depravity, from which the Unitarians inferred that since infants were born in a sinful state, they must go to hell if they died without benefit of saving grace. Like the eighteenth-century Liberals, the Unitarians found few American Calvinists on whom an unambiguous case could be built, citing extensively only Jonathan Edwards, Joseph Bellamy and the inevitable Michael Wigglesworth.[133]

Forced to back down, Beecher declared that he had meant only that American Calvinists shunned infant damnation, in particular the New England clergy since the time of Edwards. He quibbled over which theologians of the distant past had actually upheld the doctrine, even claiming that Calvin had not taught it, but he was ready to repudiate any who had done so, including Wigglesworth. Despite the insistence of the Unitarians, he would not allow contemporary Calvinists to bear responsibility for the views of remote ancestors.[134] The attack by inference presented a more difficult problem. To meet it, Beecher, who was something of a pious P. T. Barnum, indulged in sophistry. He admitted that in the traditional version of original sin infants possessed sufficient guilt to send them to hell. He then argued, quite properly, that this version did not assert that damnation actually occurred, and, most dubiously, that it did not even suggest the likelihood: "That this deserved punishment is in fact inflicted, the doctrine does not say, and does not imply."[135] Some of Beecher's own evidence showed otherwise. In the course of his discussion he referred to Joseph Bellamy's opinion that if any of the newly born "die and go into eternity with their native temper, they must necessarily be miserable,"[136] a typical example of the sort of infant damnation by implication which had once been common in New England. Beecher wanted too much; he could not be satisfied with clearing the name of contemporary Calvinists, he had to expunge the doctrine from the American record.

Emphatically rejecting infant damnation, Beecher said nothing directly about the certainty of infant salvation, leaving it to the reader to make the inference. Yet, the New Haven version of original sin seemed to provide a ready-made explanation of why heaven was guaranteed to infants, or at least those dying before the assumption of moral agency. Since they were free of guilt for Adam's crime, for their inherited nature, and for personal sins, what could bar them from heaven? Beecher's failure to develop this argument can be attributed to his fear of adding to the divisions within Calvinism. In the middle of his controversy with the Unitarians a principal figure of Andover Seminary sent a letter politely, but firmly, asking that Beecher "not use the *plural pronoun* in debate with Unitarians. You should speak for yourself only. You must be aware that on the subject of infant damnation, for example, your Calvinistic brethren would not have chosen you as an organ to express their views in many respects as you have done."[137] With such querulous allies, Beecher dared not offer positive arguments for universal infant salvation, which would have been the best way of all to demonstrate that contemporary Calvinists did not believe that any little ones were damned. As a result, the engagement with the Unitarians ended inconclusively, although the decisive repudiation of those who had explicitly consigned the newly born to hell must have improved the public standing of Beecher's brand of Orthodoxy.

Even so, disavowals of infant damnation, no matter how strongly expressed, were limited in what they could accomplish. At best, they reduced a long time stigma and diminished the tendency of people to turn away from Calvinism in revulsion. But stopping decline was a different matter from making up lost ground. Disavowals could not convert the Calvinist stand on the question of infant destiny into a substantial asset in the effort to win new friends; negatives are seldom great proselytizing devices. Only an unequivocal declaration that Calvinism upheld the salvation of all infants would do, for in the 1820s the general public would accept nothing less. And by providing positive evidence that the Orthodox no longer believed in the damnation of infants, the declaration would thwart any lingering Unitarian hopes of further exploiting this issue for major polemical advantage. (The Unitarians did continue to exploit original sin as it related to infancy, only slightly hindered by the New Haven school's revisions.)

Nathaniel W. Taylor and Chauncey Goodrich took the momentous step. In an apparent effort to mollify the conservatives, they achieved the salvation of infants by extending Christ's mediation to the entire class, rather than by using the infant's initial lack of guilt for a direct claim on heaven (as the public was doing). Taylor declared: "If then you ask, what becomes of an infant if he dies, while yet an infant?—I answer, he may be saved; in my belief he is saved, through the redemption that is in Christ Jesus."[138] The conservatives, however, refused to ignore the New Haven school's revisionist version of original sin, even when it was kept in the background. They insisted that Christ's atonement applied only to sinners, and so could be of no avail to infants if they were guiltless. A critic of Taylor inquired, "What infant, who has in fact never been under the dominion of sin, can say, Christ has redeemed him to God by his blood? . . . It still remains for the author of this sermon to tell, what becomes of that large portion of the human race who die in infancy."[139]

Ironically, the very absence of guilt which the New Haven school had used to release infants from the danger of hell threatened to keep them out of heaven. The problem proved to be too much for one member, Eleazar Fitch, who left the fate of infants unresolved.[140] To get around the dilemma, Taylor offered the explanation that Christ secured grace for infants as a preventive of sin rather than as a cure. At birth infants were innocent, but when they reached moral agency they were certain to commit transgressions and become iniquitous. By sending for infants at an earlier point and bringing them into heaven, a merciful deity saved the little ones from the inevitable fall: "What then if God, to avert these evils from one class of the human race, before they become accountable subjects of his moral government in this world, translates them to another, that they may never partake in the pollution of sin, but wake up there in the beauty of holiness."[141] This idea was similar to the popular rationalization of death which assumed that had the infant lived his innocence probably would have been to some degree corrupted by the wickedness of the world.[142] The differences were that the Calvinistic Taylor regarded the corruption as certain, as total, and as springing from human nature rather than from the environment.

A potential sinfulness did not meet conservative standards. Infants had to be full-fledged evildoers in order to take part in the processes of salvation. Consequently, some conservatives believed that they were being solicitous of infants in rejecting the revisionists' sinless interval and viewing the little ones as guilty from birth, which would make them eligible for grace. "Christ came to save sinners," Joseph Harvey insisted, "and by proving that infants are sinners, we prove that they may be saved by Christ. . . . But if they are not sinners, it is difficult, if not impossible, to find the least ground of encouragement concerning their future blessedness."[143] Original sin, long attacked for implying the damnation of infants, was now being justified on the basis that it gave the best chance for their salvation. The conservatives were not immune to the pressures of the age.

A handful did fight to retain the doctrine of infant damnation. The Reverend Alvan Hyde, an Edwardean, stated that children "are capable, while infants, of being *saved*, and liable to be *lost— eternally lost*. . . . They will have a place assigned them in the future world, and will be seen among the inhabitants of heaven or hell."[144] With the exception of Wigglesworth's *Day of Doom*, this declaration of 1830 was as explicit an avowal of the likelihood of infant damnation as had ever been made in New England. How Lyman Beecher must have been chagrined when he learned of it!

Hyde spoke for those who retained the conviction of the Puritans and of Jonathan Edwards that morally and theologically infants and adults shared the same situation. The dogged persistence of this kind of tough, unyielding Calvinism is remarkable, but those who kept it up were a minority, and a dwindling one. As the Romantic movement came into its own in the 1830s and 1840s, filling the sky with infant cherubs ascending to the kingdom of God, [145] even most conservatives were affected. Except for diehards like Hyde, they came to see that abandoning infant damnation had substantial advantages, as long as it did not entail surrendering infant sinfulness as well. They were not really giving up very much, anyway. After the turn of the nineteenth century, infant damnation had so rarely received any determined presentation, in contrast to original sin, that with some justification conservatives could refuse to recognize the doctrine as being a legitimate part of the American Calvinist heritage which they were obliged to defend.

A case in point was Gardiner Spring, an Old School Presbyterian of New York and generally a foe of the New Haven theology. Despite his conservatism, Spring was almost as optimistic as the revisionists on the question of deceased infants, while treating it far more sentimentally. In his semi-traditional defense of original sin, *A Dissertation on Native Depravity*, Spring remarked: "That the grace of God, through Jesus Christ, rescues all infants from perdition, I do not deny, but fondly hope; that it rescues untold millions, I have not a doubt. . . . This race of fallen infants is the object of his greatest love—his most distinguished and distinguishing mercy. . . . It were a higher privilege, therefore to be created an infant than an angel."[146] In this mixture of the old and the new, infants were both sinful from birth and an elevated class.

The retention in the conservative explanation of a native sinfulness disturbed the revisionists, just as its absence from the revisionist explanation had upset the conservatives. In a review of Gardiner Spring's book, Nathaniel W. Taylor criticized his version of original sin for compelling the damnation of infants. Since the very young were incapable of repenting their sinfulness or of showing faith in God, necessary conditions for receiving divine pardon and undergoing spiritual regeneration, to die soon after they entered the world as sinners made a fiery doom certain. "None of them according to Dr. Spring's principles can be saved," complained Taylor, "His scheme of making infants sinners for their own benefit, and to avoid throwing them out of the economy of redemption, throws them into the lake of fire."[147]

The final turn in the history of infant damnation had been reached: a Calvinist, who was endeavoring to save all infants, was criticizing a fellow Calvinist, who also wanted to place all infants in heaven, for not achieving it. Taylor and Spring were definitely in accord on ends, if not means. With both revisionist Calvinists and most of the conservative ones trying to keep infants out of the lake of fire, the possibility of the damnation of any of their number faded out of Calvinism itself, the intransigence of a few notwithstanding. Shortly before mid-century, Horace Bushnell asked a Sunday school body, "Is there any one of your respectable

committee, who entertains the distinction of elect and nonelect
infants at all? We may not have reasoned ourselves out of this once
familiar distinction, as pertaining to infants; but it is gone: time
has killed it."[148]

Epilogue

Pronounced dead by Bushnell and other knowledgeable witnesses at mid-century, the corpse of infant damnation nevertheless
sporadically showed deceptive signs of life. Now and then an
unreconstructed Calvinist came out of the New England hills to
create a brief flurry of controversy with the contention that "it is
most natural and proper to infer that if any of the human race are
lost, some infants may be." Even these diehards had to admit that
nearly everyone else was convinced of the contrary.[149] Others
occasionally bestowed a semblance of life on infant damnation by
reenacting the 1820s and 1830s debates between revisionists and
conservatives over which version of original sin truly provided for
the salvation of infants, and which doomed them.[150] As the
historian Paul Hazard observed in another context, "A doctrine
lives on for a long time, even when wounded, even when its soul
has fled."[151] And after death, it can persist as a ghost.

Like most eras, the mid-nineteenth century was not lacking
people eager to beat a corpse or tilt at a ghost. By doing so, they
could perhaps force some last bit of polemical advantage out of the
doctrine of infant damnation. The Unitarians by and large
refrained from such attacks, having long before obtained all the
benefits to be had from exploiting the issue, but newer foes of
Calvinism wanted their innings.[152] The most audacious were the
Swedenborgians. Borrowing heavily from the Unitarian scholarship of the 1820s, they demonstrated that infant damnation had
once been a major Calvinist doctrine.[153] In opposition to this
dogma of the past they presented their own elaborate version of
universal infant salvation, describing how the little ones mentally
and physically matured in heaven, under the tutelage of good
angels. (Swedenborg maintained that he had talked with such
angels, as well as with some who had entered heaven as babies.)[154]
Conceding that few Calvinists, if any, still professed a belief in
infant damnation, the Swedenborgians brashly claimed that the

light spread by their own sect had ended it.[155] Having flogged the corpse, they demanded credit for the kill.

The remains of infant damnation still gave an occasional twitch in the late nineteenth century. Roman Catholics, who had not been a party to the earlier debates in America, defended their traditional belief that baptism was necessary for the salvation of infants, but viewed the limbo to which the unbaptized were consigned as a "state of endless happiness, much better than anything to be found in this world," although, of course, inferior to heaven.[156] Within Protestantism, a minor incident occurred when the Lutheran theologian C. P. Krauth charged that the awful doctrine of infant damnation continued to be held by some Calvinists. A well-known Presbyterian divine, Charles Hodge, denied the slander.[157] Hodge and his colleagues at the Princeton Theological Seminary, the very seat of conservative Calvinism, had become the group most active in expunging any traces of infant damnation from both contemporary Calvinism and the recent historical record, taking on the role formerly held by New England ministers. One Princetonian wrote:

> It may seem surprising that after the death of Calvin bodies of Calvinists should have arisen in Holland and in Old and New England who taught not only the damnation of infants, but their reprobation and perdition in terms which would not now be endured in a Christian assembly. But it was not surprising that such teaching soon passed away into a merited oblivion. Nor is it surprising that at length the oblivion became so complete that consistent Calvinists, like Lyman Beecher and Charles Hodge, could declare that they never knew a Calvinist who held the doctrine.[158]

That the most significant and hotly disputed questions of one age are often irrelevant to the next, at least in the terms and manner in which they had been fought, is well known. Yet, all social groups do not necessarily participate in the change at the same time, so that to a certain extent contemporaries may be living in different ages. In mid-nineteenth-century New England, debate over the related doctrines of original sin and infant damnation was still going on, but for most people the subject had lost its meaning.

Of course, theology, in general, had long been declining as a matter of compelling importance. Benjamin Franklin's *The Way to Wealth,* a collection of Poor Richard maxims which appeared in 1757, had been considerably more popular than Jonathan Edwards's *The Great Christian Doctrine of Original Sin Defended,* which was posthumously published the next year. What made the early nineteenth century a new age for some was that groups which had traditionally been highly interested in theological discussion became indifferent to it. Writing in 1829, a conservative Calvinist lamented, "The time was, when such authors as Edwards and Bellamy, Flavel and Baxter, were more read by the body of ministers and professed Christians in our land, than they are at present." A member of the New Haven school concurred, implying that many clergymen possessed a greater desire to make a name in the expanding system of philanthropic and missionary institutions than to chop doctrine.[159] Religion *per se* was not declining; on the contrary, in the second quarter of the nineteenth century it had again become the main determinant of American culture as during Puritan times and the Great Awakening, but its intellectual expression, embodied in theology, was less important.

The 1820s and 1830s were the last period in which the theological complexities of original sin as relating to infants, and the doctrinal arguments for and against their damnation, could summon any interest from the general populace. Although in succeeding decades the Swedenborgians flayed away at the corpse of infant damnation and seminarians dueled with its ghost in the theological journals, few watched. By the time of the Civil War the debate on infancy could seem as remote as a medieval disputation. In a not unsympathetic review of Lyman Beecher's *Autobiography,* the *Atlantic Monthly* of 1865 remarked that "Whether the two-year-old baby who dashes his bread-and-butter on the floor, in wrath at the lack of marmalade, does it because of a prevailing effectual tendency in his nature, or in consequence of his federal alliance with Adam, or from a previous surfeit of plumcake" was a question with as much contemporary relevance as the scholastic conflict between Nominalism and Realism.[160] Some failed to notice, but the overdue obituary for the infant issue had been posted.

PART TWO

The Living Child

III. The Methodology of Upbringing

The Child Psychology
of Timothy Dwight

The Literature of Domestic Education

IN 1689 COTTON MATHER attempted to counsel bereaved parents by reminding them of some harsh facts: "A dead child is a sight no more surprising than a broken pitcher, or a blasted flower."[1] Few would have quareled with the statement at the time, or when *Right Thoughts in Sad Hours* was republished, over a century later, in 1811. Yet, in both Puritan days and the early national period more children lived than died. Except in the unluckier families, or in times of epidemics, for every infant who perished two or more survived.[2] Most parents knew what it was like both to lose offspring and to rear them to maturity.

By the nineteenth century mothers and fathers could turn to a substantial body of literature for help in the task of upbringing. Unlike today, this literature was not written by professionals in child care, but by philosophers, clergymen, articulate parents, and general practitioner doctors. Almost anyone who had some acquaintance with children (and even that was not an absolute necessity) could set himself or herself up as an authority on domestic education.

The influence of this literature upon the general public is hard to estimate. Works on domestic education did not have a mass circulation before the 1830s, except for some pamphlets of the American Tract Society and a few republished English books.

Much of the advice to parents was contained in periodical articles, printed sermons, and an occasional treatise; this material had a limited, although by no means negligible, audience. On the other hand, there was more child-rearing literature than ever before. And some New Englanders, eager to obtain guidance, took pains to secure the writings of recognized authorities. One purpose of the maternal societies which were organized in the early nineteenth century was to provide a way for mothers to become acquainted with the available material. Boston's Federal Street Baptist Maternal Society perused portions of "the most valuable works" on child rearing at the monthly meetings, and levied fifty cents in dues for the "formation of a select library, for the use of the members."[3] Access to expert advice on upbringing became easier in the 1830s with the appearance of a new semipopularized literature intended for a mass audience. John S. C. Abbott's *The Mother at Home* (1833) introduced the best seller to this field and the sociology of guidance in child rearing was permanently altered.

No matter how disseminated, advice on upbringing, if at all extensive, usually consisted of three levels of discussion. On the most general one, *rationale*, the overall goals of child rearing were set forth. On the second level, *psychology*, both the universal characteristics of human nature and the special characteristics of the juvenile mind were analyzed. On the last and most specific level, *methodology*, rules were given for the daily household routine on such matters as the display of affection, the manner of punishment, and the techniques of moral instruction.

As a result of this tripartite structure, child-rearing advice served both as a formal ideology and as a family guidebook. In regard to the first aspect, the more abstract one, various schools of thought can be readily discerned. In regard to the second and more concrete aspect, definite schools are less evident as eclecticism tended to be the rule. Since so many of the specific guidelines of family management were widely shared, they are most easily presented by focusing on the writings of one authority, Timothy Dwight (1752-1817), whose views were in large part typical of his era.[4] In addition, the use of biographical elements reveals how private experience, as well as the larger cultural context, helped to shape ideas about domestic education.

An Expert for His Times

During the course of a half century of adult responsibilities, which commenced at age seventeen, Timothy Dwight played a father's role in over two thousand lives.[5] Most of the brood were his students. At Yale, where Dwight was tutor from 1771 to 1777, and president from 1795 to 1817, he introduced a highly paternalistic style: "I stand as a Father to the Youths, whom I am about to address. . . . They have been wholly committed to my parental care; and are now about to receive my last parental office. . . . Let me, then, Young Gentlemen, my pupils, my children, endeared to me by many affecting considerations, address to you the following counsels."[6] He had undoubtedly used the same approach in teaching school children in New Haven, in Northampton, and in Greenfield Hill, Connecticut, where he had established a well-known academy while serving as pastor. A dozen of its students customarily boarded at his home, making for even more of a parent-child relationship.[7]

Dwight also bore the appearance of a surrogate parent towards his brothers and sisters. With the untimely death of their father in 1777, Timothy, as the eldest, had assumed responsibility for stabilizing the family finances and managing his dozen siblings.[8] Even his proud mother, a daughter of Jonathan Edwards, was said to regard him in a way which "resembled the affection of a dutiful child towards her father, rather than the feelings of a mother for her son,"[9] a relationship unlikely to be so unblushingly reported by a present-day grandson for its ambiguities are obvious. Last of Dwight's brood, and perhaps in some ways least, were his own eight sons who benefited from whatever time was left from his duties as clergyman, teacher, and administrator; his theological and literary projects; and his many travels in New England and New York.[10]

This diffusive fatherhood gave Dwight an acquaintance with children in their various stages which was as extensive as that of any man of his era. With justification, he thought of himself as an expert on the psychology of juveniles and the methods of management which were suitable to it: "I have taught many little children, and have had such experience that I know pretty well the state of their minds."[11] He was contemptuous of those who wrote about children without having observed them closely, for they merely gave "the speculations of the closet. These, however ingenious, must often err; and not being founded on facts, will frequently be found inapplicable to the real circumstances of life."[12] Today, Dwight would not be considered an expert on child psychology because he lacked rigorous training and did not use systematic techniques of observation. But each period has its own definition of who qualifies as an expert on a subject, and Dwight met the test of his times. "I have just read Dwight's sermons on the duty of parents to their children, and of children to their parents," wrote a father in 1819, "And while I find them very instructive and entertaining, I feel greatly reproved for my unfaithfulness as a parent."[13]

His influence was not confined to his publications. Most of Dwight's child psychology was presented to Yale students in the form of sermons (which were to constitute the body of his *Theology*), as well as in more informal classroom talks. Many of these undergraduates were profoundly influenced by Dwight—"had their principles, literary, political, moral, and religious, settled for life."[14] Some of them must have used his ideas in their own families (as Lyman Beecher seems to have done), and in the advice they gave to other parents.

Dwight's ideas about child psychology were representative of the mainstream of Calvinist thought in the early national period. Indeed, Dwight was at the very center of the Calvinist tradition as it entered its final epoch. Although his theology generally followed the lines laid down by his grandfather, Jonathan Edwards, he resisted what he considered to be Samuel Hopkins's extreme extensions of the Edwardean system. After Dwight's death, one of his sons remarked, "My father was very far from a zealot, & generally pleased moderate men of all parties." Having little interest in original theological speculation or doctrinal controversy, Dwight devoted himself to mining the common seams of New England Calvinism.[15]

At the same time, he was well acquainted with a number of Enlightenment ideas. He formally disagreed with some of the abstract aspects of the Enlightenment approach to child rearing (although the implications of his writings occasionally contradicted his explicit statements), but he concurred on many of the particulars of domestic management. Advice for handling the depraved child was much closer to that for the plastic child, than to Romantic precepts intended for a cherub-like being. At odds over parts of the general strategy of domestic education, Calvinism and Lockeanism harmonized very well on everyday tactics.

The scientific approach to the study of children that has become dominant in the twentieth century has shunted these earlier psychological expositions and methodological programs into an obscurity that is, on the whole, deserved. Nevertheless, today's highly trained experts have in several instances come up with the same principles. Just as a sometimes impressive understanding of the complexities of the adult mind predates the work of modern specialists, insight into the psychology of children existed in the past.[16] With or without specialized techniques, common sense could go a long way.

The Parental Mind

Timothy Dwight's child psychology began not with the mind of the child, but with the minds of its progenitors. His analyses of how children think and act were largely derived from his examination of the role parents were to play. This child psychology was not so much descriptive as programmatic, similar in connotation to the term "child psychology" in its present-day popular usage. Since he was instructing parents on the methodology of upbringing, he had to take into account their psyches, along with those of their offspring.

With his extensive practice in the duties of a parent, Dwight was not likely to underestimate the burdens that child rearing placed upon mothers and fathers. The raising of children would be the hardest task most people faced. In Dwight's best poem, the long *Greenfield Hill*, a wise farmer remarks to his fellow villagers that, "'of all your toil, and care,/ Your children claim the largest share.'"[17] Parental duties included providing children with adequate food, clothing, and shelter; instructing them in morality, religion, the three "R's" and, to some extent, general knowledge; and placing them in the employment in which they could best serve man and God. Dwight's Puritan ancestors had said almost the same thing.[18]

Given the labor and self-sacrifice that effective child rearing required, the "ten thousand supplies, cares, and tendernesses,"[19] what motivated people to fulfill this duty? Dwight believed that it was parental love. No other force could sustain the burdens. Despite afflictions like poverty, misfortune, the ingratitude or even rebellion of a child, parental love persisted.[20] Dwight was almost as effusive on this subject as a Romantic. In contrast to the Puritans, he seldom warned about the danger of the love of children overshadowing the love of God or advised limits on parental affection. The obsessive love described by Philippe Ariès was becoming the order of the day. "Parental love," exulted Dwight, "is unrivalled by any affection of the human breast in its strength, its tenderness, its patience, its permanency, and its cheerful self-denial."[21]

This master emotion was elicited by the particular nature of the human baby. Partly anticipating John Fiske's ideas about the civilizing effects of infant dependency, Dwight observed that a baby's trials and throes made him an object of great solicitude while his complete helplessness summoned extensive efforts from his guardians. The more they did for the little one, the more they loved him. As a result, parental affection was not a mere animal-like instinct, but an emotion that was both resonant and exalted. According to Dwight, "An ample reward is furnished for all the labour, expense, and suffering, undergone in their behalf, by their health, their safety, their comforts, and their smiles."[22] This linear type of psychological theorizing ignored the ambiguities of the parent-child relationship and the likelihood of some feelings of resentment—if not outright hatred—on the part of the mother or father.[23]

Dwight did make his analysis more intricate by distinguishing parental love as found in the framework of the nuclear family from the same emotion in other settings, such as a system of "promiscuous concubinage." What was strong and enduring in the former case was weak and impermanent in the latter.[24] But this opinion was less the result of study than of ethnocentric bias in favor of the Western family as opposed to other forms, which Dwight probably associated with the exoticism of Asia. Furthermore, it compounded the problem of explaining why individuals in proper monogamous marriages often turned out to be deficient in the duties of child rearing. Love for children was supposed to be "always existing, and flourishing, in Married Parents, with so few exceptions," yet this master emotion was readily thrust aside by such common vices as laziness, drunkenness, and excessive personal ambition. A father who played an important part in the upbringing of his children was offset by the one who totally consigned their care to an overburdened wife. The sons observed "'their father roam,/ And riot, rake, and reign, at home./ Too late he sees, and sees to mourn,/ His race of every hope forlorn.'"[25] Having paid tribute to the grandeur of parental love, Dwight reverted to a tone of traditional Calvinist pessimism and made the impulses of depravity and the temptations of the environment at least as potent.

To bolster a commitment to child rearing that could be overcome all too easily, Dwight, along with most other Orthodox clergymen, invoked the threat of hell for a job poorly done. Children left unrestrained and unimproved were almost certain to be damned. Dwight presented the standard vision of the Last Judgment at work, asking parents to imagine the feelings of those who must watch their offspring being condemned to eternal torment.[26] The same terrible fate threatened parents themselves. Because child rearing was a task ordained by God, to fail at it through lack of proper application was exceedingly sinful. Dwight reminded mothers and fathers who had become wearied by the endless burdens of upbringing or discouraged by the lack of success that "these reasons for their negligence will be unhappily alleged at the final day."[27] Since the saliency of hell was diminishing in the early nineteenth century, such threats were probably less intensely frightening than when Cotton Mather had employed them. But those who had remained staunch Calvinists could still be strongly moved. One mother reflected: "I have had much solicitude for my children this evening. At one time, such a sense of the everlasting consequences of the trust committed to me, in reference to their immortal souls, rushed upon me, as literally made me shudder."[28]

When Dwight talked about the nature of parental love and the duties required in child rearing, he especially had in mind the role of mothers: "The mother gives the first turn and cast to the mind. Her province is infinitely more valuable than that of the father."[29] His own mother had been the predominant force in his upbringing as Major Dwight had been too involved in agricultural and mercantile endeavors to be more than a peripheral influence. Many years later, when the Yale president spoke of Mary Edwards Dwight his eyes were said to shine with uncommon brightness. Upon her death, he declared: "All that I am and all that I shall be, I owe to my mother."[30] Since, to be conjectural, Dwight had belatedly triumphed in the Oedipal rivalry and by being "father" to his mother was really being "husband," his statement probably had implications he could not have intended.

Dwight himself had a general theory as to why women often had a larger influence within the family than men. The great dangers involved in pregnancy and birth forced females to confront the fact of their own mortality and gave extra force to the Christian message that life on earth was but a trial for the life to come. As a result, women were more likely to be "unaffectedly pious, humble, benevolent, patient, and self-denying."[31] These virtues, which "put our own sex to shame," happened to be ideal for the family situation. Since they were to a large extent the traditional Christian virtues, exercising them increased the chances of salvation. Dwight estimated that the proportion of women to men in heaven would be two to one.[32] The ladies of New England were likely to be especially well represented. During his travels, Dwight found them to be "almost universally industrious, economical, attentive to their families, and diligent in the education and government of their children."[33]

To ensure the perpetuation of female domestic virtuousness, Dwight advocated very different role conditioning for young girls and young boys. The rustic sage in *Greenfield Hill* told the villagers to train their sons to be bold in the face of danger and impervious to fear: "'Teach them each *manly art to prize,*/ And

base effem'nancy despise,/ Teach them to wrestle, leap, and run,/
To win the palm, and prize it, won.'" A contrasting regimen was
in order for the girls of the community:

> *'With gentler hand, your daughters train,*
> The housewife's various arts to gain;
> O'er scenes domestic to preside;
> The needle, wheel, and shuttle, guide;
> The peacock's gaudry to despise,
> And view vain sports with parents' eyes.'[34]

As such advice had long been common wisdom, Dwight was
telling New England what it already believed, rather than
contributing anything new. However, he was slightly ahead of the
time in his views on formal education for females. Instead of a
mere introduction to traditional learning, followed by a smatter-
ing of music, painting, and dance for the daughters of the affluent,
Dwight proposed that girls receive as thorough an academic
training as boys. Against prevailing opinion, he suggested that the
sexes were evenly matched in mental acuity: "The great doctrines
of physical and moral science are as intelligible by the mind of a
female, as by that of a male." He conducted his schools in
Northampton and Greenfield Hill on the basis of an equal
academic education for both sexes.[35] Nevertheless, Dwight was not
attempting to emancipate women from their domestic station. His
goal was simply to make them better qualified to fulfill its duties,
the most important of which was child rearing.[36] Dwight had
presaged the response to rising female aspirations that was
commonly offered in later eras: advanced training would be made
available, but only for the purpose of improving performance in
the traditional tasks.

The father's role in child rearing was also important, if
considerably less substantial than that of the mother. Without his
support, she might easily fail, as did the woman in *Greenfield Hill*
whose husband abandoned domestic duties.[37] Joint parental effort
required complete accord on the scheme of management. Along
with other experts of the time, Dwight advised parents to present a
united front to their offspring, a principle which has remained a
staple in the lore of child rearing. Mothers and fathers should

'In every plan, harmonious meet;
The conduct each of each approve.
What one commands, let both require;
In counsels, smiles, and frowns, conspire;
Alike oppose; alike befriend;
And each the other's choice commend.'[38]

Concurring upon the Calvinist theory of child rearing and allied in its practice, parents had a good chance to shape a child into an individual who was virtuous in both character and conduct. Having contributed to that accomplishment, a mother or a father could contemplate the Day of Judgment without undue alarm.

The Governing of Children: The Restrictive Phases

When parents of today consult popular works on child psychology for advice about upbringing they usually find a textual arrangement based on the child's developmental stages as correlated with chronological age. Certain things can be expected of the body and mind of a one year old, other things of a one-and-a-half year old, and so on through adolescence. Timothy Dwight and his contemporaries were far less sophisticated about development. Except for the broad categories of infancy, childhood, and youth they made relatively few distinctions about changing mental and physical phases. Instead, their expositions of child psychology were based on moral stages. They assessed development not in terms of visually-directed reaching, stranger anxiety, and parallel play, but in terms of levels of virtue or wickedness.

Calvinists like Dwight assumed that the infant possessed a high—although not the highest—level of wickedness. The practical manifestations of original sin and native depravity, far more important in the daily routine than the doctrine's complex theology, were "infantine selfishness, wrath, revenge, and cruelty. . . . Ingratitude, and rebellion. . . . Unbrotherly and unsisterly coldness and alienation."[39] The list was virtually endless, for only a few of the evil attitudes grownups indulged could not be found among children. Yet, the little ones were less iniquitous than mature sinners. Their smaller abilities drastically limited the harm they could do, and more importantly, their propensities to wickedness were weaker. Depravity was not a static property, but one which increased in strength as the individual advanced in years, unless checked by outside forces. Dwight used a standard metaphor to explain this fundamental point. Like weeds, evil tendencies grew best when left alone:

> 'So faults, inborn, spontaneous rise,
> And daily wax in strength, and size,
> Ripen, with neither toil, nor care,
> And choke each germ of virtue there.'[40]

In its own way, this perspective was a developmental one.

Dwight not only traced the course of depravity, but attempted to indicate its location in the faculties of the mind. In an earlier period depravity had been regarded as an extranatural quality, a special taint or pollution which the child inherited from his parents. Jonathan Edwards had rejected this account, substituting one in which depravity was a result of man's natural qualities. Although Dwight sometimes slipped into the old language—"a leprosy has seized the soul, & corrupted its whole constitution"[41]— he was aiming for rhetorical effect at such moments rather than theoretical precision. In his role as psychologist, Dwight repeated his grandfather's efforts to place depravity in the natural operations of the mind, but displayed considerably less skill. According to Dwight, depravity was seated in the force which activated the will, a rather vague *"Energy of the Mind"* or *"controlling Disposition,"* an *"unknown cause"* insofar as its exact operations were hidden from men.[42] He failed to use Edwards's explanation of motive, the will being moved by the strongest one, as a way of linking the temperament's disposition to evil with the specific acts of the will. As far as the blame went, the elements of the psyche most responsible for the bias towards evil were the appetites and the passions, "principles in the human mind, which perpetually prompt to wrong."[43]

By viewing the appetites and passions as the least worthy parts of the psyche, Dwight proved himself to be outside of the gathering Romantic movement whose mainstream celebrated the emotions. Of course, like virtually all Americans, he was not up-to-date on the most advanced work of European thought. While new truths and new ways of finding truth were being proclaimed, Dwight was still debating Paine and Voltaire. Yet, an increased emphasis on the nonrational elements of the mind had begun far back in the eighteenth century, the Age of Reason itself.[44] Edwards's demonstration that piety resided in the affections and not the intellect, the faculty for which Liberals like Charles Chauncy argued, was a part of this trend. Dwight even participated in it to the extent that he accepted the evangelical definition of true religion as being centered in the heart and expressed through the feelings.[45] Nevertheless, along with many of the New England Calvinists of the early national period, he remained highly suspicious of the emotions. In words that echoed the remarks of ministers and priests over many centuries, Dwight declared that "Christianity is a system of restraint on every passion, and every appetite. Some it forbids entirely: and all it confines within limits, which by the mass of mankind, both learned and unlearned, will be esteemed narrow and severe."[46] In his fundamental distrust of the emotions, Dwight was closer to the psychological views of both the seventeenth-century Puritans and their contemporary of the early Enlightenment, John Locke, than to the ideas of Romanticism which reached America soon after his death.[47]

A relentless battle had to be fought against the various vices that sprang from a child's undisciplined passions and appetites. Dwight was the very opposite of those recent child psychologists who have advised parents to take a lenient approach toward bad conduct because although a nuisance, it is just an aspect of some normal stage of development through which the child soon passes.[48] Bad conduct was not only annoying to parents, but a moral evil. Although natural and inevitable because of the defects of the human psyche, it was not to be tolerated. Nor did Dwight worry about the costs of repressing primal urges. If he saw in young children the instinctive selfishness that the Freudians later perceived, he did not possess their conviction that stifling it could result in the loss of energy and originality.[49] He insisted that depravity be stamped out, crushed, suppressed, without compromise: "Children should regularly be checked, and subdued, in every ebullition of passion; particularly of pride and anger."[50] As the weeds metaphor suggested, depravity could be most effectively "exterminated, or restrained" (Dwight was never consistent on whether parents were mainly doing the former or the latter) when it first appeared in the child. Left alone, it would become so extensive and entrenched that suppression would be all but impossible, even when severe methods were employed. Like good husbandmen examining their gardens, parents had to be aware of all their children's tendencies and be ever ready to nip the pernicious ones as soon as they surfaced. If they did not do it, probably no one ever would.[51]

The war against depravity required the establishment of firm parental authority. Unless the elders had total control, evil propensities could not be thoroughly subdued nor the path of virtue made plain. The test of authority was the degree of obedience its commands exacted from those under its domain. In reviewing civil society, Dwight, staunch Federalist that he was, stood for unwavering law and order. Similarly, his first principle of domestic management was that children be made to comply unfalteringly with parental wishes. In modern child-rearing lexicon he would be termed antipermissive. *"Children,"* he insisted, *"are bound to obey the Commands of their parents."*[52] According to Dwight's mother, he had in his own childhood perfectly fulfilled this obligation.[53] Nowadays, many would worry about a youngster who never disobeyed his parents,[54] but in Dwight's time it was a pleasing sign of a domestic regime that was as well managed as was possible.

Dwight was not so simplistic as to believe that disobedience by a child could never be legitimate. He made it clear that should a parent so forget himself as to give a command contrary to the laws of God, the duty of the child was to defy it.[55] But all told, Dwight devoted relatively little attention to the ways in which parental authority was limited. In many respects it was a difficult topic for him. As a young man he had taken part in a dramatic act of filial defiance insofar as the American Revolution, in which he served as a chaplain, was a child's assault on its progenitor. (Dwight once wrote, "NEW-ENGLAND Boasts a parent's name.")[56] At the same time, he was influenced by the Enlightenment's general mistrust of "the chains of authority." As late as 1789, he described America's cultural dependency upon Europe in terms of a too slavish obedience to a parental authority that was too long maintained.[57] With the excesses of the French Revolution in the 1790s, and especially the fear that they might be duplicated in America by Jeffersonian democrats, the Enlightenment emphasis on emancipation from fettering authority disappeared from Dwight's thought. His remarks on family government in the early nineteenth century sounded amazingly like the Loyalist presentation a generation before of the correct relationship between Mother England and her toddler colonies: the superior commanded and the subordinate obeyed. He even stressed the absolute nature of parental powers: "The parent's will is the only law to the child."[58]

As a result of his heightened emphasis on parental authority, Dwight was left in a poor position to explain the course of action to be taken by children with thoroughly depraved parents. Heir to the Reformation tradition and the Calvinist conscience, himself a one time revolutionary, Dwight could not deprive them of all rights of resistance. But as one disturbed by the execution of Louis XVI and the subsequent bloody rampages that swept France and apparently threatened America, he was hardly in the mood to make a strong case for dissent.[59] His discomfort with the subject was evident in the advice he offered. A child with sinful parents was expected to obey always, except when the commands were unlawful; to honor their status, but not their personal characters; to rebuke the elders' wickedness, while remaining submissive; and to avoid being wrongly influenced, without ceasing to be dutiful. The situation, in short, was "singularly embarrassing" (for Dwight as well as the child). He admitted that any juvenile who successfully resisted an evil environment without becoming rebellious, "may well be considered as eminently the object of the divine favour. Still it is possible."[60]

Where parental authority was properly exercised, the child had no legitimate reason for disobedience, and was not in need of an exceptional divine blessing to avoid being ruined by his upbringing. On the contrary, parents who gave lawful commands and thoroughly enforced them provided the best setting for a child's moral development. Total subordination to the parental will began as soon as the child was capable of reason. At that early moment, the necessity of complete obedience had to be "impressed so deeply, as never to be effaced." If parents correctly executed this task, acquiescence to their authority became an internalized principle in the child, a central element of his character. Controlled from within, he willingly carried out all legitimate parental commands.[61] As Dwight presented it, the process of subordination was rather subtle and complex, belying the frequent characterization of Calvinist child-rearing methodology as merely a crude effort to break the will. Sharp struggles between parent and child were the sign either of an unusual degree of depravity in the youngster, or of considerable mismanagement by the parent. Dwight was convinced that "If begun in season, the task of securing filial obedience will usually be easy"; "If children are taught effectively to obey at first; they will easily be induced to obey ever afterwards."[62] Harmony, not conflict, was to characterize the relationship between superior and subordinate.

To promote it, Dwight wanted children to act out their status inferiority in various ways. Obedience itself was not the only thing; equally important was the style in which children rendered it. They were expected to comply with parental commands immediately and cheerfully. Belated or begrudged obedience was "hypocritical; a cheat; a sin." By the same token, a deferential tone was as important in conversing with parents as what was said. Children "are required ever to speak modestly, submissively, and respectfully. . . . They are to address them, not as disputants; not as equals; but as children; as modest inferiors. Both their words, and their manner of uttering them, should bear unequivocal evidence, that they are conscious of this character." The thoughts and emotions of the child counted as well as his deeds. He was required to sustain in his mind an attitude not merely of respect for his parents, but of veneration, indeed of reverence. Once again, the likelihood of ambivalence was not even guessed at by Dwight, let alone condoned. All in all, a child could hardly pay enough tribute to those exalted beings, "appointed by God himself," who ruled over him. "Filial duties are so numerous," announced Dwight, "that many volumes might be written on this subject only, without particularizing them all."[63]

Dwight confined himself to a few pages, but his discussion still had an element of unreality to it. If children who fit his description of cheerful submissiveness were the only ones to qualify as exemplary, America seemed to be in short supply. Travelers of the early nineteenth century were usually more impressed by the undisciplined and irreverent nature of the new nation's youngsters than by their deferential meekness.[64] Such sources are, to be sure, often untrustworthy. Nevertheless, a wide variety of witnesses attested to the lapse of strict parental authority (while disagreeing as to whether it was good or bad) so that the existence of some valid evidence behind their testimony is probable. Phenomena like the waning of orthodox Calvinism, the rising spirit of egalitarianism, and the continuing development of obsessive love for offspring could have fostered a desire for greater independence on the part of young children and a reduced exercise of strict authority on the part of parents.[65]

Since Dwight referred to "the numerous complaints, so often made by parents concerning the difficulty of governing their children," he had some awareness of the situation.[66] But he offered no remedy except the standard formulas which either no longer appealed to those who were to put them into effect, or, if practiced, no longer worked. As was often evident in their approach to doctrinal issues like infant damnation, Calvinists had a great knack for faithfully adhering to past frames of reference despite vast changes in the larger culture which had made them obsolete. For one thing, a degree of abstractedness was invariably present in the true Calvinist mind which had been trained to think in terms that were both cosmic and absolutist. The events described in the Bible provided analogues for almost everything that took place afterwards, and perhaps were as psychologically real as even present happenings, while scriptural decrees set forth the rules for all circumstances. Although Dwight was more worldy-wise than some of his brethren (Nathaniel Emmons, for example), he retained much of this way of thinking.[67] When in the 1790s he wrote about the virtuous ruler, his model was King David. He asked the American public to offer homage to a leader of this type, "vice-gerent of God." The request was as unrealistic as it was inappropriate for a new republic witnessing the beginnings of political parties.[68] A man who could direct presidents to pattern themselves after an ancient monarch and the public to revere them, could demand that, in an increasingly secular, egalitarian, and capitalist society, parents and children abide by Biblical counsels.

In addition to scripture, the traditions of child psychology in New England contributed to the persistent emphasis on strong parental authority in the writings of Orthodox spokesmen like Dwight.[69] The Puritans had, of course, advocated it. Cotton Mather told parents to "keep up so much *Authority,* that your *Word* may be a *Law* unto them."[70] Such prescriptions were handed down over the decades from minister to ministerial candidate, an apostolic succession of child-rearing lore.

In the eighteenth century the Enlightenment, in the form of John Locke's *Some Thoughts Concerning Education,* reinforced the Calvinist insistence upon early and absolute parental authority. Locke has often been made out to be the proponent of a less authoritarian child-rearing regimen than the prevailing one.[71] This interpretation is correct insofar as older children were concerned, but in regard to younger ones he actually stood for a more total authoritarianism than crude methods could provide:

> A Compliance and Suppleness of their Wills, being by a steady Hand introduc'd by Parents, before Children have Memories to retain the Beginnings of it, will seem natural to them, and work afterwards in them as if it were so, preventing all Occasions of struggling or repining. The only Care is, that it be begun early, and inflexibly kept to 'till *Awe* and *Respect* be grown familiar, and there appears not the least Reluctancy in the Submission, and ready Obedience of their Minds.[72]

Locke saw what the history of colonialism was later to prove: subjugation is most effective when the subordinate believes that things cannot be otherwise and cooperates in maintaining his inferior position. He showed New England's Calvinists that parental authority had a firmer foundation if the child's will was molded rather than broken.

Locke's system of parental authority was cited approvingly in New England well into the nineteenth century.[73] His influence was also indirect, conveyed through such later English child-rearing works as the highly popular *Hints for the Improvement of Early Education, and Nursery Discipline,* by Louisa Hoare.[74] An American who was instrumental in spreading the Lockean system was the Reverend John Witherspoon, president of Princeton during the late eighteenth century. In 1816 a New England mother who was suggesting books for a maternal association's library remarked, "Upon the whole, I give the preference to Locke and Witherspoon, above any other writers I am acquainted with, on the subject of education." An article in the *Panoplist* two years earlier had rated Witherspoon's *A Series of Letters on Education* (1797) as second only to the Bible as a guide to child rearing.[75] The method of the *Letters* was a highly calculated Lockeanism. Witherspoon urged fathers deliberately to select instances in which they could emphatically teach an eight to nine month old child the complete superiority of the paternal will to his own, perhaps depriving him once a day of a favorite plaything. By the time the infant had reached fourteen months, he should be habituated to "an entire and absolute authority" and fathers could advance "from contradicting to commanding."[76]

Dwight did make some timely changes in the Calvinist-Lockean tradition of strong parental authority. Although he continued to expect from children a reverential obedience that was completely out of touch with the current realities, what he expected of parents in certain ways fit evolving family patterns. Whereas Locke and Witherspoon had regarded the father as the more important parent, Dwight gave that role to the mother. The shift reflected both his own boyhood experience and the development in the society at large of an intenser love of children, for which women served as the chief managers. As a result, Dwight's version of parental authority, severe as it may seem today, represented a softer form of autocracy than his predecessors had advocated. The obligations of parents and children were the same, but a mellower tone prevailed. With the mother in the lead, parents administered a family government uniting tenderness and authority, devotion and absolutism. The parental will remained the child's only law, yet "being steadily regulated by parental affection, is probably more moderate, equitable, and pleasing to him, than any other human government to any other subject." Dwight never realized that once parents gave free reign to their love of a child and made his happiness a major concern, they would find it hard to go on treating him as a distinct inferior.[77]

Locke, Mather, and Witherspoon had also talked about mixing love with authority—they, too, were influenced by the evolution of the family from the medieval pattern towards the modern one—but they described parent-child relationships in which the proportion of affection to intimidation was markedly lower than in Dwight's version. Cotton Mather counseled parents that "Our Authority should be so Tempered with Kindness, and Meekness, and Loving Tenderness, that our children may *Fear* us with *Delight*."[78] A century later, Dwight hoped that children would obey more out of love than out of fear. The increasingly obsessive love of parents made them uncomfortable with the knowledge that in some ways their image was a frightening one to their offspring. Instead, they desired to induce a commensurate love on the part of the child.[79] And in a society in which grownup offspring seemed more and more likely to face different situations and occupy different social strata than those of their parents, as well as to live in far removed places, such love would be one way of establishing a lifetime bond.[80] Dwight only sensed these needs, but the Romantic child-rearing literature which began to appear in America in the late 1820s turned them into a central concern. Bronson Alcott and Lydia Child were no less insistent than writers in the Calvinist-Lockean tradition that children must always obey, but they expected to win juvenile compliance to authority by having maternal love and kindness awaken corresponding affections in the child: "Gentleness, patience, and love are almost everything in education"; "Fear and coercion she keeps out of sight."[81]

Dwight was also a transitional figure in his desire to have parents become genuine friends with their child, but without relinquishing their superior station. Locke had opposed an early familiarity between father and son, although he approved of it when the boy was older.[82] Witherspoon was a little less alarmed by intimacy and even cautioned against keeping young children "at too great a distance, by a uniform sternness and severity of carriage." He did instruct parents to avoid all levity in the company of children, lest their dignity be diminished: "I would have their familiarity to be evidently an act of condescension." [83] In contrast, Dwight's advice had a distinctly more modern note:

'When round they flock, and smile, and tell
Their lambkin sports, and infant weal,
Nor foolish laugh, nor fret, nor frown;
But all their little interests own;
Like them, those trifles serious deem,
And daily witness your esteem:
Yourselves their best friends always prove.'[84]

As part of this approach, children were to be encouraged to communicate to parents their inner feelings and desires: "'Teach them, *with confidence t' impart,/Each secret purpose of the heart.'*"[85] The result would be a pleasing intimacy between parent and child, another condition that the Romantics wrote about in a more sustained and consistent way than did Dwight.[86] But intimacy, particularly of the type Dwight suggested, in which the child was expected to expose his inner self, was not an unmixed blessing. The line between intimacy and intrusion is a thin one. The medieval family unit may have made little allowance for the physical privacy of the child (or of anyone else, for that matter), but its very lack of obsessiveness about children had the unintended effect of ensuring considerable psychic privacy. The far more self-conscious modern family unit allows no sector of child life to be left unexamined.[87]

No matter how affectionate or intimate parents were with their offspring, Dwight required that they employ sharp punishments when the occasion warranted. Since native depravity made the display of some evil traits in juvenile character and conduct almost inevitable, despite the parents' preventive efforts, sooner or later this function of parental authority had to be exercised. The means of correction varied according to the age and the personality of the child. They were a formidable arsenal: reproof, disgrace, confinement, ostracism, the denial of privileges, and for younger children, the rod. Dwight was sure that "A string may almost always be struck, which will accord with the state of the heart; an effort made, which will ensure a victory."[88] On the other hand, he warned against excessive punishment. He understood how repeated chastisements only served to reinforce offending behavior: "The consciousness of having been often corrected, produces, of course, in the mind of every child, who is the subject of this discipline, an habitual sense of degradation. . . . It is commonly followed by an indifference to the crime; often, by a determination to repeat it; and, usually, by feelings of revenge towards the author of the infliction.''[89] He wisely cautioned parents against using punishments as a way to assuage their own frustrations and resentments.[90]

Some of this advice had long precedent—Locke had similarly rebuked those who believed that domestic education began and ended with fault finding[91]—but Dwight gave the entire area of punishment an uncommon amount of thought. One of his major innovations at Yale was a change in the method of discipline. In place of a comprehensive network of fines, he substituted a far more effective system of private conferences with students. During these interviews he reviewed their characters and attempted to untap the right hopes or fears for prompting reform. Saved by the closed door of the President's office from disgrace before his peers, an offender usually responded in a positive way.[92] Dwight advocated a similar routine for the family:

> '*All discipline*, as facts attest,
> *In private minister'd is best.*
> Vex'd to be seen disgrac'd, and sham'd,
> His passion rous'd, his pride inflam'd,
> Your child his guilt with care conceals,
> And pertly talks, and stoutly feels.
>
> . . . .
>
> Alone, before the parents bar,
> His conscience with himself at war,
> Of pride, and petulance, bereft,
> Without a hope, or refuge, left,
> He shrinks, beneath a father's eye,
> And feels his firm perverseness die.'[93]

Punishment worked successfully only when its administrators were in complete control of their own emotions. The raging parent alienated the child while providing him with a vivid example of the sort of indulgence of the passions that domestic education was supposed to prevent. To avoid such exhibitions, Dwight suggested that a parent not correct a child immediately after a transgression, but delay his response until anger had cooled: "His countenance ought then to be mild; his accent gentle; his words free from all unkindness."[94] Most important of all, the parental demeanor had to indicate that the main concern was for the offender's moral development. Punishment was to have the appearance of an act of solicitude rather than of an angry outburst. The sagacious farmer of *Greenfield Hill* expressed this view in a phrase which seems to belong to a later period in the history of child psychology: "'Teach them ... / You hate the fault, but love the child.'"[95]

In a well-managed home, punishment, as necessary as it sometimes was, would be relatively infrequent. While still in the cradle the child learned the necessity of complete subservience to the parental will. From that early age, his passions and appetites were kept under tight restraint. At the same time, ample parental affection encouraged the little one to behave properly as a way of pleasing those who pleased him. Only when juvenile depravity breached these devices did punishment become a vital element in upbringing. Dwight wrote that in regard to parental government, "correction, sometimes esteemed the whole of it, is usually the least part: a part, indispensable indeed, and sometimes efficacious, when all others have failed."[96] Rather than being an inner gear of a good child-rearing system, punishment was a safety brake, a last resort.

The Governing of Children: The Development of the Virtuous Individual

Timothy Dwight was less than four years old when his mother began instructing him in religion. She provided the standard fare for children in Calvinist New England: the catechisms of the *Westminster Confession,* the hymns and spiritual songs of Isaac Watts, various prayers, etc. A few days after the start of these lessons, Master Timothy alarmed his family by not returning home from school on time. He was finally discovered in an apple orchard, teaching a group of Indians about Christianity.[97] Timothy had erred by being tardy. Yet, in this case the lapse was probably excusable since the youngster was engaged in the vital task of spreading the gospel to the heathen: piety and benevolence were greater virtues than punctuality. Mary Edwards Dwight should have been pleased to see that her child-rearing methods were working: Timothy was displaying virtuous behavior not only in her immediate presence, but also when out of her sight. An upbringing that failed to prepare a child to be virtuous on his own initiative accomplished little, no matter how well he acted when under direct parental authority and restraint. As their faculties developed, children had to be "taught to think, judge, and act, for themselves," to become, in short, individuals capable of responsible self-direction.[98]

The restrictive functions of parental government helped to make it possible. By clipping or uprooting the rising weeds of depravity from the earliest years on, mothers and fathers kept them in a manageable condition. Eventually, the child did the job on his own by exerting self-restraint. To contemporaries, Timothy Dwight was himself an example of the efficacy of this method. His first biographers described the mature man as having by nature an impetuous temper (practically the only fault they cited), but "by a rigid self-discipline, he had acquired such control . . . that he never felt the evils inherent to excessive indulgence."[99]

Yet, virtue involved much more than suppression of the bad elements in one's character and conduct. The essence of virtue was active pursuit of the good: in relation to the self, to fellow men, and to God. In order to shape a child into a being who lived in this manner, domestic education had to perform other functions in addition to the restrictive ones. Parents had to make sure that the child's character contained elements which would indicate to him what the good act was in any situation, and would motivate him to perform it.

Dwight's explanation of how parents were to proceed in this essential undertaking employed the psychological language of the eighteenth century, a vocabulary verging towards obsolescence even as he wrote. Nevertheless, his discussion has a quality of enduring importance because he took up the universal questions of child rearing. What are the rules of character and conduct? How can they be taught to a child? And what will compel him to follow them? If Dwight's answers were limited by his time and place, the same is true of those provided by the writers on child psychology who preceded him, and by the ones who have followed.

The easiest question for Dwight was the one concerning the

content of the rules of character and conduct, the question that many in the culture of today find the hardest. For the answer, the Reverend Dwight had to look no further than the King James Bible resting on his desk: *"Moral knowledge is all included, as well as enjoined, in the Scriptures."*[100] As completely as Luther or Calvin, he believed the Bible to be the pure divine word. When late eighteenth-century freethinkers like Tom Paine challenged that conviction, Dwight was in the forefront of the Christian counterattack. His forceful vindications of the "genuineness and authenticity" of scripture made him a quasi saint in the eyes of the pious.[101] Dwight was not so literalistic as to feel obligated to cite chapter and verse every time he mentioned a particular moral principle that should be imparted to children, be it truthfulness, frugality, kindness to animals, or whatever, but he could undoubtedly have done so if challenged.

By putting a copy of the Bible into the hands of every child who was able to read, parents arranged for the direct absorption of its moral rules. The precocious Timothy was perusing the text before he was four.[102] To reinforce and supplement what the child learned on his own, parents provided systematic religious instruction. (Dwight was writing before Sunday schools became common, relieving parents of some of this responsibility.) The evangelical parts of Christianity—the necessity of confessing one's sinfulness, the need of faith in the Saviour, the requirement of prayer—were taught along with the moral code.[103]

As the comprehension of even the brightest child had definite limitations, religious instruction had to be fashioned to meet his capabilities. Dwight advised parents to defer discussion of complex matters until the child was older, to use simple language in teaching, and, most importantly, to show by their tone and countenance that religion was the most delightful of subjects. Unlike high-Hopkinsians whose forbidding approach did so much to give Calvinism a bad name, he believed that *"Religion should always be exhibited in a solemn, and pleasing, and never in a gloomy, and discouraging light."*[104]

Education in religion was not confined to formal instruction, but went on throughout the day. Parents had to be continually inculcating Christian moral principles. Children needed *"line upon line, and precept upon precept; here a little, and there a little."*[105] The effects might not be immediate, but would tell in the long run if parents only had the patience to stick with the task. Dwight compared parents to a silversmith who after a thousand hammering strokes,

> . . . still unform'd the work perceives;
> A thousand, and a thousand more,
> Unfinish'd leaves it as before;
> Yet, though, from each, no print is found,
> Still toiling on his steady round,
> He sees the ductile mass refine,
> And in a beauteous vessel shine.'[106]

The metaphor was apt. In Dwight's system parents did the shaping, and children were shaped. Like any thoroughgoing sensationalist, he was far from accepting the Romantic suggestion that moral education was a two-way transaction, the parent learning at least as much from the child as he taught.

In psychological terms, parents were striking deep impressions on the mind of the young child. Parents who delayed such instruction from the mistaken belief that infants were not yet ready for it risked disaster, for the mind would never again be so plastic.[107] Furthermore, that very openness to sensations allowed bad ones to enter as readily as good ones: "If the best impressions are not made, the worst will be." Dwight envisioned domestic education as a near frantic effort to preempt the infant psyche by imprinting correct notions as rapidly as possible. In the final reckoning, mothers and fathers were racing the devil, *"the enemy who never neglects to sow tares, when parents are asleep."*[108]

The psychology of moral instruction involved the two main classes of mental faculties. In the understanding, moral principles enlightened the intellect and stocked the memory, while in the heart they moved the affections and governed the conscience, the agency of moral judgment.[109] Dwight's placement of the conscience in the heart muddled his psychology as it ascribed to this faculty the kind of deductive reasoning that supposedly characterized the understanding. Dwight did not accept the common eighteenth-century idea that the conscience was an innate moral sense, operating either by intuitive reason (the view developed by Richard Price, Thomas Reid, and Dugald Stewart), or by the feelings' reflex response to certain sensations (the position taken by the Earl of Shaftesbury, Francis Hutcheson, and Joseph Butler). Like John Locke and William Paley, whose books he assigned as college texts,[110] Dwight saw conscience as an agency devoid of innate ideas or impulses. All its content came from outside; it had to be taught what was right and what was wrong.[111] By putting this intellectualistic (as opposed to intuitive or affective) agency in the heart, Dwight confused his organizational chart of the mind. The advantage of doing so was that it let him pay tribute to the heart's rising importance in psychological theory, without yielding on the substantive issue of how conscience operated.

Dwight's view of the workings of conscience is in better accord with twentieth-century opinions than with those in greatest favor in his own time.[112] Contemporary psychologists do not talk about an innate sense of right and wrong in the child, but, like Dwight, advise parents to create that sense: "A conscience, in the proper sense of the word, consists of standards and prohibitions which have been taken over by the personality and which govern behavior from within."[113] In technical Freudian language it is the superego. To claim that Dwight had anticipated Freudian theory on the conscience would be an exaggeration—his scheme of the mind is quite different—but he did have somewhat similar ideas about how conscience perpetuated the parents' moral code long after their external authority had lapsed. He believed that, "In the earliest stages of childhood may be implanted such a sense of right and wrong, of truth and falsehood, of honesty and fraud, of good will and malice . . . as will remain, influence, and govern, through every succeeding period."[114]

In order for moral instruction to make the deepest possible impressions on the conscience, as well as on the other mental agencies, the examples parents set had to harmonize with their precepts. Even the very young quickly picked up any discrepancies between what was preached and what was practiced. A bad example nullified the best principles.[115] Dwight thought that the cause of example's great influence on children was an inborn propensity to imitation which was at its height in the early periods of life.[116] Unfortunately, evil examples were sooner followed than good ones, the result of native depravity. That disproportional effect made the providing of a sanitary moral environment all the more essential. For the child to become virtuous, his parents, his companions, his books, etc., had to be unexceptionably whole-some.[117] Dwight sometimes even suggested that example, rather than merely reinforcing principles, was itself the prime means of moral training: "In family education, a good parental example instructs more than the wisest precepts, and regulates beyond the best exerted government."[118] Such statements were the sign of a tension which appeared in several places in Dwight's child psychology between mentalistic approaches to upbringing and behaviorist ones.

With precept and example in harmony, indelible moral impressions were made on the various mental faculties. Instilled so early that the child had no memory of ever having been without them, they became as intrinsic a part of him as his veins and arteries. Whenever the mind "turns a retrospective view upon the preceding periods of its existence, these truths should seem always to have been in its possession; to have the character of innate principles; to have been inwoven in its nature; and to constitute a part of all its current of thinking."[119] In the terminology of modern social science, this pattern is known as inner-direction: moral rules were to be so completely internalized in childhood that throughout an individual's life they continually provided the guidelines for behavior.[120] Children thereby served as the vehicles for carrying into the future the moral traditions of the past.

An awareness of moral guidelines was not the same as the ability to follow them. A child or an adult could know what was correct behavior in a given situation, and yet act otherwise. The urgings of the depraved parts of his psyche might sway the will to go against the dictates of conscience. Accordingly, parents had not only to instruct in Christian morality, but to present its principles in a way which raised compelling inclinations to adhere to them. The conscience needed allies in its fight to control the will.

The major form of motivation in Dwight's child psychology depended upon anticipations of the feelings of pleasure and of pain. Parents had to persuade children that the practice of Christian morality led to both greater inner satisfaction and, in most cases, greater well-being in the world.[121] Once a child realized that the virtuous person was happier than the evil one, the only sane choice was to attempt to become virtuous. This response was not a conditioned one; Dwight was not trying to fix a pattern of virtuous behavior by directly associating selected actions with pleasure-pain stimuli, as did conditioning associationalists like the English child-rearing theorists, Maria and Richard Edgeworth. Instead, the child's response was a calculated one, a utilitarian estimation of quantums of pleasure and of pain. "The only possible encouragements to Virtue are either the pleasure which Virtue gives, or the rewards which it promises," stated Dwight, "The only restraints upon Vice are the pain which it produces, or the punishment with which it is threatened."[122]

Dwight's motivational utilitarianism differed in important ways from Jeremy Bentham's famous system in which human reason executed the calculus of pleasure and pain. Although Dwight believed that moral standards were founded on utility rather than on the simple fiat of God, he did not think that men could decide which actions were in the final balance useful or nonuseful. Men were incapable of taking into account all of the collateral and long run effects. In contrast, God observed the entire pattern and read the final totals—only He could be a full-fledged utilitarian.[123] But with due regard for man's limited capacities, He had furnished the Bible as the substitute for an independent calculation of utility-virtue: "The precepts of this Sacred Volume were all formed by Him, who alone *sees the end from the beginning,* and who alone, therefore, understands the real nature of all moral actions."[124] Parents had to convince children that an adherence to the moral principles of scripture maximized the amount of pleasure and minimized the amount of pain they would experience, and had a similar result for those affected by their actions. To follow God's commands was the acme of utilitarianism!

Nowhere was this truth clearer than in regard to the afterlife. The intensity and eternal duration of the pleasure to be had in the one realm and of the pain to be undergone in the other dwarfed all temporal experience. Dwight believed that a proper understanding of these prospects was essential in establishing compelling motives for virtue. (He was blind to the possibility that a masochistic desire for hellish torment, or a neurotic inability to accept the permanent happiness of heaven, could cause a perverse evaluation of the final consequences of good or bad behavior.) The job of parents was to impress the facts of the afterlife upon the juvenile mind early and forcefully so as to ensure that they would constantly be on the edge of consciousness, and often in the center, functioning as "powerful springs of action."[125]

Training in this kind of pleasure-pain motivation may have been an effective child-rearing technique, but in relation to evangelical doctrine it was a dangerous one. According to Edwards's account of true piety, obedience to God must come from selfless adoration of His awful greatness, rather than from an estimation of the positive or negative things He could do to one's body and soul.[126] An element of mysticism, which Dwight mostly lacked, was needed to sustain the Edwardean view. Dwight's approach to religion was instead primarily rationalist: "argument [is] the only human support of true religion." Christianity was as reasonable a system to him as Deism was to freethinkers, and he warred upon these Enlightened infidels all the more intensely because they used the same syllogistic methods he employed to reach different conclusions.[127] Consequently, the God he depicted for children was not so much a being who was but dimly perceived, yet awesome in His beauty, as one who was a highly visible keeper of accounts, a God to be honored from an attitude of selfish calculation: "Every child should know, as soon as he is capable to knowing . . . that God is an eye-witness to all his secret and open conduct alike; and that every thing, which he speaks, thinks, or does, will be the foundation of his final reward"; "He records all their conduct in the book of his remembrance."[128] Such training was far more likely to result in moralism than in true piety.

To be fair, Dwight apparently was doubtful that any mortals, even regenerated ones, could exercise a piety free of all selfish motivation. In one of the most thoughtful passages in the *Theology,* he remarked:

> A Christian loves God, his Son, his Spirit, his Law. . . . Why does he love them? . . . It will be often difficult, and sometimes impossible, for him to determine whether his emotions are merely natural, wholly Evangelical, or mixed. He . . . may be unable to determine whether he loves the character of God, considered by itself; whether he loves the divine perfections for what they are; or whether he loves God, because he regards him as a friend to himself; and delights in his perfections,

because he considers them as engaged, and operating, to promote his present and eternal good. It would be difficult for most persons to determine, precisely, what views they would form of this glorious Being, if it were revealed to them, that He was their Enemy.[129]

Dwight's acceptance of selfish elements in Christian motivation was a sign of the inner decline of the Calvinist faith. His grandfather would not have liked it at all. From an Edwardean perspective, "The Calvinist gospel had degenerated into the maxim, 'Obey God, and you will be happy.' . . . Piety is the love of God because of God's own glory, and not because the laws of God are useful for the attainment of happiness."[130] But what was compromising when measured against the standards of an exacting theology and the highest forms of religious expression promised to be eminently useful in more mundane matters (always closest to Dwight's heart), like motivating children and, by extension, the general citizenry, to virtue.[131]

Dwight's practical approach was further evident in his discussion of habits. Athough not motives as such, habits of thinking, feeling, and, in particular, acting, played a major role in the exercise of virtue. They could oppose motives, complement them, or possibly even make them unnecessary.

In order for a person to be virtuous in his character and behavior over the course of a lifetime, the formation of proper habits was essential. *"The substance of all education,"* Dwight observed, *"is the establishment of good habits.* Habits extend, alike, to the body and mind; and equally influence our thoughts and affections, our language and conduct. Without them, nothing in the human character, or human life, is efficacious, permanent, or useful."[132] Habits could be formed in any period of life, but were most readily set up in the first stages when the mind was in a flexible state. Parents established good habits in their charges by giving moral instruction again and again, while making the children repeat actions which jibed with their teachings. As usual, Dwight was less than precise in explaining the details of the mental processes involved: "In early childhood the susceptibility is so great, and the feelings so tender, that a few repetitions will generate habitual feeling. Every impression at this period is deep. When these, therefore, are made through a moderate succession, the combined effect can rarely be effaced. Thus good habits are soon, and durably, established."[133] Dwight emphasized that a policy of neglect led to bad habits as well as to bad principles. A child who was allowed to exercise his depravity became settled in evil ways of thinking, feeling, and behaving that were unalterable by whatever good principles and motives he possessed.[134]

Yet, useful as habits could be, even the best ones did not completely harmonize with the mentalistic aspects of Dwight's approach to moral training. If, in one sense, habits translated virtuous principles and reinforcing motives into continual practice, in another sense they actually diminished the importance of principles and motives. The conflict between the two sectors did not revolve around the process of habit formation. For this step, Dwight relied upon repeating principles until they were understood and instilling motives founded upon calculation, rather than upon a behaviorist conditioning which made no use of the reason. But once habits had been formed, to be aware of principles and to weigh motives was really no longer necessary. The practice of virtue could be automatic, an acquired reflex. Dwight never spelled out this implication, and would not have accepted it had someone else done so in his presence. Nevertheless, the conflict between reason and habit is clearly evident in his child psychology. According to one line of emphasis, "No man is better, than his principles will make him. Virtue is nothing, but voluntary obedience to truth. Vice is nothing, but voluntary obedience to falsehood. The doctrines, which he obeys, will form his whole character." According to the other line, "Habits constitute the man. Good habits form a good man, and evil habits an evil man. Subtract these from the character; and it will be difficult to conceive what will be left."[135]

Dwight's inability to determine whether principles or habits constituted the major dimension of a person involved more than just the shortcomings of a less than rigorous thinker. Tensions between mentalistic perspectives towards life which place the most significance on the internal reflections of the individual, and behaviorist ones that stress external performance, are deeply rooted in the Western tradition itself. New England Puritanism had experienced the strain in its attempt to foster both piety and moralism. In thought about child psychology the dissonance can be detected from at least the time of Locke.[136] One perspective has the goodness of a child depend upon deliberation, a process which brings into play the special qualities separating man from the animals, but requires lengthy training and is liable to many types of error. The other perspective founds goodness on self-perpetuating habits, a mode that makes little use of the higher powers of mind, but is easier to establish, and, in being safe from fallacious reasoning and faulty motives, has the advantage of greater reliability. Society is still uncertain about which it prefers.[137]

Dwightean Man and Familial Determinism

Dwight expected a very special type of person to emerge as the product of his system of domestic education. This model individual deeply repented his sins, persistently sought the Saviour, earnestly reverenced God, and was faithful in such other religious duties as the keeping of the Sabbath and private prayer.[138] In dealings with his fellow men, he was always truthful and just. "Every child should be taught to pay all his debts and fulfil all his contracts," insisted Dwight, " . . . Every thing, which he has borrowed, he should be obliged to return, uninjured, at the time: and every thing belonging to others, which he has lost, he should be required to replace."[139]

The life style of Dwight's model individual was remarkable for its steadiness. The paragon was peaceful, orderly, and sober. Neither adventuresome frontiersman nor city sophisticate, he displayed the ideals of small town New England before it was affected by industrialism and ethnic changes. Dwight delighted in the well-known designation of Connecticut as the land of *"Steady Habits."*[140] But merely being regular and dependable was not enough. Dwightean man was highly methodical, a careful organizer of all aspects of his life. In part, this emphasis was the result of Dwight's personal experience. While a tutor at Yale he had through overwork severely strained his eyes shortly after they had been weakened by a smallpox inoculation. They never fully recovered. Unable for most of his adult life to look at books for any extended period of time, he became dependent on others to read to him and eventually on amanuenses to write down his thoughts.

With the burden of this handicap he was able to accomplish as much as he did only by the most systematic use of time. He advised Yale students to follow a similar regimen: "Make every day, and every hour, yield its advantages by unremitted diligence. . . . *Methodise*, for this end, your whole time. Appropriate its due part to recreation, to food, to sleep, and to business. Methodised time, like methodised business, goes on, not only easily, but advantageously."[141]

This formula had proved to be successful for many others besides Dwight since it obviously derived from the Protestant ethic as well as from hard-learned experience. Dwightean man maintained that ethic in relatively pure form, its cruder commercial aspects subordinated. He considered the efficient use of time to be a virtue in itself, and like all other virtuous behavior to be a way of honoring God. That it also fostered the making of money was an additional benefit (part of the utility of virtue), but not the major end. A decent prosperity was to be the goal of an individual raised according to Dwight's child psychology, not riches.[142]

His demeanor was a kindly one, reflecting the ascendancy in the mind of the gentle affections. Injuries he readily forgave.[143] In regard to manners, the polish of virtue, Dwight's paragon shunned alike the vulgar and the pompous, preferring to display a simple dignity. Although civil to all, he was no egalitarian. Social inferiors were treated with condescension and those of a higher station with deference. Among intimates, he was "familiar, yet refin'd."[144]

All in all, the characteristics of this ideal personage bore a high degree of resemblance to those of the designer. The first biographer of Timothy Dwight wrote that, "The purity of his sentiments and language was equally remarkable and exemplary. . . . He was from infancy, distinguished for the most conscientious regard to truth. . . . No less was he remarkable for the most scrupulous regard to decorum. . . . His politeness was not a mere exterior. It was the great law of kindness."[145] But there were also differences between the designer and his model. Dwight, for example, was very suspicious of ambition, warning against the selfish desire to be famous, powerful, or the subject of admiration.[146] He attacked this fault all the more emphatically because he feared that it was one of his own; his enemies had scored when they labeled him "Pope Dwight." Near the end of his life, he confessed, "I have coveted reputation, and influence, to a degree which I am unable to justify."[147] The amount of virtue in the world would be significantly increased if such desires were repressed. Unlike more extreme egoists, Dwight did not want the next generation to be exactly like himself, just very similar.

Whether Dwight would ever see his model villager become the prevailing type among the adults of New England depended upon the region's parents. Most of the qualities which Dwight wished to encourage did not originate from within a person, but came from the external forces his parents controlled. Even innate characteristics such as gentle affections had to be cultivated by outside influence in order to be effectual. As Dwight said about himself, an individual was essentially the product of his early domestic environment.

Historians have often viewed environmentalism as an emancipating concept, one that opens up possibilities for change which are precluded by hereditarian doctrines.[148] But the implications are very different for those under the control of the environment than for the ones controlling it. Dwight's environmentalism enabled parents to shape the nature of their child, his depravity notwithstanding. On the other hand, it subjected children to a severe determinism which resembled Puritan predestination. The kinds of families into which God chose to deliver the young in most cases irrevocably decided their lives and afterlives. Dwight wrote:

> One child is born of parents, devoted solely to this world. From his earliest moments of understanding, he hears, and sees, nothing commended, but hunting, horse-racing, visiting, dancing, dressing, riding, parties, gaming.... His taste is formed, his habits are riveted, and the whole character of his soul is turned, to them, before he is fairly sensible, that there is any other good.... Of JEHOVAH he thinks as little, and for the same reason, as a *Chinese* or a *Hindoo*.... Thus he lives, and dies, a mere animal; a stranger to intelligence and morality, to his duty and his GOD.
>
> Another child comes into existence in the mansion of Knowledge, and Virtue. From his infancy, his mind is

fashioned to wisdom and piety. . . . Under this happy cultivation he grows up, *like an olive tree in the courts of the Lord;* and green, beautiful, and flourishing, he blossoms; bears fruit; and is prepared to be transplanted by the Divine hand to a kinder soil in the regions above.[149]

Except for its projection into the afterlife, Dwight's familial determinism is very much like the simplistic Freudian determinism which has been a mainstay of twentieth-century child-rearing lore. Whereas his children could be saved or ruined by the way parents acquainted them with scripture, those of the present supposedly can have their futures decided by the way parents introduce them to the potty chair. A contemporary authority on upbringing speaks of the "popular fallacy, something that might be called 'Childhood as Destiny,' a belief that the experiences of early childhood determine one's fate and commit the personality to rigid patterns of behavior and that thereafter nothing short of a psychoanalysis [today's equivalent of regeneration by grace!] can modify this edifice."[150] In this instance, as in several others, contemporary perspectives on child rearing are not as new as is commonly believed.

IV. The Structure of Child-Rearing Theory

Systems of the Early National Period

The Ideological Dimension

IN 1820 THE *Christian Spectator* published a short article by the late Timothy Dwight, entitled "An Essay on Education." The piece had little to say about the details of the daily management of children. Instead, it discussed child-rearing theory as a form of ideology, examining the goals set forth in different writings on the subject, and the systems by which they were to be achieved. Its concern was with the rationale and general pattern of upbringing rather than with specific methods.[1]

The ideological aspects of child-rearing theory were not always as sharply divorced from the family guidebook aspects as in this instance. Often, a sermon, tract, or treatise on domestic education concerned itself with both. Nevertheless, the two dimensions were conceptually distinct. Authorities who shared similar opinions on a particular matter such as punishment did not necessarily agree on an overall approach to domestic education. Nor was an individual expert's methodological program always totally consistent with his ideological position. The abstract theory of child rearing had a logic of its own.

The early national period, the half century from the first years of the 1780s to the first years of the 1830s, is the last one in which Calvinist perspectives can be regarded as the predominant influence on the ideological dimension of New England child-rearing theory. After the 1830s, Calvinism was no longer a widespread faith, although it lingered for decades in vestigial forms. Emerson, who was born in 1803, recalled fifty years later how "Calvinism was still robust & effective on life and character in all the people who surrounded my childhood, & gave a deep religious tinge to manners and conversation. I doubt the race is now extinct, & cetainly no sentiment has taken its place on the new generation,— none as pervasive and controlling."[2]

As strong as Calvinism was in the early 1800s, when compared to the middle of the century, it was hardly in the position that it had once occupied. From the time of the Puritan founders until the late eighteenth century, its tenets had been almost unchallenged in systematic writings on child rearing by New Englanders. In the 1780s, however, theological Liberals began an alternative approach by presenting a theory of upbringing based on Enlightenment assumptions. Unitarians continued it in the nineteenth century. Around 1830, an even more divergent approach emerged, a Romantic one, although its fullest development was in the years ahead. Also in the future was Horace Bushnell's blending of the three views into a harmonious whole.

The Calvinist Approach: Conversion versus Moral Training

The child-rearing system set forth by Calvinist laymen and ministers—Congregationalists, Presbyterians, and some Baptists—was closely tied to their theology. Techniques for everyday management of the family could originate from direct observation, cherished maxims of folklore, lingering fragments of classical wisdom and so on. In contrast, the formal rationale and general character of domestic education had to be grounded in religious doctrine.

The element of theology that came to the fore in the Calvinist discussion was the doctrine of original sin and total depravity. A doctrine of seeming simplicity, one which could be preached to an audience so forcefully as to set hearts racing with fear, it had become in technical theology a vast and difficult subject. While the Orthodox ministry quarreled about whether the newly born infant was guilty or innocent, or quibbled over the moment when depravity first appeared, they did agree that sooner or later the child transgressed and, as a result, deserved to be punished by God. Infants might be a special case, but once past three or four years of age the moral situation of a child was essentially the same as an adult's. Without the receipt of saving grace, the depraved individual was certain to be subjected to the unending miseries of hell; with grace he was assured of the eternal bliss of heaven.

Although a person had an entire lifetime for grace to manifest itself in his soul, right up to the last moments on the deathbed, the clergy emphasized that the great event was more likely to happen in the early portions than in the middle and late ones when he had become hardened and set in sin. And since, as parents knew only too well, death could strike anyone at any time, a lad of seven being almost as threatened, it seemed, as an elder of seventy-seven, the sooner conversion with its guarantee of heaven occurred the better. The formal goal of Calvinist domestic-education theory was, perforce, the child's reception of purifying grace: "The most important object of education is unattained, so long as the heart remains unsubdued by the saving power of evangelical truth."[3]

If the major premises were accepted, this basic framework of Calvinist child-rearing theory was impressively tight. Original sin, total depravity, eternal hell, purifying grace, and eternal heaven locked together to make an imposing imperative. What robbed it of much of its force, and the overall theory of its consistency, was a supplemental element, moral education. Conceived as a support for the process of redemption, it implicitly became in Calvinist writings the real end of upbringing. In this way, the abstract parts of Calvinist child-rearing theory justified the formation of a virtuous child, which could be brought about by means of the parental techniques described in the methodological parts.

Contrary to what might be expected, moral training was not automatically assumed by Calvinists to be essential to the child-rearing process. One of the fascinations of Calvinist literature throughout its history is that it attempted to ask fundamental questions about its own endeavors, to take nothing for granted, although the answers were not always as forthright as the questions. In this instance, the child-rearing writers seemed cognizant of a possible challenge which probably few of their public would so boldly state: why should parents bother at all with developing the moral character and conduct of their children if grace and salvation, the supreme goals, cannot be gained by the most exemplary character and conduct? ("By the deeds of the law, there shall no flesh be justified." Romans 3:20.)

The easiest answer was that God required it. Endless scrutiny of the Bible brought forth a number of passages which could be interpreted as commanding a moral upbringing of children. The most popular, cited in a thousand sermons, was from Proverbs 22:6: "Train up a child in the way he should go: and when he is old, he will not depart from it." Like the rest of God's commands, this one was to be obeyed without question. As Timothy Dwight proclaimed, "To know, that any thing is the will of God, is enough."[4]

But God's naked fiat was really not enough for most men in 1800, as Dwight himself realized. The blind obedience of the first Calvinist generations was centuries behind, having given way to incessant attempts to justify to men the commands of the Lord. Dwight was therefore quick to add that God's decree was "powerfully enforced by Reason."[5]

The strongest of these additional arguments for moral training concerned the safety of society. Good citizens were expected to shudder as the authorities on child rearing described the menace to law, order, and general social stability posed by the native depravity of the younger generation. Only conversion could totally eliminate the threat. Unfortunately, even in the best of circumstances, many individuals would never receive grace while others would be in a depraved state for a considerable portion of their youth, or even maturity, before being converted. Put bluntly, grace was too sporadic for society to rely upon it as a police force. Although moral training could not expunge innate depravity, such training could keep its evil impulses under restraint, well short of the terrible extremes that were possible—it alone saved society from a tidal wave of barbarism. In the absence of moral upbringing, children "could never be governed. A generation of such children would set at defiance all the laws, and magistrates, in the Universe; and would never yield to any control, but that of the sword."[6] From this perspective, moral training was a civic responsibility of the highest order, a duty the family owed to the larger community, to the nation itself, a duty that was second only to securing the redemption of the child. A writer in a Baptist magazine observed, "If the spirit of conversion should be withheld, still the instructions and examples of a religious parent will probably have a salutary effect on the character of his offspring; and should the best result of his labours be, their becoming good members of society, this alone would be a large recompense for his toils."[7]

In depicting the threat which the unredeemed and unrestrained posed to the social body, some of the Calvinist writers on child rearing used such lurid phrases that the modern reader must wonder about ulterior motives for the hyperbole. Bernard Bailyn has shown that the similarly overwrought tracts of the American Revolution represented "real fears, real anxieties,"[8] and undoubtedly there was also a considerable degree of genuine apprehension behind the Calvinist rhetoric about the consequences of neglecting moral upbringing. Nevertheless, a suspicion of propaganda remains, supported by evidence that the New England clergy had used against Jefferson and his party much of the same sort of language, sometimes rather cynically.[9] A more charitable supposition is that the writers were swept away by their own rhetoric, carried by its momentum to exaggerated conclusions, like those of Timothy Dwight: "If children were not advised; what useful thing could they know? If they were not exhorted, and commanded; what useful thing would they do; what useful habit would they establish, or even imbibe? . . . They would evidently become mere beasts of prey; and make the world a den of violence and slaughter."[10] In any event, one suspects a *frisson* sometimes stirred these writers as they portrayed the horrors against which they heroically summoned the society, horrors which at the earliest would occur only when they were well on in years and about to depart to an assured salvation. (In a similar fashion, the most elaborate depictions of hell tended to come from those convinced that their own destination was heaven.) Descriptions of a world rife with unrestrained depravity were the Calvinist equivalents of the Gothic novel.

A further argument for moral training took the form of an old theological device. The seventeenth-century Puritans had believed that their society participated in a national covenant with God which required correct conduct on the part of the community. Success in maintaining the agreement would be rewarded by God, and failure would be punished. Pursuing the logic of this theme, the Reforming Synod of 1679 had included a lax discipline over children as among the evils which had provoked God into levying his wrath against New England.[11] Traces of the idea survived in the nineteenth century in the sermons of old men whose roots lay in an earlier period. During the 1820s, Nathaniel Emmons, still preaching in his late seventies, gave several sermons in jeremiad form on national degeneracy, sounding the ancient lament that "we have been gradually, insensibly, and perpetually backsliding from God and the purity of our forefathers. . . . Do people in general practice that strict family government, and devout family religion which were once generally practiced in this country?"; "The proper exercise of parental authority is infinitely important, as it tends to draw down the richest temporal and spiritual blessings on individual persons, private families, larger communities, and whole nations and kingdoms."[12]

As Emmons's last premise suggests, justification for the rearing of moral children could be expressed through the rhetoric of hope as well as the rhetoric of fear. Even while Emmons lamented New England's present plight, others were contemplating how properly raised children would not simply restore the region's former luster, but would make it, and indeed the entire nation, shine with an unprecedented brightness. Like the trans-Appalachian West, the younger generation raised the specter of vice and infidelity. But if moral training was successfully accomplished, a potential disaster would be turned into a consummate triumph. As early as 1812, Lyman Beecher tentatively connected improvement in child rearing with the millennial theme, arguing that if the immoral portions of society were deprived of fresh recruits from the young, they would in due time die out "and a generation of another spirit will occupy, without resistance, their fortified places."[13] By the 1830s, the theme of the redemption of mankind through correct domestic education had become more explicit as the "Protestant Counter-Reformation" evolved from defensiveness to an extravagant optimism. If parents cultivated sound character and beliefs in their offspring, it would be "among the principal means of reforming the world and introducing the day of millennial glory."[14]

Up to this point in the logic of Calvinist domestic education theory, a strong case had been made for the raising of moral children, but that objective had not supplanted conversion as the

core element in child rearing. Those who advised on family duties
every so often indicated the correct priorities. Parents had to give
"the law and the gospel each its place. . . . Impress upon the minds
of your children the excellency and reasonableness of the commands, and enjoin it upon them to obey; but lead them to Christ
for life"; "They need Christ to save them."[15]

The first stage in the encroachment of moral education was its
elevation to coequal status with evangelical training as a path to
salvation. Calvinists made an implicit distinction between the
way in which infants reached salvation and the way in which anyone else reached it, from children of a few years to adults. Infants
could be redeemed despite their inability to benefit from formal
religious instruction. For those beyond infancy, evangelical
training constituted an essential step in the process of conversion:
"It is the soul, which is thus taught, alarmed, and allured, upon
which descends the efficacious grace of the Holy Spirit; and not
the soul uninstructed, unawakened, thoughtless of its guilt." The
parent, as well as the minister, had to be an evangelical instructor
and exhorter.[16] He also had to be a moral instructor. A sustained
demonstration of good character and conduct on the part of the
child was regarded as being as important in preparing for
conversion as the realization of his depravity and the need for
grace. Children "should be taught to seek by patient continuance
in well doing, for glory, and honor, and eternal life hereafter."[17]
Moral training and evangelical training were frequently joined
together under such rubrics as "family instruction and government," "family education and order," or, simply, "Christian
education."

Nevertheless, moral guidance and evangelical guidance did not
lead in quite the same direction, and their association as coequals
raised the hoary issue of justification by faith *versus* justification
by works. There was an essential theoretical difference between
teaching the child to seek through Christ the undeserved grant of
saving faith, and teaching him to obey God's moral commands.
According to orthodox doctrine, honoring parents, showing
kindness to friends and strangers, exerting industry, and so on
made a child more likely to receive the divine grant than if he had
neglected these duties, but such exhibitions of moral character and
conduct could not earn grace. As Calvinist writers elaborated their
ideas about upbringing, they confronted the perennial problem of

how to motivate individuals to moral actions without having them believe that such actions were a claim on salvation.

Some of the writers, out of a zeal to promote moral training, took liberties with orthodox theology by obscuring the essential distinctions and depicting good character and conduct as indeed meriting salvation. Mrs. Nancy Sproat correctly pointed out in one of her published lectures to her children that they could not purchase heaven by works, but in another she told them of behavioral conditions for entry into heaven: "We wish to be happy hereafter, but we do not like to practise self-denial here; and yet when our selfish feelings rise against our duty, we *must* practise it or we cannot receive the reward of obedience."[18] At best, this language was dangerously loose, at worst, it represented out-and-out Arminianism, the granting to man of the power to earn his salvation, a position repudiated by the major varieties of American Calvinism, although sometimes implicitly suggested in the manner of Mrs. Sproat. Her remarks can, perhaps, be dismissed as those of a layperson who did not fully appreciate the complexity of the area she was discussing, except that the same pattern appeared in statements by the knowledgeable Timothy Dwight. In his systematic theology, Dwight wrote, "Our justification can in no sense nor degree, be said, with truth, to be merited by ourselves," but in his essay on child rearing in the *Christian Spectator* he maintained that, "The great business of education . . . is to take this depraved being by the hand, and lead him back to real virtue; and to Heaven, its glorious reward."[19] A theory that had initially justified the moral training of children as nothing more than simple obedience to God's fiat subsequently offered God's kingdom as the payoff for moral training correctly done. The writers on upbringing, concerned about the seeming decline in family government since Puritan days, were so eager to bolster parental incentive for the arduous task of moral education that they tremendously inflated its benefits, theology notwithstanding.

Moral training had turned out to be equal in importance to evangelical training, but at this step in the argument, it was still not the primary axis of domestic education. A child could reach heaven through either route: the traditional road of piety or the unofficial, but well-posted road of morality. The transformation of moral training into the central element of domestic education occurred in the explanation of how parents employed its methods to lead a depraved child down that path of true morality. As in the discussion of faith and works, the Calvinist program for developing moral character and conduct consisted of orthodox views on one level of theory, and on a different level, unorthodox ones which negated them. Sometimes represented as heavily dependent upon God, the process of moral training was at other times depicted as quite independent in its essential operation, a procedure that was within the control of parents. If that were so, domestic education could do much more to establish moral character and conduct in the young than to convert them, an event which God alone decreed. Success in moral training turned out to be a goal attainable through parental effort, and thus the main element in child rearing.

According to the orthodox perspective, which did not allow parents such autonomy, moral training had to reckon with a native depravity that impelled children into wrongdoing with tremendous force. When the writers employed this perspective they tended to view the child as an anarchic monster. In a passage with Freudian overtones (and also with Freudian insight) a commentator in the *Panoplist* described the young child as a being whose "object is to gratify himself; and every thing in opposition to this is assaulted with violence. . . . Were infants from birth endowed with strength and activity like the young of some animals, the most fatal effects would follow. . . . You would be compelled, for your own safety, to resort to chains and fetters. . . . In his paroxisms of rage at some disappointment in his pleasures, would he hesitate, do you think, to take your life, were you the cause of his exasperation."[20] Though moral training, if strongly exerted, could have considerable success in restricting these anarchic forces and constraining the child to a path of rectitude, such success must be fragile and transitory. The force of depravity remained undiminished within, ever ready to surge forth and sweep the child into the thickets of evil.

Ostensibly, only God could extinguish this awesome force ("grace breaking down the strong barriers of depravity").[21] Grace not only redeemed a child, but imparted a new nature that would make him thoroughly moral in his character and conduct. Conversion "will best prepare [children] for the duties of *social life*. . . . They will have fixed principles of holy action, which no change of circumstances will be likely to shake." When a child misbehaved the orthodox solution was for parents to pray to God to "change his heart, and make him good, and obedient, and submissive."[22] Such advice reasserted the superiority of evangelical training over moral training: the road of virtue might end at the gates of heaven, but no child was capable of staying on it the entire way without the aid of grace.

In this orthodox phase of child-rearing theory, parents served as God's assistants, preparing their child through both moral and religious guidance for the deity's transformation of his nature. Much of their function was negative. Parents were to do the best they could in the difficult task of restraining the child from the many sins to which his depraved nature inclined him, using whatever degree of authority and sanction might be necessary. This "negative form of virtue"[23] was an important first step because God was not likely to transform a child who was flagrantly sinful, although He, of course, had the power to do so. No one suggested that through this policy of restraint parents gave the child a new nature; they were merely bringing under rudimentary control their offspring's native depravity. The positive forms of virtue had to be imparted by another force.

What is surprising is that this other force was not always designated as a divine one. Where the orthodox parts of Calvinist child-rearing theory indicated God's hand to be at work, the unorthodox parts depicted human hands. In the creation of moral character and conduct in a child, parents had a positive function, as well as a negative one. And to this positive role the unorthodox parts of the theory attributed an efficacy virtually equivalent to that of grace itself, thereby again contravening the tenets of Calvinist theology. If almost every Calvinist writer on domestic education indicated at some point that, "It is out of the power of parents to renew the hearts of their children, and remove their depravity,"[24] at other points many of them conferred upon mothers and fathers so potent an ability to mold their young into thoroughly moral beings that the sinful heart seemed little more than a formal metaphysical concept. Parents were told: "If your children possess dispositions that lead them into sin, it surely cannot be cruel to check those dispositions, or *give them a new and better direction*"; "Moral education . . . [is] the great concern of *training* our children to right principles, dispositions, and habits"; there is "a bias in human nature, which it is the object of

Christian instruction and discipline *to correct.*"[25] For all intents
and purposes, parents *could* give children new natures. The
ideological aspects of Calvinist child-rearing advice partially
affirmed the environmentalism that the guidebook aspects presented in detail.

In making statements to this effect, Calvinists drew on Enlightenment ideas about human psychology. During the late
eighteenth century, many, although not all, American Calvinists
had adopted large portions of John Locke's psychological system.
The *tabula rasa* hypothesis had not compromised their theology
directly because these Calvinists, following the lead of Jonathan
Edwards, limited the *tabula rasa* to the rational faculties. Native
depravity, which had no place in Locke's system, could then still
be retained by situating it in such nonrational agencies as the will
and the passions, which were usually considered to be parts of the
heart.[26] However, the Lockean psychology so emphasized the
impact of the environment in forming an individual's nature that
no compartment of the mind seemed secure from that influence.
Calvinist writers who adopted this psychology were able to
assume that moral training placed impressions in the rational
faculties, and even in the heart itself, which had greater strength
than the innate impulses of depravity. The heart could not be
made holy by sensationalist means, but its native inclinations
could be regarded as flexible rather than as fixedly oriented
towards sin. In effect, the *tabula rasa* had been extended from the
rational to the nonrational faculties, resulting in a plasticity that
nullified the awesome juvenile depravity conquerable only by
God. Mothers were told that "during that period of [a child's]
existence, which God has committed to your care, the mind is most
ductile, the heart most susceptible and the memory most tena-
cious. Hence, the impressions then made are rarely if ever effaced.
. . . The soul presents itself to your hand like wax to the seal."[27]

At this juncture, Calvinist child-rearing theory had become
openly contradictory. The depraved heart image implied that
children would be extremely hostile to moral training and that it
would require strenuous parental effort; the *tabula rasa* image
suggested that children would be very receptive to good influences
and that moral character and conduct might be easily developed.

When Timothy Dwight spoke with theological overtones, he sighed, "How vast a labour to train up even one child to virtue and to duty; or even to prevent one from becoming grossly sinful, and finally lost? What toils and pains . . . before this hard task can be accomplished? How rarely is it accomplished at all? What then must be the corruption of that heart, which makes all these efforts necessary; and which can resist and overcome them all." Shifting to the psychological side of his beliefs, Dwight used a very different terminology and was as optimistic as he had previously been pessimistic: "The mind is absolutely clear from every prepossession. . . . The heart is soft, gentle, and easily won. . . . To every amiable, every good thing it is drawn comparatively without trouble or resistance."[28] The terrifying juvenile depravity which threatened cities, states, and nations had vanished, replaced by an imagery that has seldom been associated with Calvinism. The Reverend Dwight, a champion of that faith, was hardly a heretic or even an exception in his views. His shifts between polar perspectives reflected the ambivalence of Calvinism in the late eighteenth and early nineteenth centuries as it tried to believe in both native depravity and the *tabula rasa*, seeking to follow Calvin and Locke at the same time.

Dwight and the other Calvinist writers on child rearing were able to preserve a technical orthodoxy by routinely adding that even the best of parental efforts to develop moral children needed God's endorsement to succeed. This blessing took the form of something external to the basic child-rearing process. The impression was conveyed that conscientious parents automatically received the divine seal of approval: "Your faithful exertions, attended with God's *ordinary* blessing, will open to you daily new sources of enjoyment in the unfolding virtues and expanding faculties of your children."[29] In creating a new nature in a child, parents, in the end, required relatively little divine help. Viewed within the total structure of Calvinist child-rearing theory, the notion of God's necessary blessing seems, like the notion of the sinful heart, essentially formal. Divine sovereignty was readily acknowledged, but the real power and responsibility were given to parents.

Having placed so much emphasis on the parental role, the domestic education experts were worried about whether the public truly understood its efficacy and importance. Early in the period, Samuel Hopkins charged that, "The duty which parents engage to do towards their children, has been generally overlooked and disregarded, even in theory, as well as practice; and the promise of the success of faithfulness in this duty, the holiness and salvation of their children, has not been believed by the most, and they are now disposed to oppose this sentiment." Similar complaints continued well into the nineteenth century. In 1828 an article in the *Spirit of the Pilgrims* remarked that many parents "know that their children need converting grace, in order to prepare them for usefulness here and glory hereafter; but they infer, since this is the gift of God, that there is little or nothing for them to do."[30]

Whatever the reality of the charge that mothers and fathers were fatalistic about the development of morality and piety in their offspring, the anxiety of the child-rearing writers suggests an incipient awareness of their message's ambiguities. Wielding the supernaturalism of Calvinist theology in the one hand, and the naturalism of Lockean psychology in the other, they could give full play to neither. Uncertain in their own minds, they presumed that the public would be even more confused.

The Enlightenment Approach: A Fuller Sensationalism

While the Calvinists grappled with the implications of John Locke's psychology for their child-rearing views, wavering between acceptance and rejection, a minority of New Englanders more completely adopted a sensationalist system. These individuals, Arminian Liberals in the eighteenth century and Unitarians in the nineteenth, espoused a Christian version of Enlightenment child-rearing theory. Their writings about upbringing were miniscule compared to the vast Calvinist outpouring, indicative of both their lesser numbers and their lack of inclination for didactic tomes or extended series of sermons on the duties of family life. The most well-known versions of Enlightenment child-rearing theory available in New England were instead found in republished foreign manuals. For example, the stridently associationalist *Practical Education* (1798) by the British novelist Maria Edgeworth and her father had at least two New England editions. It was highly praised as late as 1830.[31] Of even greater longevity and importance was Locke's own *Some Thoughts Concerning Education,* initially published in 1693. The book seems to have been well thought of in colonial days, and continued to be popular in the early national period, the first New England edition appearing in 1830.[32]

Since Calvinists were influenced by Locke, and since Locke himself was a representative of the early moderate and Christian Enlightenment rather than of the later skeptical or revolutionary phases, a hard and fast line cannot always be drawn between their approaches to child rearing.[33] Locke, along with subsequent theorists of the moderate or didactic Enlightenment who were popular in New England, agreed with the Calvinists on parts of the basic rationale of domestic education as well as on most of the psychology and methodology. Avowedly anti-Christian schemes of upbringing, or radically unconventional ones such as that of Rousseau, were of little direct influence in New England except as objects of criticism and rejection.[34] As long as the Enlightenment outlook avoided extremes, the Orthodox as well as the Liberals could live with it and learn from it.

Despite the affinities, there remained distinct differences between Enlightenment child-rearing theory and Calvinist child-rearing theory. The formidable triumvirate of original sin, total depravity, and regeneration by grace which marched across the pages of Calvinist domestic education literature did not advance onto the leaves of Enlightenment texts.[35] Calvinists might, with varying degrees of deliberateness, find ways to mitigate the implications of these doctrines for children, as they had often done with the implications for adults. But as long as individual commentators laid claim to the title of "Calvinist," some semblance of the primal trio, no matter how attenuated, had to appear. The presence or absence of these doctrines provides a touchstone for distinguishing the Calvinist theory of domestic education from other systems.

In place of the Calvinist child, with his burden of original sin, the Enlightenment substituted a child whose native state represented neither evil nor goodness. His psyche consisted of the famous *tabula rasa* of Locke, to which Americans, following the Scots, attached an embryonic moral sense. This child's particular nature developed gradually as the environment made various impacts upon the blank-slate faculties. Locke set forth that idea at the start of *Some Thoughts Concerning Education:* "Of all Men we meet with, nine Parts of ten are what they are, good or evil, useful or not, by their Education. 'Tis that which makes the great Difference in Mankind. The little, or almost insensible Impressions on our tender Infancies, have very important and lasting consequences.... I imagine the Minds of Children as easily turn'd this way or that Way, as Water it self."[36] Depravity had become ductility.

One of the first New Englanders to adopt Lockean assumptions about children was the mid-eighteenth-century religious Liberal, Charles Chauncy. The vitriolic assault upon the Calvinist doctrine of original sin and native depravity he and his fellow Arminians had launched in the 1750s did not include a fully worked out alternative version of child nature. This lacuna was filled in 1785 when Chauncy published in London his *Five Dissertations on the Scripture Account of the Fall; And its Consequences*, a book written about twenty years earlier. *Five Dissertations* confronted New England's Calvinist majority with the picture of an infant who, upon entrance into the world, had only "naked capacities," a being with the potentiality of inclining towards either sinfulness or holiness, but as yet disposed to neither.[37] In presenting the infant mind as neutral and as plastic, Chauncy's debt to John Locke was clear.

Chauncy was rather tardy in incurring this debt. His arch-foe, Jonathan Edwards, had been reading Locke long before Chauncy had even heard of the philosopher and was attempting to co-opt Enlightenment psychology and epistemology for the Calvinist system. Edwards, however, departed from the Englishman's tenets by holding that the young mind, although a blank slate in regard to ideas, was rife with predetermined inclinations which forced the unregenerate individual into rampant sinfulness.[38] If Chauncy was a late convert to the new thought, and generally a less profound student of it than Edwards, at least on this issue he was the better Lockean. He insisted upon the total plasticity of the *tabula rasa* as well as its emptiness of innate ideas.[39] Human nature did not inevitably lead to rampant sinfulness. Ever since Adam's fall, mankind lived in a world of toil and sorrow where the many stresses and anxieties compelled everyone to sin in at least some small degree. But there were always a few who were able to escape the gross sinfulness that characterized the majority. Although most children became morally corrupt as they developed beyond the neutral state in which they were born, some proceeded directly toward holiness as the result of a truly Christian upbringing which prevented the introduction of habits of sin.[40]

The implications of this position were far-reaching: sanctification could be achieved without a definite act of grace. Chauncy refrained, however, from a universal application of his radical conclusion. It was valid for the lucky few who had an exemplary domestic education, but the others would need special grace. They had not started out depraved, as in the Calvinist system, but they had developed a similar corruption through the mismanagement of their upbringing and now only God could purge it.[41] Chauncy's turn to the supernatural may have been based on a belief that sensationalism had limitations and was incapable of changing a *tabula rasa* through good impressions once it had been filled with bad ones. Or he may have merely assumed that after childhood, individuals would never again be in a situation where they could receive a steady stream of favorable impressions. In either case, he ended up relying as much on special grace for most individuals as the Calvinists did in their orthodox stance (although they asserted its necessity for *all* individuals, a major distinction), and his outlook on child rearing was only partly an Enlightenment one.

A fuller Enlightenment position emerged in early nineteenth-century Unitarianism. Its disciples encouraged parents to view their infants as unwarped and unblemished, possessors of a plasticity that responded to whatever pressures they transmitted.[42] The next step—the big one on which Chauncy faltered—was to claim that human agency unaccompanied by divine grace could always produce an individual who was steadfastly moral in character and conduct: "We believe, therefore, most fully in man's entire moral ability to make himself what he pleases."[43] The goal of Unitarian domestic education became the acquisition of a virtuous nature rather than the facilitation of conversion, a stance Calvinists had likewise taken, but more covertly and at the expense of their theology.

When the entire scope of Unitarian writings about upbringing is taken into account, the various differences between their approach and the Calvinist one are not necessarily obvious.

Especially in the first decade and a half of the nineteenth century, Unitarians tended to use shrill tones which simultaneously beseeched and threatened parents in the time-honored Calvinist manner. The differences were often less in what was said than in what was not said—no mention of depravity, conversion, special grace—omissions which might have been easily overlooked given the frequent similar discussions by both groups of such topics as parental example, scriptural lessons, and household authority. The Unitarians sometimes even seemed to insist on the necessity of divine agency in creating a moral child as strongly as did the Calvinists in their theological posture: God "is as strictly the author of virtue and salvation, if they are affected by the means of his appointment, as he would be, if they were effected by miracles. . . . His agency and blessing are as necessary to the *growth of corn* in our fields, as the *growth of virtue* in the hearts of our children." Only a sophisticated reader would realize that the statement merely affirmed that an omnipotent God ultimately determined every event, which was not at all the same as asserting in the Calvinist manner that He directly regenerated an individual through special grace.[44] By 1820, Unitarianism had found its own voice, as demonstrated in Henry Ware's *Letters Addressed to Trinitarians and Calvinists*. Devoid of vestiges of Calvinist rhetoric, this book emphasized with a cheery tone the doctrine that the child was born morally neutral, or perhaps even inclined to the good, and that his character would be formed solely by natural means.[45]

Although Ware was among the first of Unitarians explicitly and firmly to take such a stance on child rearing, he had been presaged by a Congregationalist minister writing thirty years earlier, Enos Hitchcock of Providence, Rhode Island. Strongly influenced by the Enlightenment, Hitchcock substituted Arminianism for the traditional Calvinism of his denomination and also moved towards a rejection of the divinity of Christ. When he served as a Revolutionary War chaplain his fellow New Englanders considered him to be something of a heretic.[46] The stricter Calvinists amongst them would not have been conciliated by his *Memoirs of the Bloomsgrove Family*, an immense tome published in 1790, the one Enlightenment child-rearing work written by a New

Englander that is a full-scale treatise. This book ignored both depravity and conversion and instead presented in great detail a system whereby children could be trained to true virtue through domestic education alone. Put out at a propitious time—the "Protestant Counter-Reformation" against Enlightenment influence in America had not yet commenced—*The Bloomsgrove Family* was well received by elements of the public. "I am much pleased with [it] as a system of education"; "I proceeded upon a similar plan in educating mine," remarked Ebenezer Hazard, businessman, Presbyterian elder, and member of the American Philosophical Society.[47] The resurgence of orthodoxy and evangelicalism in the nineteenth century submerged the book, and it seems to have been of little influence in later decades. Ware, who had attained roughly the same point in 1820 that Hitchcock had reached in 1790, drew on writings other than *The Bloomsgrove Family*.

If Hitchcock's followers were obscure or nonexistent, his predecessors were obvious. The "great Mr. Locke," writing a century earlier, and saying a great deal more in fewer pages, was a kind of intellectual grandfather, for there were areas of strong resemblance between *The Bloomsgrove Family* and *Some Thoughts Concerning Education*. A still closer likeness was to *Loose Hints upon Education, Chiefly Concerning the Culture of the Heart* (Edinburgh, 1781), by a more immediate intellectual ancestor, Lord Kames, an eighteenth-century Scottish philosopher. Indeed, in some ways Hitchcock seemed like a twin of Kames rather than an offspring. (*The Bloomsgrove Family* "is indebted *much* to Lord Kaimes [sic]," the Reverend Jeremy Belknap noted dryly.)[48] Insofar as the theory of child rearing was concerned, the major differences between Locke on one side and on the other, Kames and Hitchcock (and, later, the American Unitarians), concerned modifications of the *tabula rasa* hypothesis.

In its pure form, Locke's idea of the *tabula rasa* was so radically iconoclastic that many of its advocates, including the originator himself, frequently felt compelled to qualify it. Otherwise, they appeared to be denying not only traditional psychological theories and strongly held folk beliefs, but even the testimony of common sense. Although Locke did describe children as "white Paper," as ductile liquid, as "Wax, to be moulded and fashioned as one pleases,"[49] he sometimes used opposing images which gave more weight to the congenital qualities of a child's faculties than to the influence of environment: "God has stamp'd certain Characters upon Men's minds, which like their Shapes, may perhaps be a little mended, but can hardly be totally alter'd and transform'd into the contrary." More commonly, Locke qualified the *tabula rasa* hypothesis by viewing the majority of children as having strong undesirable tendencies that reduced their ductility without completely negating it: "Few of Adam's Children are so happy, as not to be born with some Byass in their natural Temper, which it is the Business of Education either to take off, or counterbalance."[50] The language suggests, perhaps, a residual Calvinism, but congenital predilection of this sort fell far short of the supposedly irresistible depravity of Calvinist theology.

The successors of Locke also conceded that particular children might have undesirable inclinations, but they generally modified the white paper image in the opposite way. While holding onto the doctrine that the impressions of sensation were the major influence in domestic education, they undercut it by endowing all children with certain desirable natural tendencies and even some innate ideas. Of these universal characteristics, the most important were related to the moral sense.

As originated by Lord Shaftesbury and Francis Hutcheson, the theory of the moral sense held that moral knowledge was not innate, but that the motivation for moral acts did come from an innate impulse, the reflex response of an individual's natural feelings to certain sensations. A later version, the one adopted by Kames and Hitchcock, was advanced by Thomas Reid and Richard Price. They claimed that both moral knowledge and moral motivation were innate, the products of an intuitive faculty.[51] Either of these versions of the moral sense qualified Locke by establishing in his neutral child, equally pliant towards good or towards evil, a primal impulse towards the good. In rebuttal, Locke wrote: "That the soul has such a tendency to what is morally good and from evil has not fallen under my observation, and therefore I cannot grant it."[52] The second version, which was a major element in the Scottish common sense philosophy, further qualified Locke by making moral ideas an important exception to the rule that sensation was the source of all knowledge.

The pure *tabula rasa*, hollow and passive, thus gave way to the inborn moral knowledge and moral motivation of Kames's and

Hitchcock's child. This youth's natural impulses led towards cleanliness, sympathy, gratitude, candor, and even religious devotion, for he had an innate notion of God's existence.[53] Kames and Hitchcock were not very rigorous, however, in applying the moral sense theory to child rearing, for they were reluctant to get too far from the realm of sensation. Whereas Calvinists seesawed between the power of depravity and the power of domestic training, they alternated between having all knowledge come from sensation and having some knowledge come from within. Hitchcock proclaimed both that, "Children acquire their knowledge by perception only," and that, "When the innate sense of right and wrong begins to exert itself, . . . conscience imposes that as a duty which convenience had dictated before."[54] The inconsistency indicates the basic attachment of Kames and Hitchcock to the Lockean scheme of child rearing; their approach represented a modification of it rather than an alternative system.

This allegiance was evident even in those instances in which Kames and Hitchcock unwaveringly upheld the innateness of moral knowledge and moral impulses. In order to be of efficacy, this native heritage needed bolstering from external sources. Kames stated that a child's heart naturally possessed the principle of gratitude, and that gratitude should also be taught him. Similarly, Hitchcock advised parents "to stamp on [children's] docile minds, an impression of a benevolent Deity. . . . Second the voice of nature (which has engraven on the mind the being of God . . .) by more explicit instruction."[55]

In the final balance, then, Kames and Hitchcock advocated, along with Locke, a system based upon implanting in the child's mind impressions from external sensations rather than upon releasing forces already present, as the Romantics were to attempt. "Virtue. . . . This is the solid and substantial Good which . . . the Labour and Art of Education should *furnish* the Mind with, and fasten there" (Locke). "You owe to your children, the *making* of them virtuous" (Kames). The parent should *"instil* those virtuous principles into his children, which form their principal glory and happiness in life" (Hitchcock).[56] Mothers and fathers were clearly putting more into the child than they drew out.

A reliance upon external forces characterized Calvinist as well as Enlightenment child-rearing theory. The Calvinists depended upon such forces both when they adopted the Enlightenment's psychological language and talked about the parental molding of a plastic child, and when they spoke in the rhetoric of theology about the necessity of divine grace. However, the need for grace, even if it was not consistently upheld, created an unbridgeable gap between the Calvinist theory and that of the Enlightenment. In the Enlightenment formulation, God functioned as the primal source of moral standards, and as the judge who determined an individual's fate in the afterlife on the basis of his fidelity to them, but not as a supernatural agency directly operative at any point in the child-rearing process.

Having dispensed with both total depravity and divine grace, the Enlightenment writers were able to be more consistent than the Calvinists in ascribing to the domestic environment the preponderant influence over the child. In effect, parents were given an even greater burden of responsibility. Failure in child rearing was never to be blamed on native corruption, nor success made to wait upon an uncertain holy influx. Some parents may not have welcomed the increased accountability. The fatalistic attitude which could be drawn from the theological vein in the Calvinist child-rearing system, a fatalism which the New England public had so often found at the bottom of Calvinism, did not necessarily repulse parents. For those who were lazy, indulgent, preoccupied with other matters, or simply uncaring about their offspring, a fatalistic attitude offered, as the ministry feared, a welcome rationalization. Since Enlightenment writings started from very different premises, they presented little in the way of sympathetic response to that parental attitude. It was flatly dismissed rather than subtly counterbalanced. A more convincing case against parental fatalism eventually would be made in the work of Horace Bushnell, the result of combining Enlightenment elements with those from both traditional Calvinism and the new Romanticism.

The Early Romantic Approach: Inborn Goodness

Romantic child-rearing theory made its initial appearance in New England at the end of the early national period, two generations after its development in Europe. The leading advocate was Bronson Alcott, the self-educated Transcendentalist whose chosen mission was to reveal to the world the true nature and importance of childhood.[57] Alcott's best known work with children was from 1834 to 1838 in the radically innovative Boston Temple School, but he was also concerned with domestic education and he expressed some of his ideas on this subject in the late 1820s and early 1830s.

The incredibly tangled sources of Alcott's thought on child rearing included close observation of his infant daughters ("The progress of my little girl is deeply interesting to me. I have kept a record of her progressive development which has already extended to more than 40 pages in manuscript"), and an immense potpourri of readings (among others, Plato, Pythagoras, Boehme, Swedenborg, Coleridge, and Wordsworth).[58] Of especial influence were the ideas of the Swiss educator Johann Heinrich Pestalozzi whose theories of domestic education were first presented in English in 1827 and were published in Boston soon thereafter. Alcott allied himself with Pestalozzi by writing an approving article about the new theories for the *American Journal of Education* in 1829.[59]

The goal of domestic education for Alcott and for Pestalozzi was to help the child secure the certainty of eternal salvation. Divine grace was not required in order to reach the necessary moral and spiritual state. The Romantic child possessed as part of his native endowment praiseworthy tendencies which had only to be developed to make him fit for heaven. Alcott enthusiastically explained Pestalozzi's method of accomplishing this evolution: "Assured that God is ever present . . . the feelings of reverence, and gratitude, and devotion, and love, spontaneously rise in [the infant's] breast, accompanied by a sense of the divine approbation, which leads to the constant, and cheerful, and conscientious performance of duty."[60]

This view of juvenile nature was the antithesis of the one upheld by Calvinist theology, which insisted that, "Mankind are born like the wild ass's colt, ignorant of God and divine things, and unwilling to learn their duty to God and man."[61] In an emotional passage in his observational journals on infancy, Alcott explicitly repudiated the degrading Calvinist doctrines of original sin and total depravity and rejoiced "that nobler views are gaining currency. Infancy is beginning to be respected."[62] His approach to domestic education also conflicted with the Enlightenment scheme. Along with Pestalozzi, he emphasized the growth of latent forces rather than a passive absorption of external impressions. Even late eighteenth-century modifiers of Locke's *tabula rasa,*like Kames and Hitchcock, had not stressed the natural inner development of the child's psyche to the extent of these Romantics.

Sometimes, Alcott went further than Pestalozzi in exalting the status of the child. Drawing on Wordsworth, he suggested that infants had their origin in heaven. Freshly arrived on earth from the realm of God, the little ones longed to go back and would eventually do so (unlike twentieth-century infants, who will never return to the comforts of the womb for which they supposedly yearn). Alcott asserted, "The newly-born soul [has] . . . visions of bliss, which bring home before the mind the remembrance of the joys of previous existence"; "The human soul has had a primordial experience in the Infinite Spirit. . . . The finite is but the return of the soul on the path of the infinite."[63] From this perspective, the task of the parent would seem to be more to maintain and conserve the residual elements of heaven than to develop unripened powers, to ward off infection and decay rather than to open a bud: "Her infant, now in paradise, she will endeavour to sustain there, by removing forbidden fruit from its view."[64]

Whether an inconsistency exists between Alcott's talk about developing latent characteristics and his talk about preserving lingering traits is not of fundamental importance. Unlike the Calvinists who struggled mightily (if often unsuccessfully) to achieve consistency, out of their respect for logic and because their ideas had to be harmonized with a received intellectual structure, Alcott and the other Transcendentalists sought to apprehend truth by direct spiritual vision. Accordingly, they neglected system and consistency in domestic education theory as in other spheres. In any case, the main directions of Alcott's thought were evident to contemporaries. The Unitarian William Ellery Channing recoiled in horror in 1837 when Alcott made pantheistic statements about "the connexion of the Divine and Human Nature [and] attempted to show the identity of the human soul, in its diviner action, with God."[65]

Another early example of Romanticism in domestic education literature was *The Mother's Book* of 1831 by Lydia Maria Child. Like Alcott, she described the infant as a "little image of God" newly arrived from heaven.[66] Her Romanticism, however, was more timid than that of the Transcendentalist. She apparently did not regard children as actually possessing a memory of their origin for she described the infant mind as "empty," although this blank mind seemed as much akin to Emerson's "transparent eyeball" as to Locke's *tabula rasa*. She even believed in a kind of genetic depravity in individual cases: "No doubt bad temper, as well as other evils, moral and physical, are often hereditary."[67]

Nevertheless, Lydia Child's basic position was the Romantic one of preserving and fostering the infant's splendid native endowment: "They come to us from heaven, with their little souls full of innocence and peace; and, as far as possible, a mother's influence should not interfere with the influence of angels."[68] She even spoke of the child as a "little cherub," [69] a phrase which in the early 1830s was probably unprecedented in New England in a full-scale work on child rearing. Appellations of this sort had long been used in ephemeral magazine poetry, as when death in infancy was rationalized as being a fortunate escape from the corruption that would have tarnished the innocent child had he remained on earth. For someone taking a systematic view to describe living children as cherubs, and to formulate a theory of domestic education on the hypothesis that they could remain so, was a revolutionary act.

Although the Romantic plan would be further elaborated in subsequent decades,[70] the writings of Alcott and Child had set forth enough of it during the early national period to provide some variety in the current theories of domestic education. This new Romantic view regarded children as envoys from heaven with desirable native endowments which should be preserved and gently stimulated. In contrast, the Enlightenment scheme emphasized the filling of the mostly empty mind and the shaping of the flexible disposition through powerful external influences. The Calvinist system was similar to the Enlightenment's in its basic operation, but was laced with tokens of orthodoxy which portrayed the child as thoroughly reformable only by God. The variety in the child-rearing theories of the early 1830s was limited in extent, but the very fact of any variety at all is of fundamental importance. Contrary to some present-day opinions which contrast contemporary parents, confronted by a multiplicity of child-rearing theories, with parents of earlier generations who supposedly were spared the difficulties of decision because they knew of only a single approach,[71] a real choice did exist for the literate classes of New England by the end of the early national period.

Synthesis

In 1833, at the close of the era, the Reverend Horace Bushnell, a young graduate of Yale College and Divinity School, was ordained pastor of the North Church of Hartford. Deeply interested in domestic education, he spent ten years brooding over what he considered to be defects in the contemporary beliefs and practices.[72] In his famous *Views of Christian Nurture,* published in 1847,[73] Bushnell put forth a remedy by combining elements from the Calvinist, Enlightenment, and Romantic theories. Although the book came out well after the early national period, the child-rearing theories of the 1780s through the early 1830s can be better understood when seen in the light of this subsequent work, and *Views of Christian Nurture* can be thoroughly appreciated only in the context of those theories. Bushnell's relation to this period is that of Rousseau to the eighteenth century: his work at once rejects, extends, and shifts to a new basis the thought of his predecessors.[74]

Like many clergymen before him, Bushnell believed that the evangelical public doubted the ability of parents to foster the moral development and conversion of children. Although a long line of Calvinist writers on domestic education had advocated a positive and active approach, a fatalistic attitude could be drawn from certain elements in their work. With that danger in mind, Bushnell deliberately sought to eliminate from his own child-rearing advice potential theoretical justifications for fatalism, while retaining, as the Enlightenment approach had not, a role for divine grace.

He began by insisting that the extraordinary receptivity of the young made domestic education highly efficacious, allowing parents to shape their offspring in whatever way they desired: "There goes out in the whole manner of the parent . . . an expression of feeling, and that feeling expressed streams directly into the soul, and reproduces itself there. . . . To this power the infant is passive as wax is to the seal."[75] The child was to be treated as a plastic form which external forces molded, a view in accord with the Calvinist theory of domestic education insofar as it had adopted the Lockean psychology. There was an obvious conflict with the Romantic scheme which treated the child as self-propelled rather than as inert.

Bushnell went further than earlier Calvinist spokesmen for domestic education by arguing that genuine holiness, and not just morality, could be developed in a child from his first years: "The child is to be trained, not for conversion at some advanced age, but [is] expected to *'grow up a Christian'*. . . . God offers a grace to make it possible." The divine blessing was not a kind of payment after parents had made a conscientious effort in domestic education, but was an integral part of the domestic education process itself. Grace became a present reality in upbringing instead of a future goal.[76]

The chronology of conversion underwent a corresponding change. For the Puritan, with his doctrines of preparation for grace and of imperfect sanctification after grace, and his characteristic doubts about the authenticity of his regeneration, conversion lay in the middle of an individual's spiritual pilgrimage. For the revivalist of the Second Great Awakening, especially one with perfectionist leanings, conversion lay toward the end of the spiritual pilgrimage. For Bushnell, conversion lay at the very beginning of the pilgrimage. Along with the divine blessing which made it possible, conversion was inseparably merged with the rearing of the child. It was to be a gradual process rather than the sudden, searing experience which had become archetypal in the era of the Second Great Awakening: "The child . . . is to open on the world as one that is spiritually renewed, not remembering the time when he went through a technical experience"; "Christian education, or training in the families, is to be itself a piece of domestic conversion."[77]

Underlying these alterations in the Calvinist system of domestic education—indeed, making them possible—were two of the major themes of mid-nineteenth-century American Romanticism. Bushnell had not accepted the Romantic idea that the parental task was to develop the child's native goodness, but he did accept certain Romantic emphases. If he insisted that character was put into the child rather than drawn out, his plan for accomplishing it was closer to the Romantic approach of gently encouraging an extant goodness than to the Calvinist and Enlightenment approach of strenuously stamping impressions on a *tabula rasa*. The basic process remained sensationalist, but of a softer and more diffuse sort. The impressions made by a Christian nurture came less from formal moral and religious training than from "the look, the voice, the handling." Children are "connected by an organic unity, not with your instructions, but with your *life*. . . . Your character is a stream, a river, flowing down upon your children, hour by hour." Bushnell was enveloping the child in the family in the same organic way that his Transcendentalist contemporaries were enveloping the individual in nature or in the Oversoul: "Embosomed for a season in nature, whose floods of life stream around and through us," wrote Emerson.[78] An organicism which made the character, conduct, and spiritual life of the child a product of the entire home environment let Bushnell overcome the tendency of evangelical Protestantism to place everything on individual supplications to an unpredictable deity. The covenants and divine promises that had been used for this purpose in the past were no longer necessary.

A second Romantic theme enabled Bushnell to avoid the Arminianism which his predecessors had so often approached, and to which his own theory of regeneration from infancy by means of Christian nurture seemed even more liable. Bushnell did not have to oscillate between an advocacy of parental ability and an avowal of divine sovereignty because he visualized Christian mothers and fathers as so infused with the divine spirit that God could be represented as directly operative when they formed the juvenile character. The deity did not use domestic education as a mere secondary instrument, perfunctorily placing a stamp of approval on its proper employment. God instead literally worked *through* a genuinely Christian domestic education; His actual spirit inhabited it. Here was the Romantic theme of the super-natural pervading the natural, of higher powers pulsating in common forms: "The house, having a domestic Spirit of grace dwelling in it, should become the church of childhood, the table and hearth a holy rite." Emerson had said, "The invariable mark of wisdom is to see the miraculous in the common."[79]

The language of *Views of Christian Nurture* also contributed to its force. Not only did the book possess an eloquent lucidity, a rare quality in latter-day Calvinist literature, but it repeatedly employed the same sort of imagery as was appearing in contemporary Romantic writing. In describing domestic education, Bushnell used metaphors and similes found upon images of ambient air ("The spirit of the house is breathed into his nature"); of warming light ("The loveliness of a good life . . . glowing about the young soul"); and, especially, of liquid motion ("The soul of the parent streaming into his eyes and ears").[80]

As Ann Douglas has pointed out, the declining status of the ministry in mid-nineteenth-century America, and the related increase in the proportion of women to men in their audience, led to a "softening of Protestant theology" and the "sentimentalization of Northern culture."[81] In both what he said and the way that he said it, Bushnell certainly fits into this context. However, the term "sentimentalization" is appropriate in his case in its more generic sense of an emphasis upon the feelings, particularly those of a warm and tender sort, rather than in its more specific sense of mawkishness. In contrast to many of his contemporaries, Bushnell was able to discipline Romanticism by subjecting it to a tough-minded perspective, drawn from the Calvinist elements of his thought. The power of his message lay in its graceful combination of the old and the new.

To ward off the inevitable charges of heterodoxy which arose from the defenders of traditional theology, Bushnell deliberately placed himself in the tradition of Samuel Hopkins and Timothy Dwight, "respected and prominent divines . . . [who] have given their testimony for Christian nurture, in a manner perfectly coincident with the doctrine, by which I have frightened, so uncomfortably, the cautious orthodoxy of some."[82] Bushnell emphasized his predecessors' insistence that God had promised to bless the properly raised children of believing parents; their conviction that domestic education could therefore bring a child to a relatively early piety; and their optimism, reinforced by the Enlightenment, about juvenile susceptibility to good impressions. As Bushnell acknowledged, the psychological rhetoric Timothy Dwight had employed could sound especially similar to his own language.[83] Bushnell also may have drawn from the work of the Reverend John S. C. Abbott who wrote the well-known *The Mother At Home* at the start of the Romantic era and anticipated some of his themes.

Bushnell's system, however, was more cohesive than the one his Calvinist predecessors had put forward. His view of child rearing as a means of grace was consistent with his theory of conversion as a gradual process set in a social matrix. His forerunners, holding a similar view of child rearing, had often emphasized in their general theology the sudden conversion of isolated sinners by an unpredictable God.[84] Bushnell's system was also better integrated in that he did not talk on occasion about an obdurate depravity which made moral cultivation extremely difficult, but unwaveringly held that good impressions easily formed ductile children into virtuous individuals. Although he clung to a belief in juvenile depravity, in describing this characteristic he avoided the fearsome terms earlier Calvinists had sometimes used. According to Bushnell, "It is not sin which [the child] derives from his parents; at least not sin in any sense which imports blame, but only some prejudice to the perfect harmony of his mold."[85] *Views of Christian Nurture* never portrayed the child as a monster, an immense advantage at a time when many were coming to believe that "children are simple—loving—true: 'Tis Heaven that made them so."[86]

All in all, Bushnell was neither a full-blooded Calvinist nor a full-blooded Romantic, but a hybrid—a Romantic-Calvinist.[87] The ways in which he employed the rhetoric of Romanticism and its themes of organicism and the pervasion of the natural by the supernatural challenged the lingering Orthodox perspective. Yet, his retention of the idea of a defective nature inherited from parents, and his description of the child as a passive lump formed by external influences, clearly separated his theory of domestic education from outright Romanticism. He was aware of the difference and wished to maintain it:

> There are many who assume the radical goodness of human nature, and the work of Christian education is, in their view, only to educate, or educe the good that is in us. Let no one be disturbed by the suspicion of a coincidence between what I have here said and such a theory. The natural pravity of men

is plainly asserted in the Scriptures, and, if it were not, the familiar laws of physiology would require us to believe, what amounts to the same thing. . . . There is no so unreasonable assumption, none so wide of all just philosophy, as that which proposes to form a child to virtue, by simply educing or drawing out what is in him.[88]

Bushnell's synthesis of Calvinist, Enlightenment, and Romantic child-rearing theories was thus only a partial one, but it was the most complete fusion that New England domestic education literature achieved.

Obsolescence

Within two generations the entire tradition for which *Views of Christian Nurture* was the summit began to be displaced. The creation of a class of professional advisers on familial matters reduced the earlier commentators to nonauthorities. As the philosopher, clergyman, and pious layman gave way to the pediatrician, psychologist, and social worker, the older types of child-rearing theory lapsed. John Locke's seventeenth-century *Some Thoughts Concerning Education* had been republished in New England in 1830 as a still relevant work, but what child-rearing book of 1830 could be so republished today?

The new authorities greatly expanded knowledge about the child's body, intellect, and emotions. The levels of discussion most directly affected by their studies, psychology and methodology, generally became far more complex and sophisticated than they had been during the early national period. What was often lost was an interest in the rationale of child rearing. Although not always successful, the earlier authorities had tried to give parents a clear sense of the general goals of upbringing, the ends for which psychological expositions and methodological programs served as means. The specialists who displaced them have not, for the most part, been as concerned with elaborating the overall purposes of child rearing. And even when they have been, the decline in the present century of big beliefs about the meaning of human life has made it increasingly difficult to formulate higher ends. Dr. Benjamin Spock, the Nestor of contemporary child management, observes that, "The rearing of children is more and more puzzling for parents in the twentieth century because we've lost a lot of our old-fashioned convictions about what kind of morals and ambitions and characters we want them to have. We've even lost our convictions about the purpose of human existence. Instead we have come to depend on psychological concepts. They've been helpful in solving many of the smaller problems but they are of little use in answering the major questions."[89] The older child-rearing theories were displaced not simply because they were deficient in specialized knowledge and empirical data, but also because they embodied ideologies of life and of death which were no longer believed.

CODA

From the Puritans to Bushnell

Coda: From the Puritans to Bushnell

TWO HUNDRED YEARS SEPARATED the mid-seventeenth century, when the Puritans were at their height, from the mid-nineteenth century, the time of Horace Bushnell. There is no evidence that the physical and mental characteristics children brought with them into the world changed during those years in a discernible way. But the adult outlook on children, both when they died and when they lived, did undergo substantial alterations.

The Dead Child

Puritan grief for deceased infants, genuine as it seems to have been, was restrained in comparison to nineteenth-century reactions. In all likelihood, New Englanders of the later period loved their offspring with greater intensity so that the loss of a child was more psychologically devastating to the parent. At the least, the bereaved felt freer about expressing the extent of their sorrow. Unlike the Puritans who had struggled, not always successfully, to control their emotions closely during mourning, as during all life experiences, people in the Romantic era of the nineteenth century gave their feelings fuller play. When, in 1827, the Calvinist minister John Todd delivered a sermon while his baby lay at home dying, as Cotton Mather had done in similar circumstances in 1701, he broke down in the pulpit and many of the congregation wept along with him.[1] Displays of what the Puritans would have considered immoderate grief were the counterparts in bereavement to the flowing emotionality of religious revivalism.

Except for the diminishing group of devout Calvinists, people no longer worried about the chances of their deceased infants ending up in hell. The lavish outpourings of sorrow were channeled into exclusively optimistic reflections on infant prospects in the afterlife. This change was part of the larger transformation whereby "innocence replaced sinfulness as the first attribute of the American character."[2] As a result of many different factors—the Enlightenment, the individualism spawned by capitalism, the rise of Romanticism—mothers and fathers in nineteenth-century New England placed a higher value than the Puritans had on the moral worth of both their infants and their own selves. The consequent waning of the Calvinist sense of sinfulness and guilt, coupled with the rise of obsessive love (which was linked to the same developments and the declining birth rate), allowed the mourner to focus on a vision of heaven without even momentary interruption by a vision of hell.

By the mid-nineteenth century, the majority of the Orthodox clergy had accepted the new sensibility regarding infants and no longer asserted, directly or by implication, that some of them would spend eternity in the nether world. The handful who refused to give up infant damnation could not sustain the doctrine as a matter of general interest. They did not even dramatize the issues in ways that at least might have aroused the public's fascination with what it considered to be abhorrent, as accounts of atrocities have done in the twentieth century. Bushnell found himself in the rare position of being able to witness the expiration in New England of a doctrine which had been in existence for almost two millennia.

The Living Child

Although free of some of the anxieties that the death of infants had once provoked, parents in the nineteenth century, especially mothers, were beset by new anxieties about the rearing of children who survived. They could ignore Michael Wigglesworth's *The Day of Doom*, but those who read books and magazines could not ignore the growing literature on child rearing. As is so evident in our own times, the very existence of a body of expert writings on upbringing could create apprehensions among the public. Susan

Huntington observed to herself, "There is scarcely any subject concerning which I feel more anxiety, than the proper education of my children. It is a difficult and delicate subject; and the more I reflect on my duty to them, the more I feel how much is to be learnt by myself. The person who undertakes to form the infant mind . . . ought to possess a deep and accurate knowledge of human nature." Resolving to exhibit "the most persevering industry in the acquisition of necessary knowledge, [and] the most indefatigable application of that knowledge to particular cases," Huntington kept up-to-date on important works in domestic education, as though she were a member of The Book-of-the-Month Club.[3] The conviction that parents were remiss if they did not obtain and study an expanding body of literature on child rearing was a new phenomenon.

Behind the growing interest in such literature was the continuing intensification of love for children. Parents who had an obsessive type of emotional attachment to their offspring were most eager to use all available means to do right by them. Such love especially characterized mothers. A mother was expected by the society at large—fathers, bachelors, single women, childless couples, and, of course, other mothers—to act as the main agency for displaying the culture's heightened estimation of children. To rely upon the mother rather than the father for this role was the easiest path for society to follow since she had traditionally done more of the routine handling of children. This approach also served as a way of keeping within bounds the culture's heightened estimation of women themselves, caused by some of the same factors that had elevated children. Steered into intensely emotional parent-child relationships, women would not be likely to nourish hopes for participation in spheres which custom defined as the male domain. In supposed compensation, they were told that the role of loving mother was the most important one in the society.[4]

The child psychology of Timothy Dwight exemplified these trends, without carrying them to the fullest extension. From the perspective of the late twentieth century, or even the Romantic mid-nineteenth century, his methods for the everyday management of children seem to have no lack of austerity and rigor, but from the perspective of the Puritan seventeenth century a definite relaxation had occurred. He grounded parental authority less on fear than on love, and in a related shift emphasized the mother's part in the socialization process. In ideas like these Dwight was responding to the emergent modern notions of the family and at least in that regard was not the anachronistic mediocrity that Vernon Louis Parrington depicted.[5]

The more abstract levels of child-rearing theory were also influenced by broad cultural developments. The same emphasis on human worth and ability which had contributed to the purging of the infant damnation issue from the reflections of the bereaved tended to diminish the role of divine agency in upbringing. Even in the Calvinist writings of the early national period, parents were given the power, ostensibly reserved for God, to form children into beings who were thoroughly virtuous in character and conduct. The fatalistic aspects of Calvinism, which offered a convenient excuse for failure at the job, were subordinated, although not eliminated until the work of Horace Bushnell.

The Old Expertise and the New

Bushnell's partial synthesis of Calvinist, Enlightenment, and Romantic ideas brought New England's traditional religious-philosophical approach to the study of children as far towards modernity as it would go before Darwinism transformed almost all categories of thought.[6] Like Timothy Dwight, Bushnell used a different vocabulary and a different method of arriving at conclusions than contemporary child study experts employ, but presented some of the same insights. However, their ideas have had little influence on modern theories about upbringing. In 1965, a well-respected psychologist could write: "The personality of a child is colored by the emotional atmosphere of his home. This truth seems self-evident, yet it is only recently that we have come to recognize the relation between a parent's character and a child's conduct."[7] Dwight and other early national period commentators on child rearing certainly saw the connection and Bushnell made it the heart of his theory of Christian nurture. But these earlier insights have not been remembered because the experts on the family severed their links with the older approaches when the field became professionalized and specialized towards the end of the nineteenth century.[8] The sound ideas of the tradition that Dwight and Bushnell represented were forgotten, along with the unsatisfactory ones, and have had to be rediscovered.

Notes

Preface

1. I want to emphasize that I am writing as an intellectual historian, which means that the kinds of materials I use and the sorts of analyses I perform will often be quite different from those of the "new" social historians, a group that has made impressive contributions to family history in recent years. In the words of John Higham, "To understand the encounter of ideas with action in a massive way, we need a systematic view of the ideas." See "American Intellectual History: A Critical Appraisal," *American Quarterly*, XIII (Summer, 1961), 232.

2. "Developmental Perspectives on the History of Childhood," in *The Family in History: Interdisciplinary Essays*, eds. Theodore K. Rabb and Robert I. Rotberg (New York: Harper paperback, 1973), p. 139; see also pp. 127-28. Similar remarks are put forth by C. John Sommerville in another essay in this collection, "Bibliographic Note: Toward a History of Childhood and Youth," pp. 234-35. See also Jay Mechling, "Advice to Historians on Advice to Mothers," *Journal of Social History*, 9 (Fall, 1975), 55-56; and Michael Zuckerman, "Dr. Spock: The Confidence Man," in *The Family in History*, ed. Charles E. Rosenberg (Philadelphia, 1975), pp. 180-82.

3. Arnold Gesell, Frances Ilg, and Louise Bates Ames, *Infant and Child in the Culture of Today* (New York, 1974, rev. ed.), p. ix.

4. Lloyd deMause, "The Evolution of Childhood," in *The History of Childhood,"* ed. Lloyd deMause (New York, 1974), p. 1.

I. "From the Cradle to the Coffin"

1. Fitzhugh Dodson, *How to Parent* (New York: Signet paperback, 1971), p. 32.

2. John Eliot, *A Brief Answer to a Small Book written by John Norcot*

Against Infant-Baptisme (Boston, 1679), p. 16; Cotton Mather, *Right Thoughts in Sad Hours* (Dunstable, 1811, orig. ed., London, 1689), pp. 50-52; Cotton Mather, *Help for Distressed Parents* (Boston, 1695), p. 13.

3. Jeannine Hensley, ed., *The Works of Anne Bradstreet* (Cambridge, 1967), p. 236; "Diary of Samuel Sewall," *Collections of the Massachusetts Historical Society*, 5th Series, V (Boston, 1878), 399; "Diary of Cotton Mather," *Massachusetts Historical Society Collections*, 7th Series, VII (Boston, 1911), 380-82.

4. John Demos, "Families in Colonial Bristol, Rhode Island: An Exercise in Historical Demography," *William and Mary Quarterly*, XXV (Jan., 1968), 40; John Demos, *A Little Commonwealth: Family Life in Plymouth Colony* (New York, 1970), pp. 65-66; Philip J. Greven, Jr., *Four Generations: Population, Land, and Family in Colonial Andover, Massachusetts* (Ithaca, 1970), pp. 25, 26.

5. Greven, *Four Generations*, pp. 25, 106-8; Susan L. Norton, "Population Growth in Colonial America: A Study of Ipswich, Massachusetts," *Population Studies*, 25 (Nov., 1971), 442-43; Maris A. Vinovskis, "Angels' Heads and Weeping Willows: Death in Early America," pp. 7, 9-10. I am grateful to Professor Vinovskis for allowing me to read the manuscript of this article, which is to be published in *The Proceedings of the American Antiquarian Society*. John Demos estimates that in seventeenth-century Plymouth the rate of infant and child mortality was 25%. See "Notes on Life in Plymouth Colony," *William and Mary Quarterly*, XXII (April, 1965), 271. See also Demos, *A Little Commonwealth*, p. 66. Infant mortality rates in present-day America vary greatly in relation to socioeconomic class, but even at their highest (such as 41.5 per 1000 in Central Harlem in 1966-1967) are well below the colonial figures. Contemporary rates are given in Urie Bronfenbrenner, "Reality and Research in the Ecology of Human Development," *Proceedings of the American Philosophical Society*, 119, Number 6 (Dec. 5, 1975), 452-54.

6. For demographic investigations of the average number of children per complete family, see Daniel Scott Smith, "The Demographic History of Colonial New England," *Journal of Economic History*, XXXII (March, 1972), 177, 179n.; Greven, *Four Generations*, pp. 30-31, 111-12, 200-4; Robert Higgs and H. Louis Stettler, III, "Colonial New England Demography: A Sampling Approach," *William and Mary Quarterly*, XXVII (April, 1970), 287-91; Demos, *A Little Commonwealth*, p. 192; and Norton, "Population Growth in Colonial America: A Study of Ipswich, Massachusetts," 444.

7. "Diary of Cotton Mather," VIII (Boston, 1912), 260-61. The number of Mather's children is given incorrectly as fourteen in Joseph E. Illick, "Child-Rearing in Seventeenth-Century England and America," in *The History of Childhood*, ed. Lloyd deMause (New York, 1974), p. 325. One of the seven children of Sewall who died in infancy was a stillborn. For tombstones marking multiple deaths, see Dickran and Ann Tashjian, *Memorials for Children of Change; The Art of Early New England Stonecarving* (Middletown, Conn., 1974), pp. 238, 239. The highest rates of infant mortality in seventeenth or eighteenth-century New England

probably occurred during the diphtheria ("throat distemper") scourge of 1735-1740, which is after the Puritan era as I have defined it. But this disease, as well as some of the other common ones, took heavy tolls of young children in various communities in the earlier years of the eighteenth century and in the seventeenth century. See Ernest Caulfield, "Some Common Diseases of Colonial Children," *Publications of the Colonial Society of Massachusetts: Transactions, 1942-1946*, XXXV, 15; Ernest Caulfield, *A True History of the Terrible Epidemic Vulgarly Called the Throat Distemper Which Occurred in His Majesty's New England Colonies Between the Years 1735 and 1740* (New Haven, 1939), p. 102; and John Duffy, *Epidemics in Colonial America* (Baton Rouge, 1953), pp. 45, 178, 216.

8. Samuel Willard, *The Mourners Cordial Against Excessive Sorrow* (Boston, 1691), p. 72.

9. Samuel Willard, *Impenitent Sinners Warned of their Misery and Summoned to Judgment* (Boston, 1698), pp. 36, 37, 39; Increase Mather, *Meditations on the Glory of the Heavenly World* (Boston, 1711), p. 100; Cotton Mather, *Meat out of the Eater; or Funeral-Discourses Occasioned by the Death of Several Relatives* (Boston, 1703), pp. 27-28, 84, 89, 97.

10. The Puritans did not offer strict definitions of infancy, and the age limit implied in different documents varies. I have therefore interpreted the term broadly, relying upon the criteria set forth by Samuel Willard in *The Mourners Cordial:* "Concerning Children that dye in their infancy. I understand all that age wherein they are not grown up to these years of knowledge, wherein they are able to improve the word of God, and the ordinances of the Gospel, for the good of their own Souls" (p. 75). Even in a society that emphasized precocity, the average child would not be expected to meet such conditions in a substantial way much before four.

11. For examples, see "Dr. Beecher's Letters," *Christian Examiner*, V (May, July, Nov., 1828), 241-63, 316-40, 506-42; "Examination of a Note by Dr. Beecher," *Christian Examiner*, IV (Sept.-Oct., 1827), 432-46; and "State of the Calvinistic Controversy," *Christian Disciple*, V (May-June, 1823), 220-22.

12. In taking this approach I have been influenced by the work of John Demos. He states: "The demand for certainty—or at least for 'proof'— while reasonable and laudable as a long-range goal, need not be rigidly maintained at every stage of historical inquiry. . . . Scholars should never, in my opinion, dismiss an important problem because of 'insufficient data.' . . . We must be ready to ponder what is *likely* to have happened— when more certain knowledge is lacking." See *A Little Commonwealth*, p. xiii.

13. "Deacon John Paine's Journal," *The Mayflower Descendant*, IX (1907), 139; "Diary of Rev. Samuel Dexter, of Dedham," *New England Historical and Genealogical Register*, XIV (1860), 204; "Diary of Lawrence Hammond," *Proceedings of the Massachusetts Historical Society*, 2nd Series, VII (1891, 1892), 151. Cf. Illick, "Child-Rearing in Seventeenth-Century England and America," p. 326. There were also diaries that merely mentioned the fact of an infant's death without comment, but the

same terseness can be found in regard to the death of a mother, father, or spouse.

14. "The Autobiography of Thomas Shepard," *Publications of the Colonial Society of Massachusetts: Transactions, 1927-1930*, XXVII, 381.

15. "Diary of Cotton Mather," VIII, 642; Samuel Kettell, ed., *Specimens of American Poetry*, I (Boston, 1829), 14; Robert Middlekauff, *The Mathers; Three Generations of Puritan Intellectuals, 1596-1728* (New York, 1971), pp. 201-2. Edmund Morgan was the first historian to emphasize the strength of parental love among the Puritans. See *The Puritan Family* (New York: Harper paperback, rev. ed., 1966), pp. 173, 185-6. David Stannard has recently confirmed the "Puritan parent's genuine love for his children," calling it "the most common, normal and expected attitude." See "Death and the Puritan Child," in *Death in America*, ed. David E. Stannard (Philadelphia: University of Pennsylvania Press paperback, 1975), p. 15.

16. John F. Walzer, "A Period of Ambivalence: Eighteenth-Century American Childhood," in *The History of Childhood*, ed. Lloyd deMause, p. 380, n. 100. David Hunt, *Parents and Children in History; The Psychology of Family Life in Early Modern France* (New York, 1970), pp. 125, 185.

17. Charles F. Adams, Jr., "Abstract of John Marshall's Diary," *Proceedings of the Massachusetts Historical Society*, 2nd Series, I (1884-85), 156; "Diary of Cotton Mather," VII, 163; "Diary of Samuel Sewall," V, 469. See also "Letter-Book of Samuel Sewall," *Collections of the Massachusetts Historical Society*, 6th Series, I (Boston, 1886), 51, 112.

18. For example, see "Comment by John Walzer," *History of Childhood Quarterly*, I (Summer, 1973), 58; and Christopher Lasch, "What the Doctor Ordered," review of Edward Shorter's *The Making of the Modern Family*, in *New York Review of Books*, XXII (Dec. 11, 1975), 50.

19. Edward Shorter, *The Making of the Modern Family* (New York, 1975), pp. 203-4.

20. Maris A. Vinovskis, "Mortality Rates and Trends in Massachusetts Before 1860," *Journal of Economic History*, XXXII (March, 1972), 200; Norton, "Population Growth in Colonial America: A Study of Ipswich, Massachusetts," 442-43.

21. These distinguishing features of family types are elaborated in Shorter, *The Making of the Modern Family*, pp. 5, 17, 169.

22. Ibid., pp. 169, 191-92, 204. Needless to say, parental love was only one of the variables that determined the death rate of infants. In eighteenth-century New England, epidemics, especially of diphtheria, caused the infant death rate to increase markedly in some communities. See Greven, *Four Generations*, pp. 186-88.

23. Shorter, *The Making of the Modern Family*, p. 199.

24. The discussion of the Augustino-federal version of original sin is mainly drawn from the following works, although I have departed from each of them at particular points: George P. Fisher, "The Augustinian and the Federal Theories of Original Sin Compared," *New Englander*,

XXVII (July, 1868), 470-74, 504-5; Perry Miller, *The New England Mind: The Seventeenth Century* (New York, 1939), pp. 400-1; H[ilrie] Shelton Smith, *Changing Conceptions of Original Sin: A Study in American Theology since 1750* (New York, 1955), pp. 2-4; Nathaniel W. Taylor, *Concio ad Clerum; Sermon Delivered in the Chapel of Yale College, September 10, 1828* (New Haven, 1828), pp. 25-26; and [Peter Clark], *Remarks on a Late Pamphlet, Intitled "The Opinion of One that has Perused the Summer-Morning's Conversation"* (Boston, 1758), p. 8.

25. Cotton Mather, *A Family Well-Ordered* (Boston, 1699), p. 11; Deodat Lawson, *The Duty and Property of a Religious Householder* (Boston, 1693), p. 42; Willard, *The Mourners Cordial*, p. 85; Thomas Paine, *The Doctrine of Original Sin Proved and Applyed* (Boston, 1724), p. 13.

26. Charles Strickland, "A Transcendentalist Father: The Child-Rearing Practices of Bronson Alcott," *History of Childhood Quarterly*, I (Summer, 1973), 11.

27. Rev. of *A Practical View of Christian Education in its Earliest Stages*, by T. Babington, *Christian Disciple*, N.S. I (March-April, 1819), 150.

28. Crispus, "On the Education of Children," *Panoplist*, X (Sept., 1814), 394.

29. Cotton Mather, *Right Thoughts in Sad Hours*, pp. 52-53; Donald E. Stanford, ed., *The Poems of Edward Taylor* (New Haven, 1960), p. 54.

30. *Silentarius* (Boston, 1721), p. 30.

31. "Diary of Samuel Sewall," V, 369; "Diary of Cotton Mather," VII, 179, 239-40.

32. Samuel E. Morison, ed., "The Commonplace Book of Joseph Green," *Publications of the Colonial Society of Massachusetts: Transactions, 1937-1942*, XXXIV, 236.

33. *Help for Distressed Parents*, p. 2.

34. I am aware of Edmund Morgan's convincing demonstration that the Puritans approved sexual activities within marriage. See "The Puritans and Sex," *New England Quarterly*, XV (Dec., 1942), 592-93. It does not rule out an element of ambivalence in their attitude. Robert Middlekauff notes that "Despite Puritans' frank discussions they felt uneasiness, even guilt, over lawful sexual intercourse" (*The Mathers*, pp. 202, 194). See also Richard Crowder, *No Featherbed to Heaven; A Biography of Michael Wigglesworth, 1631-1705* ([East Lansing, Michigan], 1962), p. 93.

35. "Diary," VIII, 118; Willard, *The Mourners Cordial*, p. 85.

36. Demos, *A Little Commonwealth*, p. 50.

37. *Baby and Child Care* (New York: Pocket Books paperback, 1968, rev. ed.), pp. 21-22.

38. *The Works of Anne Bradstreet*, p. 54; Willard, *The Mourners Cordial*, p. 77.

39. "The Sunday-School," in *The Works of William E. Channing* (Boston, 1845), IV, 358.

40. "Nature," in *The Collected Works of Ralph Waldo Emerson*, I (Cambridge, 1971), 42; Sherman Paul, "Alcott's Search for the Child," *Boston Public Library Quarterly*, 4 (Jan., 1952), 91; Strickland, "A Transcendentalist Father," 21, 32, 33, passim.

41. Cotton Mather, *Perswasions from the Terror of the Lord* (Boston, 1711), pp. 24, 34; Mather, *Help for Distressed Parents*, p. 53.

42. Samuel Smith, *The Great Assize: Or, Day of Jubilee* (Boston, 1727), p. 40; Cotton Mather, *Perswasions from the Terror*, p. 22.

43. *The Mourners Cordial*, pp. 71-72 (emphasis deleted); Mather, *Perswasions from the Terror*, p. 23; John Flavel, *A Token for Mourners* (Boston, 1725), p. 68.

44. *The Divine Right of Infant-Baptisme Asserted and Proved from Scripture and Antiquity* (Boston, 1680), p. 8. A long-held view among historians, which still has its adherents, is that the Puritans saw young children as little adults. But the Puritans did recognize major differences between children and grownups, as the infant damnation issue reveals. For a review of recent discussions of this question and an argument against the "little adult" interpretation, see Ross W. Beales, Jr., "In Search of the Historical Child: Miniature Adulthood and Youth in Colonial New England," *American Quarterly*, XXVII (Oct., 1975), 379-91.

45. Henry Flynt, *The Doctrine of the Last Judgment* (Boston, 1714); Increase Mather, *A Plain Discourse, Shewing Who Shall & Who Shall not Enter into the Kingdom of Heaven* (Boston, 1713); John Webb, *Practical Discourses on Death, Judgment, Heaven, and Hell* (Boston, 1726).

46. *Perswasions from the Terror*, pp. 20, 22-23; Increase Mather, *The Divine Right of Infant-Baptisme*, pp. 7-8.

47. William B. Hayden, *The History of the Dogma of Infant Damnation* (Portland, 1858), pp. 6-7.

48. Percy Dearmer, *The Legend of Hell* (London, 1929), p. 53; Benjamin Warfield, *The Development of the Doctrine of Infant Salvation* (New York, 1891), pp. 7-8.

49. Dearmer, *The Legend of Hell*, p. 54; Warfield, *The Development of the Doctrine of Infant Salvation*, pp. 10-11.

50. Warfield, *The Development of the Doctrine of Infant Salvation*, pp. 14-15; J. Bellamy, "Baptême (Sort des enfants morts sans)," in *Diction-narie de Théologie Catholique*, II, Part 1 (Paris, 1910), 364-78.

51. Warfield, *The Development of the Doctrine of Infant Salvation*, pp. 23-24; Hayden, *The History of the Dogma of Infant Damnation*, pp. 7-8; John Calvin, *Institutes of the Christian Religion* (Edinburgh, 1846), III, Bk. IV, chapter XVI, sec. 17; Calvin, *Tracts and Treatises in Defence of the Reformed Faith* (Edinburgh, 1958), III, 109-10, 351, 354-55.

52. C. P. Krauth, *Infant Baptism and Infant Salvation in the Calvinistic System* (Philadelphia, 1874), pp. 15-16, 18-21, 34-35, 47, 52; Warfield, *The Development of the Doctrine of Infant Salvation*, pp. 40-41. Zwingli was one of the major exceptions as he worked towards a position holding that death in infancy was itself a sign of salvation (Warfield, pp. 37-38).

53. Charles Eugene Edwards, "Calvin on Infant Salvation," *Bibliotheca Sacra*, 88 (1931), 328. By "innocent" Calvin meant that infants had not yet committed actual sin. But original sin was in itself sufficient to damn them. Through a very tortured process of reasoning, Edwards uses this citation and similar other ones to claim that Calvin rejected the doctrine of infant damnation. Most of his argument is taken from Charles

W. Shields, "The Doctrine of Calvin Concerning Infant Salvation," *Presbyterian and Reformed Review*, I (Oct., 1890), 634-51. See also Hayden, *The History of the Dogma of Infant Damnation*, pp. 9-10, 31.

54. Hayden, *The History of the Dogma of Infant Damnation*, pp. 30, 13-14 (I have deleted the capitals in the last clause of the Twiss citation); Richard Baxter, *The Practical Works* (London, 1707), I, 641, 642.

55. *The Practical Works*, I, 642.

56. The public's sensitivity is suggested in Willard, *The Mourners Cordial*, pp. 76-77. The moderation of the English presentation of infant damnation as compared to the continental one can also be accounted for by changing family patterns. A love of children developed earlier in English families than in those across the channel. See Shorter, *The Making of the Modern Family*, p. 199. C. John Sommerville has discussed this concern of the English Puritans for children in relation to the role of the Puritans as an organized reform movement. In "The English Puritans and Children: Psychohistory or Cultural History?" he argues that "Puritans were more thoughtful parents than others" and brought to children "a new sympathy and understanding" (p. 15). I am grateful to Professor Sommerville for a copy of this paper which was delivered at the meeting of the American Historical Association, Atlanta, December, 1975.

57. C. Mather, *Help for Distressed Parents*, p. 13; C. Mather, *Meat out of the Eater*, pp. 99-100; Willard, *The Mourners Cordial*, p. 82.

58. *The Presbyterian and Independent Visible Churches in New-England and else-where Brought to the Test* (Philadelphia, 1689), pp. 78, 85, 89. Another denial of infant damnation was contained in the creed of the General Baptists of Rhode Island, an Arminian sect. The statement originated in London and was republished in Newport. See *A Confession of Faith, Set Forth by Many of Those Baptists, Who Own the Doctrine of Universal Redemption*, [1730?], pp. 3-4.

59. James Allen et al., *The Principles of the Protestant Religion Maintained* (Boston, 1690), pp. 78, 79.

60. Kenneth Murdock, ed., *The Day of Doom* (New York, 1929), pp. vi, ix; John M. Murrin, "Review Essay," *History and Theory*, XI (1972), 237.

61. *The Day of Doom*, verses 22-25.

62. Ibid., verses 27-34.

63. Ibid., verse 166.

64. Ibid., verses 166-68.

65. Ibid., verses 171-73, 180-81.

66. Ibid., verse 213.

67. Gerhard T. Alexis discusses the probable theological sources of the "easiest room" idea in "Wigglesworth's 'Easiest Room,'" *New England Quarterly*, 42 (Dec., 1969), 573-83. He sees Wigglesworth's position as more gentle and humane than I do.

68. Kenneth B. Murdock, *Literature and Theology in Colonial New England* (Cambridge, 1949), pp. 145-46.

69. "Dr. Beecher's Letters," 537; Murdock, ed., *The Day of Doom*, p. iii; Moses Coit Tyler, *A History of American Literature, 1607-1765* (New York, 1878), II, 34. According to Alice Morse Earle, *The Day of Doom*

"was sold in such large numbers that it is safe to assert that every New England household, whose members could read, was familiar with it. . . . Children committed it to memory; teachers extolled it; ministers quoted it." See *Child Life in Colonial Days* (New York, 1899), pp. 252-53. Perry Miller said that the initial edition, which he regarded as "the first American best-seller," was literally "read to pieces." See *The American Puritans; Their Prose and Poetry* (New York: Doubleday paperback, 1956), p. 282. There were seven editions of the poem between 1662 and 1730.

70. *The Poems of Edward Taylor*, p. 476.

71. Morgan, *The Puritan Family*, p. 174.

72. *The Barren Fig Trees Doom* (Boston, 1691), p. 114; *The Mourners Cordial*, pp. 87, 88.

73. *Help for Distressed Parents*, pp. 13, 38.

74. "Diary," VII, 382-83. See also *Right Thoughts in Sad Hours*, pp. 52, 57; *Meat out of the Eater*, p. 97; [Cotton Mather], *The Tribe of Asher* (Boston, 1717), p. 17; Increase Mather, *Meditations on the Glory of the Heavenly World*, pp. 94-95; Increase Mather, *The Believers Gain By Death* (Boston, 1713), p. 32.

75. "The Marrow of Puritan Divinity," *Publications of the Colonial Society of Massachusetts: Transactions, 1933-1937*, XXXII, 295.

76. *The Mourners Cordial*, p. 71.

77. The Canons on the Sacrament of Baptism promulgated by the Council of Trent stated: "If anyone shall say that baptism is optional, that is, not necessary for salvation: let him be anathema." See Henry Denzinger, *The Sources of Catholic Dogma* (St. Louis, 1957), pp. 264, 247-50.

78. William Rounseville Alger, *A Critical History of the Doctrine of a Future Life* (Philadelphia, 1864), p. 414.

79. According to Dr. Pinchas Noy, an Israeli psychiatrist who dealt with civilian anxieties in the wake of the Yom Kippur War of October, 1973, "It is easier to convey that a soldier is dead than to tell the family that he is missing. In case of death it is final. Missing is something uncertain, and it is always harder to cope with the uncertain." Quoted in Henry Kamm, "Israel Sees to War's Hidden Wounds," *New York Times*, Nov. 2, 1973, p. 19.

80. "The Confession of Faith, Agreed upon by the Assembly of Divines at Westminster," in *The Confession of Faith, The Larger and Shorter Catechisms* (Edinburgh, 1773), chapter XXVIII, sec. V; Baxter, *The Practical Works*, I, 645; Samuel Willard, *A Compleat Body of Divinity* (Boston, 1726), pp. 848, 850; E. Brooks Holifield, *The Covenant Sealed: The Development of Puritan Sacramental Theology in Old and New England, 1570-1720* (New Haven, 1974), pp. 46, 92, 150, 153, 154, 192.

81. "Diary," VII, 163-64.

82. Holifield, *The Covenant Sealed*, pp. 76, 79-87, 102-3; Moses Mather, *The Visible Church in Covenant with God* (New York, 1769), p. 59; Cyprian Strong, *An Inquiry; Wherein, the End and Design of Baptism . . . are particularly considered* (Hartford, 1793), p. 75. Mather and Strong are

late eighteenth-century sources, but it is probable that the belief they described existed in earlier New England, at least among the less informed. Edward Eggleston came to a similar conclusion in *The Transit of Civilization from England to America in the Seventeenth Century* (New York, 1901), pp. 201-2.

83. John Calvin, *Commentaries on the Book of Genesis* (Edinburgh, 1847), vol. I, chap. XVII, sec. 7; "The Confession of Faith," chap. VII, secs. II-VI, chap. XXVIII, secs. IV, VI; "The Larger Catechism," in *The Confession of Faith, The Larger and Shorter Catechisms* (Edinburgh, 1773), Answer 166; [C. Mather], *The Tribe of Asher*, p. 14; Holifield, *The Covenant Sealed*, pp. 149, 189-90; Lewis B. Schenck, *The Presbyterian Doctrine of Children in the Covenant* (New Haven, 1940), pp. 6-10, 13-19.

84. Richard Mather quoted in Sandford Fleming, *Children and Puritanism* (New Haven, 1933), p. 73; Calvin, *Tracts and Treatises*, III, 109-10; "The Larger Catechism," Answer 165; Cotton Mather, *Cares about the Nurseries* (Boston, 1702), p. 66; Holifield, *The Covenant Sealed*, pp. 151, 159; Schenck, *The Presbyterian Doctrine*, pp. 13, 14, 18.

85. *Meat out of the Eater*, p. 100. See also *Perswasions from the Terror*, p. 23; I. Mather, *Meditations on the Glory of the Heavenly World*, pp. 94-95; Eliot, *A Brief Answer to a Small Book*, p. 16; Willard, *The Barren Fig Trees Doom*, p. 32; Peter Bulkeley, *The Gospel-Covenant* (London, 1651), p. 159.

86. Baxter, *The Practical Works*, I, 643.

87. Allen et al., *The Principles of the Protestant Religion Maintained*, p. 79; Willard, *The Mourners Cordial*, p. 82; Benjamin Colman and William Cooper, *Two Sermons Preached in Boston* (Boston, 1723), p. 24; William Williams, *An Essay to Prove the Interest of the Children of Believers in the Covenant* (Boston, 1727), p. 15; Holifield, *The Covenant Sealed*, pp. 68, 153-54; Perry Miller, *The New England Mind; From Colony to Province* (Cambridge, 1953), pp.88-89, 96; Fleming, *Children and Puritanism*, pp. 74-75; Robert G. Pope, "New England Versus The New England Mind: The Myth of Declension," *Journal of Social History*, III (Winter, 1969-1970), 107-8.

88. *Pray for the Rising Generation* (Cambridge, 1678), p. 12.

89. Warfield, *The Development of the Doctrine of Infant Salvation*, pp. 42-44.

90. Willard, *The Mourners Cordial*, p. 79.

91. Richard G. Dumont and Dennis C. Fox, *The American View of Death: Acceptance or Denial?* (Cambridge, 1972), p. 88; Robert Kastenbaum and Ruth Aisenberg, *The Psychology of Death* (New York, 1972), p. 98. Compare the remarks of Philippe Ariès in *Western Attitudes Toward Death* (Baltimore, 1974) about a death-related phenomenon: "This phenomenon did not occur in the world of real, acted-out events which the historian can easily collect and measure. It occurred in the obscure and extravagant world of phantasms, and the historian studying it ought to transform himself into a psychoanalyst" (p. 56).

92. Joseph M. Natterson and Alfred G. Knudson, "Observations Concerning Fear of Death in Fatally Ill Children and Their Mothers,"

Psychomatic Medicine, XXII (Nov.-Dec., 1960), 461. David Hunt writes about seventeenth-century France: "In spite of the presence of friends and relatives, and beyond the ministrations of the midwife, women had to pass through the ordeal of childbirth completely alone. . . . Childbearing was probably the single experience which made the heaviest demands on the courage and fortitude of the participant" (*Parents and Children in History*, p. 88). As a result of this unique experience, the feelings of mothers toward their children most likely differed in fundamental ways from those of fathers.

93. Joseph C. Rheingold, *The Mother, Anxiety, and Death: The Catastrophic Death Complex* (Boston, 1967), p. 9; Dumont and Fox, *The American View of Death*, p. 87.

94. Greven, *Four Generations*, p. 16; Demos, *A Little Commonwealth*, pp. 62, 63.

95. Charles E. Orbach, Arthur M. Sutherland, Mary F. Bozeman, "Psychological Impact of Cancer and Its Treatment; III. The Adaptation of Mothers to the Threatened Loss of Their Children through Leukemia: Part II," *Cancer*, 8 (Jan.-Feb., 1955), 23, 25; Mary F. Bozeman, Charles E. Orbach, and Arthur M. Sutherland, "Psychological Impact of Cancer and its Treatment; III. The Adaptation of Mothers to the Threatened Loss of their Children through Leukemia: Part I," *Cancer*, 8 (Jan.-Feb., 1955), 15.

96. Orbach et al., "Psychological Impact of Cancer," 29.

97. Kastenbaum and Aisenberg, *The Psychology of Death*, p. 107.

98. Ibid., p. 44; Charles E. Orbach, "The Multiple Meanings of the Loss of a Child," *American Journal of Psychotherapy*, 13 (Oct., 1959), 906; David Moriarty, *The Loss of Loved Ones* (Springfield, Ill., 1967), passim.

99. Demos, *A Little Commonwealth*, p. 12.

100. *Silentarius*, p. 29. For instances of sudden death see "The Diaries of John Hull," *Transactions and Collections of the American Antiquarian Society*, III (1857), 162-63; Francis G. Walett, ed., "The Diary of Ebenezer Parkman," *Proceedings Of the American Antiquarian Society*, 71 (1961), 166, 167; and "Diary of Rev. Samuel Dexter," 204.

101. *Works*, p. 236; A. V. Neale, "The Changing Pattern of Death in Childhood: Then and Now," *Medicine, Science and Law*, 4 (Jan., 1964), 36-37.

102. "The Commonplace Book of Joseph Green," 252-53; "Diary of Rev. Samuel Dexter," 202; "The Diary of Ebenezer Parkman," 195. See also "Deacon John Paine's Journal," *The Mayflower Descendent*, VIII (1906), 183, IX, 98; Mather, "Diary," VII, 304-5.

103. Cotton Mather, *The Valley of Hinnan: The Terrours of Hell Demonstrated* (Boston, 1717), p. 22.

104. For instances see "Diary of Lawrence Hammond," 151; "Diary of Rev. Samuel Dexter," 204; "Diary of Rev. William Homes of Chalmark, Martha's Vineyard," *New England Historical and Genealogical Register*, XLVIII (Oct., 1894), 448; and "The Diary of Ebenezer Parkman," 173.

105. Albert Solnit and Morris Green, "Psychologic Considerations in the Management of Deaths on Pediatric Hospital Service; 1. The Doctor and the Child's Family," *Pediatrics*, 24 (July, 1959), 109; Marion

Steinmann, "Crib Death: Too Many Clues?" *New York Times Magazine*, May 16, 1976, p. 41.

106. For an example see Kenneth Silverman, ed., *Selected Letters of Cotton Mather* (Baton Rouge, 1971), p. 125.

107. Paul Chodoff, Stanford Friedman, and David Hamburg, "Stress, Defenses and Coping Behavior: Observations in Parents of Children with Malignant Disease," *American Journal of Psychiatry*, 120 (Feb., 1964), 747-48; Erich Lindemann, "Symptomatology and Management of Acute Grief," *American Journal of Psychiatry*, 101 (Sept., 1944), 147-48.

108. Natterson and Knudson, "Observations Concerning Fear of Death in Fatally Ill Children and Their Mothers," 462.

109. Geoffrey Gorer, *Death, Grief, and Mourning in Contemporary Britain* (London, 1965), p. 68; Solnit and Green, "Psychologic Considerations in the Management of Deaths on Pediatric Hospital Service," 109; C. Mather, *Right Thoughts in Sad Hours*, pp. 53-54.

110. *The Poems of Edward Taylor*, p. 469; "Diary of Rev. William Homes," 448; "The Diaries of John Hull," 163; "Diary of Rev. Samuel Dexter," 204; "Letter-Book of Samuel Sewall," I, 181; "The Rev. John Eliot's Record of Church Members, Roxbury, Mass.," *New England Historical and Genealogical Record*, XXXV (July, 1881), 244; Kastenbaum and Aisenberg, *The Psychology of Death*, pp. 206-7.

111. David K. Switzer, *The Dynamics of Grief* (Nashville, 1970), pp. 12, 49. "Death is always a shock no matter what the preparation." See Solnit and Green, "Psychologic Considerations in the Management of Deaths on Pediatric Hospital Service," 112.

112. "Diary of Samuel Sewall," V, 443; "Letter of John Cotton to Mary Hinckley," in John Demos, ed., *Remarkable Providences, 1600-1760* (New York, 1972), p. 165; "The Winthrop Papers, Part IV," *Collections of the Massachusetts Historical Society*, 5th Series, VIII (Boston, 1882), 419. See also "The Autobiography of Thomas Shepard," 382, 391; C. Mather, *Right Thoughts in Sad Hours*, pp. 50-51; and *The Poems of Edward Taylor*, p. 469.

113. The classic discussion of this subject is Helene Deutsch, "Absence of Grief," *Psychoanalytic Quarterly*, VI (1937), 12-22.

114. Henry Gibbs, *Bethany: or, The House of Mourning* (Boston, 1714), p. 12; John Barnard, *Two Sermons: The Christians Behavior under Severe and Repeated Bereavements and the Fatal Consequence of a Peoples Persisting in Sin* (Boston, 1714), p. 4; Willard, *The Mourners Cordial*, p. 35.

115. [Cotton Mather], *Wholesome Words: A Visit of Advice Given unto Families that are Visited with Sickness* (Boston, 1713), p. 23; Willard, *The Mourners Cordial*, pp. 42, 119, 121; Gibbs, *Bethany*, p. 12; Barnard, *Two Sermons*, p. 4. For a discussion of acute grief, see Lindemann, "Symptomatology and Management of Acute Grief."

116. For evidence that the deaths of adults were felt more acutely than those of children see *The Poems of Edward Taylor*, p. 472; and C. Mather, *Meat out of the Eater*, p. 185.

117. Willard, *The Mourners Cordial*, p. 46; Gibbs, *Bethany*, p. 12.

118. Gibbs, *Bethany*, p. 13; [C. Mather], *Wholesome Words*, pp. 22, 24.

119. Barnard, *Two Sermons*, pp. 20, 10; C. Mather, *Help for Distressed Parents*, p. 39; C. Mather, *Meat out of the Eater*, pp. 24-26.

120. "The Winthrop Papers," 419; *The Poems of Edward Taylor*, p. 469. See also "The Commonplace Book of Joseph Green," 250; Kettell, *Specimens of American Poetry*, I, 14-15; and "Letter-Book of Samuel Sewall," I, 22. Some individuals continue to find these attitudes personally viable. See Chodoff et al., "Stress, Defenses and Coping Behavior," 747.

121. "The Autobiography," 354. See also M. G. Hall, ed., "The Autobiography of Increase Mather," *Proceedings of the American Antiquarian Society*, 71 (1961), 314; "Diary of Increase Mather," *Proceedings of the Massachusetts Historical Society*, 2nd Series, XIII (1899-1900), 342, 367; Middlekauff, *The Mathers*, p. 94; and "Diary of Rev. Samuel Dexter," 202.

122. Chodoff et. al., "Stress, Defenses and Coping Behavior," 748. An example of the unreliability of medical prognosis in Puritan times can be found in the "Diary of Cotton Mather," VII, 376-77: "The Illness of the Child went on; and in the Evening [of Saturday] one of the Physicians, unable to do any more, left the Child, concluding it would certainly dy.... Well, on the Lord's-day in the Forenoon, the Child was diverting herself, and running and laughing the whole Forenoon, about the House, and at Noon, sat at the Table with me. The Physician was astonished, at so sudden a Recovery of the Child!"

123. Bozeman et al., "Psychologic Impact of Cancer and its Treatment," 7.

124. Ibid., 5; Natterson and Knudson, "Observations Concerning Fear of Death in Fatally Ill Children and their Mothers," 462.

125. "Diary," VII, 179, 258-59, 303-5, 336-37, 378, VIII, 258, 261, 362, 374.

126. These feelings and hopes for the child are suggested in C. Mather, *Silentarius*, p. 29, and "Diary of Samuel Sewall," V, 399. David E. Stannard has shown a parallel situation among Puritan adults facing their own deaths as they struggled to reconcile their fear of dying with the expected attitude of acceptance. See "Death and Dying in Puritan New England," *American Historical Review*, 78 (Dec., 1973), 1312, 1317, 1330.

127. Edmund S. Morgan, ed., "The Diary of Michael Wigglesworth," *Publications of the Colonial Society of Massachusetts: Transactions, 1942-1946*, XXXV, 415-16; "Diary of Cotton Mather," VIII, 374, 187; "Diary of Increase Mather," 341-42.

128. *The Poems of Edward Taylor*, p. 469; "Diary of Samuel Sewall," V, 331, VII (Boston, 1882), 343-44. See also Bert Roller, *Children in American Poetry, 1610-1900* (Nashville, 1930), p. 14.

129. "An increase of meaning produces a reduction of grief response.... The lack of meaning would tend to increase grief." See Switzer, *The Dynamics of Grief*, p. 166.

130. Willard, *The Mourners Cordial*, pp. 82, 83, 67; *The Works of Anne Bradstreet*, pp. 235, 236; I. Mather, *Meditations on the Glory of the Heavenly World*, pp. 94-95; C. Mather, *Right Thoughts in Sad Hours*, p. 57.

131. Orbach, "The Multiple Meanings of the Loss of a Child," 912; Marc Oraison, *Death—And then What?* (Paramus, N. J., 1969), pp. 71-72.

132. "Deacon John Paine's Journal," IX, 139; *The Poems of Edward Taylor*, p. 470; "The Autobiography of Thomas Shepard," 391.

133. *The Works of Anne Bradstreet*, p. 235. Cotton Mather used a different metaphor to depict the deaths of infants, but the meaning was the same: "The lamps but just litt up, and blown out again." Quoted in Richard Harrison Shryock, *Medicine and Society in America: 1660-1860* (New York, 1960), p. 110.

134. *Help for Distressed Parents*, pp. 39-40; C. Mather, *Right Thoughts in Sad Hours*, pp. 56-57; Willard, *The Mourners Cordial*, p. 86. This attitude can still be found today. See Orbach, "The Multiple Meanings of the Loss of a Child," 910.

135. C. Mather, *Right Thoughts in Sad Hours*, p. 51; Switzer, *The Dynamics of Grief*, pp. 60, 173, 177; Rheingold, *The Mother, Anxiety, and Death*, p. 30; Solnit and Green, "Psychologic Considerations in the Management of Deaths on Pediatric Hospital Service," 108. Increase Mather told his children, "all of you [are] so many parts of myself and dearer to me than all things which I enjoy in this world." Quoted in Kenneth Murdock, *Increase Mather, The Foremost American Puritan* (Cambridge, 1925), p. 73.

136. Natterson et al., "Observations Concerning Fear of Death in Fatally Ill Children and their Mothers," 461; Switzer, *The Dynamics of Grief*, pp. 116, 146.

137. *The Poems of Edward Taylor*, p. 470; C. Mather, *Right Thoughts in Sad Hours*, pp. 49, 53; C. Mather, *Meat out of the Eater*, pp. 26, 96; Kettell, *Specimens of American Poetry*, I, 14; *The Works of Anne Bradstreet*, p. 236.

138. "Letter-Book of Samuel Sewall," II (Boston, 1888), 70; "Letter of John Cotton to Mary Hinckley," p. 165. See also C. Mather, *Right Thoughts in Sad Hours*, pp. i, iii; and Tashjian, *Memorials for Children of Change*, p. 46.

139. I. Mather, *The Folly of Sinning, Opened & Applyed* (Boston, 1699), pp. 38, 39. There is no doubt that the murder of a soul meant its damnation: "The soul that's damned is killed" (p. 30). The second instance is from John Rogers, *Death The Certain Wages of Sin to the Impenitent* (Boston, 1701), p. 137.

140. One Puritan mother, driven to distraction by this threat, drowned her child in the belief that by doing so she would save it from damnation. See Miller, *The New England Mind: The Seventeenth Century*, p. 56. See also Stannard, "Death and the Puritan Child," pp. 26-27; and Middlekauff, *The Mathers*, p. 50. In contrast, Kastenbaum and Aisenberg judge that of death-related fears in contemporary society the fear of "what happens to the *other* person in his after-life" is the least thought about and important (*The Psychology of Death*, p. 46). Without a proper understanding of the intensity the threat of hell once possessed, past perspectives towards death will be seriously distorted. For an example, see

Eric Bermann, *Scapegoat; The Impact of Death-Fear on an American Family* (Ann Arbor, 1973): "In the past, religion seemed to neatly obtund death's bite, at least as the common man endured it, by positing a fine, active postlife. Conceptions of this hereafter were sufficient to belie the very possibility that death was anything greater than a catnap followed by a trip into pastoral existence" (p. 253). A similar view is presented in James J. Naglack, "Death in Colonial New England," *Historical Journal of Western Massachusetts*, 4 (Fall, 1975), 32.

141. "Diary," VII, 217, 282-83, 295, VIII, 234.

142. Cotton Mather, and probably other ministers, referred to tormented infants in elaborating scriptual and historical references: "The Diabolical Idolaters offered up their Children to *Molock* there; and employed the Noise of Drums to drown the doleful Cry of the Infants while they were *Burning Alive* unto the *Devil*" (*The Valley of Hinnam*, p. 25). These barbarities of the Valley of Hinnam had nothing to do with Puritan infants, but the description might have served as a reinforcement of Wigglesworthian imagery. See also Willard, *A Compleat Body of Divinity*, p. 234.

143. Cotton Mather, *Seasonable Thoughts upon Mortality* (Boston, 1712), p. 7; Cotton Mather and Thomas Foxcroft, *Two Funeral Sermons Preach'd upon Mournful Occasions* (Boston, 1722), Foxcroft sermon, p. 15; Cotton Mather, *Golgotha; A Lively Description of Death* (Boston, 1713), p. 15.

144. Vinovskis, "Angels' Heads and Weeping Willows: Death in Early America," p. 16.

145. Moriarty, *The Loss of Loved Ones*, p. 97; Erich Lindemann found that individuals with "obsessive personality makeup" were likely to develop serious depressions during bereavement ("Symptomatology and Management of Acute Grief," 146). One suspects that this personality type was highly common among the Puritans.

146. Willard, *The Mourners Cordial*, p. 120. For particular instances of depression see "The Winthrop Papers," 419; and "Letter of John Cotton to Mary Hinckley," p. 165.

147. Quoted in Cotton Mather, *Ecclesiastes; The Life of the Reverend & Excellent Jonathan Mitchel* (Boston, 1697), p. 103.

148. Switzer, *The Dynamics of Grief*, p. 111.

149. *The Day of Doom*, verses 199-200. See also "The Autobiography of Thomas Shepard," 355; and "The Autobiography of Increase Mather," 315-16.

150. John Bowlby, "Processes of Mourning," *International Journal of Psycho-Analysis*, XLII (July-Oct., 1961), 321.

151. Switzer, *The Dynamics of Grief*, p. 95; Walzer, "A Period of Ambivalence: Eighteenth-Century American Childhood," p. 352.

152. *The Works of Anne Bradstreet*, p. 53; Demos, *A Little Commonwealth*, p. 131; Rheingold, *The Mother, Anxiety, and Death*, p. 126; Adrienne Rich, *Of Woman Born: Motherhood As Experience and Institution* (New York, 1976), pp. 24, 261, 263, 276-79; Hunt, *Parents and Children in History*, pp. 121-22. Hunt adds that the father would often

resent the child's usurpation of the mother's body during nursing (p. 106).

153. *Totem and Taboo* (London, n.d.), pp. 102, 107. See also Switzer, *The Dynamics of Grief*, p. 29; Oraison, *Death—And then What?*, pp. 79-80.

154. Freud, *Totem and Taboo*, p. 104.

155. Natterson and Knudson, "Observations Concerning Fear of Death in Fatally Ill Children and their Mothers," 462; Solnit and Green, "Psychologic Considerations in the Management of Deaths on Pediatric Hospital Service," 109; Lindemann, "Symptomatology and Management of Acute Grief," 142; Bozeman et al., "Psychologic Impact of Cancer and Its Treatment," 4.

156. "Diary," V, 443. Medical thought in the Puritan era was a mixture of modern elements and medievalisms; among the latter was the ascription of diseases to moral causes. See Shryock, *Medicine and Society in America, 1660-1860*, pp. 49-54. In a study of vital registers in New England towns, H. Louis Stettler, III, found that the causes assigned to death were from the modern standpoint often "ludicrous." See "The New England Throat Distemper and Family Size," in *Empirical Studies in Health Economics; Proceedings of the Second Conference on the Economics of Health* (Baltimore, 1970), p. 20.

157. Willard, *The Mourners Cordial*, p. 81; "Diary of Cotton Mather," VIII, 20.

158. "The Autobiography of Thomas Shepard," 381; "Diary of Increase Mather," 341-42; Kettell, *Specimens of American Poetry*, I, 14; Gibbs, *Bethany*, p. 14. Similar reactions can be found in some modern parents. See Bozeman et al., "Psychologic Impact of Cancer and Its Treatment," 4-5.

159. Bowlby, "Processes of Mourning," 321; Chodoff et al., "Stress, Defenses and Coping Behavior," 746-47; Solnit and Green, "Psychologic Considerations in the Management of Deaths on Pediatric Hospital Service," 109; Bozeman et al., "Psychologic Impact of Cancer and Its Treatment," 5; Orbach et al., "Psychological Impact of Cancer and Its Treatment," 27.

160. "Diary of Rev. Samuel Dexter," 108; C. Mather, *Meat out of the Eater*, p. 29; "Diary of Samuel Sewall," VI (Boston, 1879), 221; *Selected Letters of Cotton Mather*, p. 230. Joseph Rheingold writes that "The psychology of death and the psychology of aggression are interwoven Separation, loss, and trauma, although admitted to be of possible impersonal or inevitable nature, are conceived unconsciously as acts of aggression" (*The Mother, Anxiety, and Death*, p. 20).

161. Willard, *The Mourners Cordial*, pp. 76-77, 120. For this type of reaction in modern parents see Chodoff et al., "Stress, Defenses and Coping Behavior," 747.

162. Caulfield, *A True History of the Terrible Epidemic Vulgarly Called the Throat Distemper*, p. 6; Mary Caroline Crawford, *Social Life in Old New England* (Boston, 1915), pp. 453-54.

163. "The Commonplace Book of Joseph Green," 250; C. Mather, *Right Thoughts in Sad Hours*, p. 46.

164. "Diary," VII, 283. See also the citation from Richard Mather in Morgan, *The Puritan Family*, p. 92.

165. "Diary of Lawrence Hammond," 15; "Letter-Book of Samuel Sewall," I, 22; "The Autobiography of Increase Mather," 300; "Diary of Rev. Samuel Dexter," 202, 203; "Deacon John Paine's Journal," VIII, 183; "The Commonplace Book of Joseph Green," 253.

166. "The Commonplace Book of Joseph Green," 252, 253.

167. *Right Thoughts in Sad Hours*, pp. 56-57; "Deacon John Paine's Journal," IX, 139.

168. C. Mather, *Silentarius*, pp. 29-30; C. Mather, *Right Thoughts in Sad Hours*, p. 56.

169. Solnit and Green, "Psychologic Considerations in the Management of Deaths on Pediatric Hospital Service," 109; Switzer, *The Dynamics of Grief*, p. 50; Lindemann, "Symptomatology and Management of Acute Grief," 142, 143, 147.

170. Kastenbaum and Aisenberg, *The Psychology of Death*, pp. 193, 201.

171. Thomas D. Eliot, "The Adjustive Behavior of Bereaved Families: A New Field for Research," *Social Forces*, 8 (June, 1930), 546; Bowlby, "Processes of Mourning," 331.

172. Bowlby, "Processes of Mourning," 319; Glenn M. Vernon, *Sociology of Death: An Analysis of Death-Related Behavior* (New York, 1970), p. 175; Edgar N. Jackson, *Understanding Grief* (Nashville, 1957), p. 75.

173. "The Diaries of John Hull," 143. C. Mather, *Meat out of the Eater*, pp. 25-26.

174. Stettler, "The New England Throat Distemper and Family Size," p. 18 and n.

175. Lindemann, "Symptomatology and Management of Acute Grief," 147.

176. *The Mourners Cordial*, pp. 73-74.

177. Cf. Stannard, "Death and the Puritan Child," pp. 27-28; Tashjian, *Memorials for Children of Change*, pp. 132, 135.

178. On the horrific aspect of tombstone figures, see Tashjian, *Memorials for Children of Change*, pp. 62, 170, passim.

II.   *"Unsullied Back to Heaven"*

1. William Patten, *Reminiscences of the Late Rev. Samuel Hopkins, D. D., of Newport, R.I.* (Providence, 1843), p. 124.

2. Ibid.

3. An example of the Freudian child as the Calvinist child redivivus can be found in Isabel Paterson's introduction to Richard Hughes's engaging novel, *A High Wind in Jamica* (New York, 1932): "Young children are amoral. . . . Viewed objectively, and disregarding their charm, they are

nuisances and bores. To a harassed guardian, original sin is a convenient definition of the motive of their activities. Translated into terms of impulse and environmental resistance, original sin is a fact" (pp. x-xi). A more recent novel which makes this point is William Golding's well-known *Lord of the Flies.*

4. Conrad Wright, *The Beginnings of Unitarianism in America* (1955; rpt. Hamden, Conn.: Archon Books, 1976), pp. 9, 57-58; William G. McLoughlin, *Isaac Backus and the American Pietistic Tradition* (Boston, 1967), pp. 84, 86-87;Edwin Scott Gaustad, *The Great Awakening in New England* (Gloucester, Mass., 1965), pp. 114-15, 120-21, 126-28, 134.

5. Wright, *The Beginnings of Unitarianism.* p. 10.

6. *The Scripture-Doctrine of Original Sin Proposed to Free and Candid Examination* (London, 1750, 3rd. ed.), pp. 93, 95, 128, 145-46, 187-88, 244, Supplement, 146. For a fuller treatment, see Smith, *Changing Conceptions of Original Sin,* pp. 13-19.

7. *A Winter Evening's Conversation Upon the Doctrine of Original Sin* (Boston, 1757), pp. 7-10, 28.

8. Ibid., p. 26.

9. Ibid., pp, 6, 28, passim.

10. Ibid., pp. 6, 27, 28.

11. *The Winter Evening Conversation Vindicated* (Boston, [1758]), pp. 14, 29, 68.

12. *A Winter Evening's Conversation Upon the Doctrine of Original Sin,* p. 9.

13. *The Winter Evening Conversation Vindicated,* pp. 12, 13, 20.

14. *The Opinion of One that has perused the Summer Morning's Conversation* (Boston, 1758), p. 3.

15. *Remarks on A Late Pamphlet,* p. 27.

16. *A Winter Evening's Conversation Upon the Doctrine of Original Sin,* p. 7.

17. *The Opinion of One that has perused the Summer Morning's Conversation,* p. 4.

18. *The Scripture-Doctrine of Original Sin, Stated and Defended. In a Summer-Morning's Conversation* (Boston, 1758), pp. 8, 96.

19. Ibid., pp. 8n, 50, 51, 97, 115.

20. Ibid., preface.

21. *The Opinion of One that has perused the Summer Morning's Conversation,* pp. 5, 7, 16, 20-26.

22. *Remarks on a Late Pamphlet,* p. 19.

23. Ibid., pp. 19, 23, 29, 39-40.

24. *A Defence of the Principles of the "Summer-Morning's Conversation"* (Boston, 1760), pp. 19-20; *Remarks on a Late Pamphlet,* p. 27.

25. *Remarks on a Late Pamphlet,* pp. 33, 42.

26. *A Letter to the Reverend Author of the Winter-Evening Conversation on Original Sin* (Boston, 1758), pp. 6-7. The same point is even better made in Samuel Macclintock, *The Justice of God in the Mortality of Mankind* (Portsmouth, N.H., 1759), p. 10n.

27. *A Letter to the Reverend Author of the Winter-Evening Conversation,* p. 15.

28. For Calvinist acclaim of Edwards's work as the answer to the attack on original sin, see [Bellamy], *A Letter to the Reverend Author of the Winter-Evening Conversation*, pp. 13-14, and Macclintock, *The Justice of God*, p. 11n.

29. "An Humble Inquiry into Rules of the Word of God, Concerning the Qualifications Requisite to a Complete Standing and Full Communion in the Visible Christian Church," in *Works* (Worcester, 1808-9), I, 155.

30. "Doctrine of Original Sin Defended," in *Works*, VI, 460-62, 252; "Misrepresentations Corrected, and Truth Vindicated," in *Works*, I, 497-98.

31. "Doctrine of Original Sin," 475.

32. Wright, *The Beginnings of Unitarianism in America*, p. 83.

33. "Doctrine of Original Sin," 284, 301.

34. *The Scripture-Doctrine of Original Sin, Stated and Defended*, p. 42.

35. "Doctrine of Original Sin," 437-39, 439n; Perry Miller, *Jonathan Edwards* ([New York], 1949), pp. 279-80.

36. "Doctrine of Original Sin," 458.

37. Ibid., 427-31.

38. Calvin had taught that "not only has punishment passed from [Adam] upon us, but pollution instilled from him is inherent in us, to which punishment is justly due." Quoted in Fisher, "The Augustinian and the Federal Theories of Original Sin Compared," 485.

39. *Five Dissertations on the Scripture Account of the Fall; and Its Consequences* (London, 1785), pp. 186-88, 247-48. The book was written about 1765.

40. "Doctrine of Original Sin," 427-28.

41. William B. Sprague, ed., *Memoir of the Rev. Edward D. Griffin, D.D.* (New York, 1839), p. 39.

42. "Doctrine of Original Sin," 325-26.

43. Miller, *Jonathan Edwards*, p. 278. In Harriet Beecher Stowe's *Oldtown Folks*, ed. Henry F. May (Cambridge, Mass., 1966, 1st ed., 1869), one of the characters states: "I hold Jonathan Edwards to have been the greatest man, since St. Augustine, that Christianity has turned out. But when a great man, instead of making himself a great ladder for feeble folks to climb on, strikes away the ladder and bids them come to where he stands at a step, his greatness and his goodness both may prove unfortunate for those who come after him" (p. 416).

44. For example, John Murray, *The Original Sin Imputed* (Newburyport, 1791), pp. 6, 9, 22.

45. Dwight to Dr. Ryland, March 16, 1805, Dwight Family Papers, Yale University Library; Dwight, *Travels; in New-England and New-York* (New Haven, 1821-22), IV, 323-25; Charles E. Cunningham, *Timothy Dwight, 1752-1817* (New York, 1942), pp. 327-28.

46. Dwight, *Theology: Explained and Defended, in a Series of Sermons* (Middletown, Conn., 1818-19), II, 2-4; Jacob Ide, ed., *Works of Nathaniel Emmons* (Boston, 1842), IV, 488-90; Hopkins, *The System of Doctrines* (Boston, 1793), I, 319-20.

47.*Works*, IV, 356-57; Dwight, *Theology*, II, 5. Hopkins's rejection of inherited depravity is implicit. For a discussion of his views on this issue, see Frank Hugh Foster, *A Genetic History of the New England Theology* (Chicago, 1907), p. 182.

48, *System of Doctrines*, I, 309-10.

49. *Works*,IV, 487-88.

50. Ibid., 357, 508.

51. *Theology*, I, 532, II, 8.

52. Ibid., II, 5.

53. Edward D. Griffin, *A Series of Lectures, Delivered in Park Street Church, Boston* (Boston, 1813), pp. 11, 13, 16, 18; John Smalley, *Sermons, on Various Subjects, Doctrinal and Practical* (Middletown, Conn., 1814), p. 295.

54. *Five Dissertations*, pp. 171, 175.

55. "Doctrine of Original Sin," 159-61.

56. For example, Dwight, *Theology*, V, 414.

57. *Works*, IV, 510. Emmons had once believed that children were moral agents from birth. See *Sermons on Some of the First Principles and Doctines of True Religion* (Wrentham, Mass., 1800), pp. 190-92. He later thought more of the view that they were not, but never completely made up his mind.

58. *Works*, IV, 510.

59. Ibid., n.

60. Murray, *The Original Sin Imputed*, p. 78; Isaac Foster, *The Holiness of Infants Explained and Improved* (Boston, 1766), p. 10; Jonathan Parsons, *Infant Baptism from Heaven* (Boston, 1765), pp. 34-35.

61. George Beckwith, *The Infant Seed of Visible Believers, Their Right to Church Membership and Baptism* (New London, 1770), pp. 22-23; Thomas Worcester, *Little Children in the Kingdom of Heaven, Only by the Blessing of Christ* (Concord, N.H., 1803), pp. 7-12, 26-31; Thomas Worcester, *Two Sermons on the Government and Religious Education of Children* (Concord, N.H., 1804), p. 25, and n.

62. *Infant Baptism from Heaven* (Boston, 1767, 2nd ed.), p. 108.

63. *The Original Sin Imputed*, pp. 78-79.

64. For examples, see Peter Powers, *A Humble Enquiry into the Nature of Covenanting with God* (Newburyport, 1796), p. 31; and Patten, *Reminiscences of the Late Rev. Samuel Hopkins*, p. 125.

65. Griffin,*A Series Of Lectures*, pp. 13-14; McLoughlin, *Isaac Backus*, p. 228.

66. Patten, *Reminiscences of the Late Rev. Samuel Hopkins*, p. 130.

67. For example, Zabdiel Adams, *Our Lapse in Adam, and Redemption by Christ Considered* (Boston, 1791), p. 6.

68. Maris Vinovskis, "Angels' Heads and Weeping Willows: Death in Early America," p. 9 and Graph No. 5; Yasukichi Yasuba, *Birth Rates of the White Population in the United States, 1800-1860*, The Johns Hopkins University Studies in Historical and Political Science, Series LXXIX (Baltimore, 1962), pp. 96, 100.

69. Franklin B. Dexter, ed., "Inscriptions on Tombstones in New

Haven Erected prior to 1800," *Papers of the New Haven Colony Historical Society* (New Haven, 1882), III, 509, see also, 484.

70. Tashjian, *Memorials for Children of Change*, p. 257.

71. Benjamin B. Wisner, ed., *Memoirs of the Late Mrs. Susan Huntington, of Boston, Mass.* (Boston, 1826), pp. 66-67, 138, 139-40, 305, 314; Sprague, *Memoir of the Rev. Edward D. Griffin*, p. 144.

72. *Memoirs of the Late Mrs. Susan Huntington*, pp. 136-37, 223, 254, 314.

73. Ibid., pp. 304. 307, 363, 408; Barbara M. Cross, ed., *The Autobiography of Lyman Beecher* (Cambridge, Mass., 1961), I 319.

74. Mr. Hough, "On the Birth of an Infant," *American Baptist Magazine and Missionary Intelligencer*, N.S. I (Sept., 1817), 209.

75. *Memoirs of the Late Mrs. Susan Huntington*, p. 140; Sarah Connell Ayer, *Diary of Sarah Connell Ayer* (Portland, Maine, 1910), p. 209, 336.

76. "Letter-Book of Samuel Sewall," II, 70; Dexter, "Inscriptions on Tombstones in New Haven," 538; Kettell, *Specimens of American Poetry*, I, 14-15; Roller, *Children in American Poetry*, pp. 14, 16-17.

77. For an example, see Elias Nason, *A History of the Town of Dunstable, Massachusetts* (Boston, 1877), p. 251.

78. *The Boston Magazine*, I (Aug., 1784), 438; See also Julian D. Mason, Jr., ed., *The Poems of Phillis Wheatley* (Chapel Hill, 1966), pp. 31-32, 43-44.

79. Lydia H. Sigourney, "Death of an Infant," in Kettell, *Specimens of American Poetry*, II, 209; L[ydia] H. S[igourney], "The Dead Twins," *Ladies' Magazine and Literary Gazette*, III (Feb., 1830), 71.

80. N. P. Willis, "Thoughts While Making a Grave for A First Child, Born Dead," in Rufus Wilmot Griswold, ed., *The Poets and Poetry of America* (Philadelphia, 1842), p. 285; Caroline May, ed., *The American Female Poets* (Philadelphia, 1848), pp. 95-96.

81. Ann Douglas, "Heaven Our Home: Consolation Literature in The Northern United States, 1830-1880," in *Death in America*, ed. David E. Stannard (Philadelphia: University of Pennsylvania Press paperback, 1975), p. 57. The entire essay is highly perceptive about bereavement.

82. This attitude is described, and opposed, in Powers, *A Humble Inquiry*, pp. 30-31.

83. Crispus, "On the Education of Children," 394.

84. For examples from these various periods, see "The Mother," *Merrimack Magazine and Ladies' Literary Cabinet*, I (Oct. 12, 1805), 36, and "An Address to a Fond Mother," I (Dec. 28, 1805), 80; J.N.M., "A Visit to the Grave of a Child," *Ladies' Magazine*, II (Sept., 1829), 418-19; Kettell, *Specimens of American Poetry*, II, 73-74, 279; and May, *The American Female Poets*, pp. 103-4, 397-402.

85. *The Works of Anne Bradstreet*, pp. 235, 207.

86. William Cullen Bryant, "Innocent Child and Snow-White Flower," *The Poetical Works*, ed. Parke Godwin (New York, 1883), I, 216.

87. *History of the United States of America during the Administrations of Thomas Jefferson and James Madison* (New York, 1921), I, 81-82.

88. Donald Meyer, "The Dissolution of Calvinism," in *Paths of*

American Thought, eds. Arthur M. Schlesinger, Jr. and Morton White (Boston, 1963), p. 79.

89. Philippe Ariès, *Centuries of Childhood* (New York, 1962), pp. 402-3, 412-13. The manifestations of this new sensibility in European philosophy, literature, pedagogy, etc., are discussed in George Boas, *The Cult of Childhood* (London, 1966).

90. Yasuba, *Birth Rates of the White Population in the United States, 1800-1860,* pp. 70-72. Yasuba believes that before 1840 urbanization and industrialization were not significant causes of the lessening birth rates (pp. 22, 141-42). His argument has been supported by Colin Foster and G. S. L. Tucker, *Economic Opportunity and White American Fertility Ratios, 1800-1860* (New Haven, 1972), pp. 87-88, 91, 100.

91. Caulfield, *A True History of the Terrible Epidemic Vulgarly Called the Throat Distemper,* p. 15.

92. Yasuba, *Birth Rates of the White Population in the United States, 1800-1860,* pp. 57, 61, 68; Forster and Tucker, *Economic Opportunity and White American Fertility Ratios, 1800-1860,* p. 5.

93. Patten, *Reminiscences of the Late Rev. Samuel Hopkins,* p. 126.

94. *Letters Addressed to Trinitarians and Calvinists* (Cambridge, 1820), pp. 21, 41.

95. Ibid., pp. 20, 26, 30-31.

96. "Likeness to God," in *Works,* III, 247; "The Sunday-School," in *Works,* IV, 357.

97. *A Reply to Dr. Ware's Letters to Trinitarians and Calvinists* (Andover, 1821), pp. 13-15, 35; *Remarks on Dr. Ware's Answer* (Andover, 1822), pp. 9-10.

98. *A Reply to Dr. Ware's Letters,* pp. 45-46.

99. Ibid., pp. 13, 19, 20, 40.

100. Ibid., p. 78.

101. "Dissertation on the Sinfulness of Infants," *Christian Disciple,* II (Aug., 1814), 246, 248.

102. "The Dying Child," *Christian Examiner,* V (Jan., 1828), 13-14; "Lines Addressed to a Lovely Infant, Expiring in its Father's Arms," *Christian Disciple,* N.S. III (July - Aug., 1821), 280; "Lines, Addressed to a Mother, on the Death of Two Infants," *Christian Examiner,* II (Jan., 1825), 33-34; "The Voices of the Dead," *Christian Examiner,* IV (Nov. Dec., 1827), 462-64.

103. John E. Todd, ed., *John Todd, The Story of His Life* (New York, 1876), p. 176.

104. For a contemporary example, see Charles Briggs, "On Hereditary and Total Depravity," *The Liberal Preacher,* II (Jan., 1829), 107-8. At Groton, the Calvinist clergyman John Todd fought bitterly with the Unitarians, who employed against him unfavorable rumors, among other devices. "I lately attended the funeral of a child, and in the course of my remarks I said to the parents they must soon follow their child into eternity. One of the Unitarians spread the report that I said the child had gone to hell, and the parents must soon follow it." See *John Todd,* p. 166.

105. *Works,* II, 425.

106. Sidney Earl Mead, *Nathaniel William Taylor, 1786-1858, A Connecticut Liberal* (1942; rpt. Hamden, Conn.: Archon Books, 1967), pp. 99, 153-57.

107. Smith, *Changing Conceptions of Original Sin*, pp. 97-98; *The Autobiography of Lyman Beecher*, I, 348-49.

108. Taylor, *Concio ad Clerum*, pp. 5-6, 14, 25-26; [Nathaniel W. Taylor], "Review of Norton's Views of Calvinism," *Christian Spectator*, V (April, 1823), 206-7, 213; Eleazar T. Fitch, *Two Discourses on the Nature of Sin* (New Haven, 1826), pp. 27-28; [Chauncey Goodrich], "Review of Taylor and Harvey on Human Depravity," *Quarterly Christian Spectator*, N.S. I (June, 1829), 349-51; Lyman Beecher, "Future Punishment of Infants not a Doctrine of Calvinism," *Spirit of the Pilgrims*, I (Feb., 1828), 80, 158.

109. *Correspondence between Rev. Dr. Taylor and Rev. Dr. Hawes from the Connecticut Observer* (n.p., 1832?), p. 4; Fitch, *Two Discourses on the Nature of Sin*, pp. 23-24; Beecher, "Future Punishment of Infants not a Doctrine of Calvinism," 158.

110. *Concio ad Clerum*, p. 14; Fitch, *Two Discourses on the Nature of Sin*, pp. 15-16; *The Autobiography of Lyman Beecher*, I, 348-49, II, 15-16.

111. *The Autobiography of Lyman Beecher*, I, 348-49.

112. Ibid., II, 117.

113. [Bennet Tyler], *Letters on the Origin and Progress of the New Haven Theology* (New York, 1837), pp. 8-9.

114. "Remarks on a Letter to the Editors, Respecting the Review of Dr. Taylor and Mr. Harvey," *Quarterly Christian Spectator*, N.S. I (Sept., 1829), 549.

115. Lyman Beecher, "The Native Character of Man," *The National Preacher*, II (June, 1827), 11, 12.

116. Dr. _____ to Dr. Nettleton, Jan. 17, 1822, in *The Autobiography of Lyman Beecher*, I, 350.

117. *Concio ad Clerum*, p. 24; [Nathaniel W. Taylor], *An Inquiry into the Nature of Sin* (New Haven, 1829), p. 30; Fitch, *Two Discourses on the Nature of Sin*, pp. 44-46; Eleazar Fitch, *An Inquiry into the Nature of Sin* (New Haven, 1827), p. 81; [Goodrich], "Review of Taylor and Harvey on Human Depravity," 367, 374-75; Beecher, "The Native Character of Man," 11-12.

118. In addition to theological matters, personal and practical considerations contributed to the strife. See Mead, *Nathaniel William Taylor*, pp. 217-21.

119. [Ashbel Green], "Fitch's Discourses on the Nature of Sin," *The Christian Advocate*, V (April, 1827), 162-65; Bennet Tyler, *Remarks on Rev. Dr. Taylor's Letter to Dr. Hawes* (Boston, 1832), pp. 5-8; Joseph Harvey, *A Review of a Sermon, Delivered in the Chapel of Yale College, September 10, 1828 by Nathaniel Taylor* (Hartford, 1829), pp. 24-25.

120. [Green], "Fitch's Discourses on the Nature of Sin," 136-37; Harvey, *A Review of a Sermon*, pp. 5-6. Harvey changed his views somewhat after criticism from the New Haven school, and rejected imputation. See *An Examination of a Review of Dr. Taylor's sermon on Human Depravity, and Mr. Harvey's Strictures on that Sermon* (Hartford, 1829), p. 6.

121. Gardiner Spring, *A Dissertation on Native Depravity* (New York, 1833), pp. 10-11, 28, 34-37; Alvan Hyde, *Essay on the State of Infants* (New York, 1830), pp. 4-6, 11; Harvey, *An Examination of a Review*, pp. 34-35; Leonard Woods, *An Essay on Native Depravity* (Boston, 1835), pp. 162, 168-73.

122. Schenck, *The Presbyterian Doctrine of Children in the Covenant*, pp. 110-13.

123. My interpretation opposes that of Sidney Mead on this point for I believe that he has exaggerated Taylor's practicality. See *Nathaniel William Taylor*, pp. 62n, 62-64, 158. Mead's view does serve as a useful balance to that of Meyer in "The Dissolution of Calvinism," pp. 77, 79-80.

124. *An Inquiry into the Nature of Sin*, p. 33.

125. Spring, *A Dissertation on Native Depravity*, p. 17. Another conservative complained that "In all the annals of theological discussion, I have seen no match for Dr. Taylor's obscurity." See Dr. Porter to Lyman Beecher, May 22, 1829, in *The Autobiography of Lyman Beecher*, II, 119-20.

126. *The Autobiography of Lyman Beecher*, II, 15.

127. Ibid., II, 106.

128. Ibid., I, 400, 402.

129. Parsons, *Infant Baptism from Heaven* (1st. ed.), pp. 34-35; Foster, *The Holiness of Infants*, p. 26; Mead, *Nathaniel William Taylor*, p. 90. For an example of Baptist use of the infant damnation charge, see "Beauties of Free Salvation," *Rhode-Island Baptist*, I (August, 1824), 243-48.

130. Andrews Norton, "Views of Calvinism," *Christian Disciple*, IV (July - Aug., 1822), 257, 258-59n; "State of the Calvinistic Controversy," 220-22.

131. Taylor attempted a limited rebuttal in "Review Reviewed," *Christian Spectator*, VI (July, 1824), 361.

132. This passage was a note in the seventh edition (1827) of Beecher's sermon, "The Goverment of God Desirable." It can be found in *Sermons Delivered on Various Occasions* (Boston, 1828), p. 17, and in *The Autobiography of Lyman Beecher*, II, 103, where the opinion of Charles Beecher is given.

133. "Examination of a Note by Dr. Beecher," 431-48; "Dr. Beecher's Letters," 229-63, 316-40, 506-42. The latter article was separately published, with additions, as [F. Jenks], *Reply to Three Letters of the Rev. Lyman Beecher, D.D. Against the Calvinist Doctrine of Infant Damnation* (Boston, 1829).

134. "Future Punishment of Infants Not a Doctrine of Calvinism," 44-45, 82-87, 91-92, 150-51, 163; Lyman Beecher, "Dr. Beecher's Reply to the *Christian Examiner*," *Spirit of the Pilgrims*, III (April, 1830), 190, 192-95.

135. "Future Punishment of Infants not a Doctrine of Calvinism," 46.

136. Ibid., 90.

137. Ebenezer Porter to Beecher, May 22, 1829, in *The Autobiography of Lyman Beecher*, II, 124.

138. *Concio ad Clerum*, p. 24; [Goodrich], "Review of Taylor and Harvey on Human Depravity," 374.

139. Harvey, *A Review of a Sermon*, pp. 19-20.

140. *An Inquiry into the Nature of Sin*, pp. 80-82.

141. "Spring on Native Depravity," *Quarterly Christian Spectator*, V (June, 1833), 324; [Goodrich], "Review of Taylor and Harvey on Human Depravity," 374.

142. For examples, see May, *The American Female Poets*, pp. 95-96; Thomas Buchanan Read, ed., *The Female Poets of America* (Philadelphia, 1849), pp, 272-73; and [F. Parkman, ed.], *An Offering of Sympathy to Parents Bereaved of their Children* (Boston, 1830), pp. 58, 59.

143. [Harvey], *An Examination of a Review of Dr. Taylor's Sermon*, pp. 11-12, 22; Woods, *Native Depravity*, pp. 105-7.

144. *Essay on the State of Infants*, pp. 5, 7, 12. Hyde was pastor in Lee, Massachusetts. For another example, see Gilbert H. Barnes, *The Anti-Slavery Impulse, 1830-1844* (New York, 1933), p. 5.

145. In addition to poems cited earlier, see George B. Cheever, ed., *The American Common-Place Book of Poetry* (Boston, 1831), pp. 376-77; James R. Lowell, *The Poetical Works* (Boston, 1871), I, 221; and Henry Wadsworth Longfellow, *The Complete Poetical Works* (Boston, 1893), p. 107.

146. *A Dissertation on Native Depravity*, pp. 52, 86-87. See also Edward D. Griffin, *Sermons* (New York, 1839), I, 313-14; Leonard Woods, *Works* (Andover, 1850), II, 340-41; and Nehemiah Adams, *The Friends of Christ in the New Testament* (Boston, 1855, 5th ed.), pp. 142-49.

147. "Spring on Native Depravity," 325-26.

148. *Views of Christian Nurture, and of Subjects Adjacent Thereto* (Hartford, 1848, 2nd ed.), p. 64. See also Edwards A. Park, "Unity Amid Diversities of Belief, Even on Imputed and Involuntary Sin," *Bibliotheca Sacra*, VIII (July, 1851), 634.

149. This statement is that of an unidentified letter writer to the *Congregational Journal* (Dec. 17th or 18th, 1857), quoted in Hayden, *The History of the Dogma of Infant Damnation*, pp. 28-29; "Infants—How Affected by the Sin of Adam," *Congregational Journal*, XXXIX (Dec. 24, 1857), 206; "Perdition of Infants," *Christian Register*, XXXVI (Dec. 26, 1857), 206. For discussion of the infant issue in other sections of the country during this period, see George W. Bethune, *Early Lost, Early Saved, An Argument for the Salvation of Infants* (Philadelphia, 1846); Thomas Smyth, *Infants Die to Live: Solace for Bereaved Parents* (New York, 1848); N. L. Rice, "Infant Damnation," *Presbyterian Expositor*, I (June 15, 1858), 357-61; and J. H. A. Bomberger, *Infant Salvation in its Relation to Infant Depravity, Infant Regeneration, and Infant Baptism* (Philadelphia, 1859).

150. Enoch Pond, "The Character of Infants," *Bibliotheca Sacra*, IX (Oct., 1852), 748-49, 752; Bennet Tyler, *Lectures on Theology* (Boston, 1859), p. 210; Alvan Tobey, "The Salvation of Infants," *Bibliotheca Sacra*,

XVIII (April , 1861), 392-94, 399-400; Joseph Haven, "Sin, As Related to Human Nature and to the Divine Purpose," *Bibliotheca Sacra*, XX (July, 1863), 469-71.

151. *European Thought in the Eighteenth Century, from Montesquieu to Lessing* (Cleveland, 1963), p. 322.

152. An example of late Unitarian use of infant damnation is in Orville Dewey, "Why I am a Unitarian," in *The Pitts-Street Chapel Lectures* (Boston, 1858), pp. 305-6.

153. B. F. Barrett, *Beauty for Ashes; Or, The Old and the New Doctrine, Concerning the State of Infants after Death, Contrasted* (New York, 1855), pp. 16-55; Hayden, *The History of the Dogma of Infant Damnation*, pp. 6-17, 29-32.

154. B. F. Barrett, *A Discourse on the State of Infants in the Spiritual World* (New York, 1841), pp. 8-14; Barrett, *Beauty for Ashes*, pp. 64-83; Hayden, *The History of the Dogma of Infant Damnation*, pp. 17, 20-21.

155. Barrett, *A Discourse on the State of Infants*, p. 13; Barrett, *Beauty for Ashes*, pp. 12, 15, 53, 62, 98-99; Hayden, *The History of the Dogma of Infant Damnation*, pp. 6, 18.

156. A. F. Hewit, "Future Destiny of Infants," *Catholic World*, 51 (Aug., 1890), 576, 577, 582, 583; James F. Loughlin, "The Fate of Unbaptized Infants," *Catholic World*, 51 (July, 1890), pp. 461, 465. A veiled attack on the Catholic position occurred in D. W. Griffith's 1920 film, *Way Down East*. The young heroine, Anna Moore (played by Lillian Gish), has given birth to an illegitimate child. In the boardinghouse where Anna is staying, the cold-hearted proprietess tells her, "If your baby dies without being baptized, it will never see God." The crucifix above the boarding-house bed—unlikely in a Protestant establishment in New England—and the proprietess' name, Maria Poole, suggest that this unsympathetic woman is a Catholic.

157. C. P. Krauth, *Infant Baptism and Infant Salvation in the Calvinistic System*, pp. 10, 56-57; Charles Hodge, *Systematic Theology* (New York, 1877), III, 605n; "Infant Salvation," *American Church Review*, 26 (Oct., 1874), 519-25.

158. Shields, "The Doctrine of Calvin Concerning Infant Salvation," 650; Hodge, *Systematic Theology*, I, 26-27; Warfield, *The Development of the Doctrine of Infant Salvation*, pp. 49, 60-61.

159. Harvey, *An Examination of a Review of Dr. Taylor's Sermon*, p. 3; Fitch, *An Inquiry into the Nature of Sin*, p. 5; Dwight, *Theology*, V, 564-65; Perry Miller, *The Life of the Mind in America; From the Revolution to the Civil War* (New York, 1965), pp. 59-60.

160. "Reviews and Literary Notices," *Atlantic Monthly*, XV (May, 1865), 632. According to Leonard Bacon, a well-known minister of mid-century, Nathaniel W. Taylor "came to be regarded as a kind of relic of a bygone era, who devoted his lectures at Yale Divinity School to the discussion of forgotten issues." Quoted in Mead, *Nathaniel William Taylor*, p. 223n. See also Nahum Gale's "Memoir" of Bennet Tyler in Tyler, *Lectures on Theology*, pp. 109-10.

III.   The Methodology of Upbringing

1. *Right Thoughts in Sad Hours,* p. 52.

2. Stannard, "Death and the Puritan Child," p. 18.

3. "Maternal Societies," *American Baptist Magazine,* IX (Aug., 1829), 285-86; A Mother, "Maternal Association," *Panoplist,* XII (June, 1816), 278; *Memoirs of the Late Mrs. Susan Huntington,* pp. 143-45.

4. To avoid excessive documentation, I have not tried to record every instance in which Dwight's views were also set forth by his contemporaries. Some of his ideas were such commonplaces of the day that a page of sources could be listed. Instead, I have provided supplementary documentation only in selected cases. Additional examples can be found in Peter Gregg Slater, "Views of Children and of Child Rearing During the Early National Period: A Study in the New England Intellect," Diss. University of California, Berkeley, 1970, 159-309.

5. [Sereno Dwight], "Memoir of the Life of President Dwight," in *Theology,* I, lviii.

6. *Sermons* (New Haven, 1828), I, 290; See also Anon., *Incidents in the Life of President Dwight, Illustrative of his Moral and Religious Character* (New Haven, 1831), p. 73.

7. Cunningham, *Timothy Dwight,* pp. 144, 149-50.

8. [Sereno Dwight], "Memoir," I, xvii-xviii.

9. Ibid., xviii.

10. In reading the accounts of Timothy Dwight written by two of his sons, one is struck by how little was said about him as their parent. Benjamin Dwight was silent on the matter in the manuscript, "Biographical Hints & Facts, Respecting the Late Rev. Timothy Dwight" (Dwight Family Papers, Yale University Library), and Sereno Dwight was perfunctory in his "Memoir." Dwight's friend and colleague, the noted scientist Benjamin Silliman, observed that, "Although, ardently loving his children he never solicited favours for them, or enlisted his friends to do it; while, he constantly gave his influence for the advancement of others." See *A Sketch of the Life and Character of President Dwight* (New Haven, 1817), p. 36.

11. Theodore Dwight, Jun., comp., *President Dwight's Decisions of Questions Discussed by the Senior Class in Yale College, in 1813 and 1814* (New York, 1833), p. 243.

12. "An Essay on Education," *Christian Spectator,* II (July, 1820), 349; William J. McTaggart and William K. Bottorff, eds., *The Major Poems of Timothy Dwight* (Gainesville, Florida, 1969), p. 537.

13. Cyrus Yale, ed., *The Godly Pastor. Life of the Rev. Jeremiah Hallock, of Canton, Conn.* (New York, [1854]), p. 258. The core of Dwight's child psychology was contained in the five volumes of his *Theology.* This work was quite popular in both Europe and America for several decades after its publication in 1818-1819, going through over twelve editions. See Stephen Berk, *Calvinism vs. Democracy: Timothy Dwight and the Origins of American Evangelical Orthodoxy* (Hamden, Conn., 1974), p. 195. Dwight's other publications also had much to say

about children in the family. Since his opinions on the subject did not change greatly once they had been formed in early manhood, I have analyzed his writings as a single unit. Detailed accounts of Dwight's changing views about other matters, such as literary canons, political issues, or the American future, can be found in the above mentioned book by Berk; in Leon Howard, *The Connecticut Wits* (Chicago, 1943); in Ernest Lee Tuveson, *Redeemer Nation; The Idea of America's Millennial Role* (Chicago, 1968), pp. 103-12; and in Kenneth Silverman, *Timothy Dwight* (New York, 1969). The only modern biography is Cunningham's *Timothy Dwight.*

14. Howard, *The Connecticut Wits,* pp. 399-400.

15. To Mary Woolsey Dwight, Feb. 22, 1817. See also Timothy Dwight to Dr. Ryland, March 16, 1805. Both letters are in the Dwight Family Papers, Yale University Library. Dwight's differences with the Hopkinsians are well covered in Berk, *Calvinism vs. Democracy,* pp. 72-73, passim. For a discussion of Dwight's theology as a common denominator, see Foster, *A Genetic History of the New England Theology,* pp. 361-62; and Howard, *The Connecticut Wits,* pp. 355, 363-64.

16. Cf. Philip J. Greven, Jr., ed., *Child-Rearing Concepts, 1628-1861* (Itasca, Illinois: F. E. Peacock paperback, 1973), pp. 5-6.

17. *Major Poems,* p. 489.

18. *Theology,* IV, 102-4, 198, 231; Willard, *A Compleat Body of Divinity,* pp. 601-4; Robert H. Bremner, ed., *Children and Youth in America: A Documentary History* (Cambridge, Mass., 1970-1971), I, 35, 39-42; Morgan, *The Puritan Family,* pp. 65-66, 87-90; James Axtell, *The School Upon a Hill: Education and Society in Colonial New England* (New Haven, 1974), pp. 10-13, 101-4, 135-36.

19. *Theology,* IV, 231.

20. Ibid.; *Sermons,* II, 74.

21. *Theology,* IV, 96-97; *Sermons,* II, 153.

22. *Sermons,* I, 439-40.

23. A brilliant treatment of some of these ambiguities can be found in Joseph Heller's novel, *Something Happened* (New York: Ballantine paperback, 1975). See also Rich, *Of Woman Born,* pp. 21-22.

24. *Theology,* IV, 231.

25. Ibid., IV, 121, 216, 231; *Major Poems,* pp. 499-500.

26. "An Essay on Education," 352. For other examples, see Joel Harvey Linsley, *Lectures on the Relations and Duties of the Middle Aged* (Hartford, 1828), p. 98; John Stevens Cabot Abbott, *The Mother at Home* (Boston, 1834, 4th ed.), pp. 113-16; [Daniel Huntington], *Hints on Early Religious Education,* American Tract Society General and Occasional Series, V, No. 143 (New York, [c. 1830]), pp. 15-16; and Cyrus Comstock, *Essays on the Duty of Parents and Children* (Hartford, 1810), pp. 45-46.

27. *Theology,* IV, 121, V, 127; *The Charitable Blessed* (New Haven, 1810), p. 15.

28. *Memoirs of the Late Mrs. Susan Huntington,* p. 98.

29. *President Dwight's Decisions,* p. 41; *Travels,* IV, 476.

30. [Sereno Dwight], "Memoir," I, v; *Incidents in the Life of President Dwight,* pp. 13-14; Cunningham, *Timothy Dwight,* pp. 10, 103.

31. *Theology*, I, 483-84; *Travels*, IV, 474.

32. *Theology*, IV, 484; *Travels*, IV, 474; *President Dwight's Decisions*, p. 43.

33. *Travels*, IV, 474.

34. *Major Poems*, pp. 490-91.

35. *Travels*, IV, 475-76; *President Dwight's Decisions*, pp. 41-43; Cunningham, *Timothy Dwight*, p. 154.

36. *Travels*, IV, 476.

37. *Major Poems*, pp. 499-500.

38. Ibid., p. 501; *Theology*, IV, 126. For other examples, see Noah Webster, *A Collection of Essays and Fugitiv Writings* (Boston, 1790), p. 16; John Witherspoon, *A Series of Letters on Education* (New York, 1797), pp. 5-7; Comstock, *Essays*, pp. 186-88; and Gesell et al., *Infant and Child*, p. 190.

39. *Theology*, I, 532, II, 8.

40. *Major Poems*, 493; *Theology*, I, 375-76, V, 115-16.

41. "Long Life Not Desirable," Dwight Family Papers, Yale University Library.

42. *Theology*, I, 527, II, 15.

43. *The True Means of Establishing Public Happiness* (New Haven, [1795]), p. 14; *Sermons*, II, 25.

44. Ernst Cassirer, *The Philosophy of the Enlightenment* (Princeton, 1951), pp. 105-8; Ronald S. Crane, "Suggestions Toward a Genealogy of the 'Man of Feeling,'" *Journal of English Literary History*, I (Dec., 1934), 207, 214, 230; Peter Gay, *The Enlightenment: An Interpretation*, Vol. II, *The Science of Freedom* (New York, 1969), 187-89.

45. Miller, *Jonathan Edwards*, pp. 183-84; "The Work of Salvation," Dwight Family Papers, Yale University Library; *Theology*, II, 548-49, 558-60; [Sereno Dwight], "Memoir," I, lxxv.

46. *The Nature, and Danger, of Infidel Philosophy* (New Haven, 1798), p. 50; *The True Means of Establishing Public Happiness*, p. 14. For examples of a similar message from other Calvinists, see A Mother, "Maternal Association," 279; and [Goodrich], "Remarks on a Letter to the Editors," 551.

47. Miller, *The New England Mind: The Seventeenth Century*, p. 253; John Locke, *Some Thoughts Concerning Education*, ed. R. H. Quick (Cambridge, England, 1884), sections 33, 107.

48. Gesell et al., *Infant and Child*, p. 23; Dodson, *How to Parent*, p. 116; Selma H. Fraiberg, *The Magic Years; Understanding and Handling the Problems of Early Childhood* (New York: Scribner paperback, 1959), pp. 65-66.

49. Anna Freud, *Psycho-Analysis for Teachers and Parents, Introductory Lectures* (New York, 1935), pp. 74, 75, 98.

50. *Theology*, IV, 107, 108, 110.

51. Ibid., IV, 120, 237, V, 117.

52. Ibid., IV, 90.

53. [Sereno Dwight], "Memoir," I, lxxiv.

54. For example, see Dodson, *How to Parent*, pp. 237-38; and Haim G.

Ginott, *Between Parent and Child: New Solutions to Old Problems* (New York, 1965), pp. 184-85.

55. *Theology*, IV, 90.

56. *Major Poems*, p. 4. For an extensive analysis of this theme, see Edwin G. Burrows and Michael Wallace, "The American Revolution: The Ideology and Psychology of National Liberation," *Perspectives in American History*, VI (1972), pp. 167-306.

57. *A Valedictory Address to the Young Gentlemen, Who Commenced Bachelor of Arts, at Yale-College, July 25th, 1776* (New Haven, 1776), p. 12; "The Friend," *American Museum*, V (May, June, 1789), 445-46, 567.

58. *Theology*, IV, 118. On the Loyalist presentation, see Burrows and Wallace, "The American Revolution," 218-25.

59. Gary B. Nash has shown that the hostile reaction of the New England clergy to the French Revolution did not occur during the height of the turbulence in the early 1790s, but a few years later when the domestic situation seemed to be deteriorating. See "The American Clergy and the French Revolution," *William and Mary Quarterly*, XXII (July, 1965), 392-412. Dwight was typical in this regard. Not until 1798 did he publish a major attack upon the "Jacobin phrenzy"—*The Nature, and Danger, of Infidel Philosophy*. His subsequent writings have many references to the French Revolution.

60. *Theology*, IV, 88, 90, 93-95.

61. Ibid., IV, 119-20, 235-36. An example of early and total authority in practice was the family of Dwight's student, Lyman Beecher. His daughter, Catharine, later recalled, "With most of his children, when quite young, he had one, two, or three seasons in which he taught them that obedience must be exact, prompt, and cheerful, and by a discipline so severe that it was thoroughly remembered and feared. Ever after, a decided word of command was all-sufficient. . . . Words of command [were] obeyed with almost military speed and precision." See *The Autobiography of Lyman Beecher*, I, 104.

62. *Theology*, IV, 120. William G. McLoughlin has analyzed perceptively an instance in which an extensive struggle was necessary to secure obedience. In 1831 the Baptist clergyman, moral philosopher, and college president, Francis Wayland, literally starved his recalcitrant fifteen month old son into submission. Wayland, whose views on authority were similar to those of Dwight, believed that this child had an "unusually unyielding temper." See "Evangelical Childrearing in the Age of Jackson: Francis Wayland's Views on When and How to Subdue the Willfulness of Children," *Journal of Social History*, 9 (Fall, 1975), 22-23, 36, passim.

63. *Theology*, IV, 86-91; *The True Means of Establishing Public Happiness*, p. 36.

64. Bremner, ed., *Children and Youth in America*, I, 343-45; Burrows and Wallace, "The American Revolution," 264-66; Arthur Calhoun, *A Social History of the American Family from Colonial Times to the Present* (New York, 1945, rev. ed.), II, 55, 64-66; Frank F. Furstenberg, Jr., "Industrialization and the American Family: A Look Backward," *American Sociological Review*, 31 (June, 1966), 334-35.

65. Cf. William J. Goode, *World Revolution and Family Patterns* (New York, 1963), pp. 77-78, 372. Other commonly assigned causes are the related increases in economic opportunity and geographical mobility which made children restless with parental apron strings and eager to be on their way. But these influences could not have had much effect on children under twelve.

66. *Theology*, V, 21.

67. Note Dwight's telling remark about "our own history, which after that of the scriptures, is better known to us than any other." See *Virtuous Rulers a National Blessing* (Hartford, 1791), p. 28. His long poem, *The Conquest of Canaan*, was an epic account of scriptural scenes, into which contemporary events were occasionally interpolated. According to Harriet Beecher Stowe, "No New-Englander, brought up under the *régime* established by the Puritans, could really estimate how much of himself had actually been formed by this constant face-to-face intimacy with Hebrew literature." See *Oldtown Folks*, p. 296.

68. *Virtuous Rulers*, pp. 8-11, 34-35. Leon Howard aptly characterizes Dwight's mind as "rather pedantic, theory-ridden," and refers to his "lifelong habit of carrying his principles to their logical conclusion." See *The Connecticut Wits*, pp. 95, 228.

69. For contemporary examples, see Emmons, *Works*, II, 478-81; Thomas H. Gallaudet, "Preliminary Essay" in Thomas Babington, *A Practical View of Christian Education* (Hartford, 1831, 4th American ed.), p. 3; and Abbott, *The Mother at Home*, pp. 25-26.

70. *A Family Well Ordered*, p. 22; Willard, *A Compleat Body of Divinity*, pp. 603-7, 648. Excerpts from seventeenth-century Massachusetts and Connecticut laws which supported parental authority are given in Bremner, ed., *Children and Youth in America*, I, 37-39. The belief in such authority is discussed in Axtell, *The School Upon A Hill*, pp. 89-91, 143-44, 147-50; and Emory Elliott, *Power and the Pulpit in Puritan New England* (Princeton, 1975), pp. 66-68, 120-21. An emphasis on strong parental authority had been part of English Puritanism. See Levin L. Schücking, *The Puritan Family; A Social Study from the Literary Sources* (New York, 1970), pp. 72-74; and Lawrence Stone, "The Rise of the Nuclear Family in Early Modern England," in *The Family in History*, ed. Charles E. Rosenberg (Philadelphia, 1975), pp. 34-36, 43-44.

71. For example, Merle Curti, "The Great Mr. Locke," *Huntington Library Bulletin*, No. 11 (April, 1937), 111; Burrows and Wallace, "The American Revolution," 260-62. A contrary interpretation, one which I have found instructive although not in all aspects convincing, is presented in Daniel Calhoun, *The Intelligence of a People* (Princeton, 1973), pp. 139-44.

72. *Some Thoughts Concerning Education*, sections 40, 42, 44, 100.

73. For example, B. N., "On Early Religious Education," *Christian Spectator*, IV (Aug., 1822), 398-99.

74. *Hints for the Improvement of Early Education and Nursery Discipline* (Salem, 1827, 1st ed., London, 1820), pp. 34-37, 41-42. This book was republished in New England at least a half dozen times in the 1820s, and was reissued as late as 1847. There is a New York edition of 1887.

75. *Memoirs of the Late Mrs. Susan Huntington*, p. 144, also, p. 99; Crispus, "On the Education of Children," 402. See also Samuel R. Hall, *Practical Lectures on Parental Responsibility and the Religious Education of Children* (Boston, 1833), p. 77, passim; and Comstock, *Essays*, pp. 144, 147-48, 168 and n., 185, 186.

76. *A Series of Letters on Education* (New York, 1797), pp. 25-35. For examples of parents practicing the Witherspoon method, see Robert Sunley, "Early Nineteenth-Century American Literature on Child Rearing," in *Childhood in Contemporary Cultures*, eds. Margaret Mead and Martha Wolfenstein (Chicago, 1955), p. 160.

77. *Theology*, IV, 118, 123. Bernard Farber has attempted to correlate the social class of families with the degree to which parents stressed tenderness or authority. See *Guardians of Virtue; Salem Families in 1800* (New York, 1972), pp. 186-88, 197-98, 205.

78. Mather, *A Family Well Ordered*, pp. 22-23; Locke, *Some Thoughts Concerning Education*, sections 34, 42; Witherspoon, *A Series of Letters*, pp. 7-8, 42-44.

79. *Major Poems*, p. 491; *Theology*, IV, 235-36, V, 139; *Virtuous Rulers*, pp. 16-17. Even President Francis Wayland of Brown, who starved his infant son into obedience, was eager to believe that this method fostered a greater love: "The agony was over. He was completely subdued. He repeatedly kissed me, and would do so whenever I commanded. He would kiss any one when I directed him, so full of love was he to all the family. Indeed, so entirely and instantaneously were his feelings towards me changed, that he preferred me now to any of the family. As he had never done before, he moaned after me when he saw that I was going away." Both the tone of the passage, and its depiction of Wayland insisting that the child repeatedly demonstrate affection, are indicative of what a contemporary psychologist terms his "tremendous sense of guilt" for having used such fearsome tactics. See McLoughlin, "Evangelical Childrearing in the Age of Jackson," pp. 36, 40.

80. This point is suggested in Bernard Wishy, *The Child and the Republic; The Dawn of Modern American Child Nurture* (Philadelphia, 1968), p. 33.

81. Lydia M. Child, *The Mother's Book* (Boston, 1831), p. 2; Bronson Alcott, "Maternal Instruction. . . . In the Spirit of Pestalozzi's Method," *American Journal of Education*, IV (Jan., 1829), 55. See also Johann Heinrich Pestalozzi, *Letters of Pestalozzi on the Education of Infancy*, trans. James Greaves (Boston, 1830), pp. 44-49. In *The Wish to be Free; Society, Psyche, and Value Change* (Berkeley and Los Angeles, 1969), Fred Weinstein and Gerald M. Platt attribute the development of a child-rearing pattern founded on maternal manipulation of the emotions to "the economic revolution" which, by creating "highly industrialized, technical societies," removed the father from the home (see pp. 182-83). But Dwight and the American Romantics, as well as the Swiss Pestalozzi, were writing before these developments were very far along. Either they had anticipated the outcome, which is unlikely, or were influenced by other factors, some of which I have tried to suggest. For discussions of the

causes behind changes in the structure of the family, see Goode, *World Revolution and Family Patterns*, pp. 2-3; William L. O'Neill, *Divorce in the Progressive Era* (New Haven, 1967), p. 17; Shorter, *The Making of the Modern Family*, pp. 255-56, 263-65; Christopher Lasch, "What the Doctor Ordered"; Furstenberg, "Industrialization and the American Family," 326-27; and Robert V. Wells, "Family History and Demographic Transition," *Journal of Social History*, 9 (Fall, 1975), 6-9, 12, 14.

82. *Some Thoughts Concerning Education*, section 95.

83. *A Series of Letters*, pp. 41-43.

84. *Major Poems*, p. 491. Unfortunately, the degree to which Dwight followed these counsels in his home cannot be determined. His student, Lyman Beecher, frolicked with his own offspring daily and was remembered by Catharine "more as a playmate than in any other character during my childhood." See *The Autobiography of Lyman Beecher*, I, 104. Another moderate Calvinist who saw no conflict between parental authority and playfulness was Francis Wayland. This aspect of his home life is described in McLoughlin, "Evangelical Childrearing in the Age of Jackson," 32.

85. *Major Poems*, p. 491.

86. For example, Child, *The Mother's Book*, pp. 155-57.

87. This point is suggested in Ariès, *Centuries of Childhood*, pp. 393-415.

88. *Theology*, IV, 118, 372; *Major Poems*, 492.

89. *Theology*, IV, 353-54.

90. Ibid., IV, 121-23.

91. *Some Thoughts Concerning Education*, sections 43, 44, 46, 47, 51.

92. [Sereno Dwight], "Memoir," I, xxix-xxx; Cunningham, *Timothy Dwight*, pp. 148-49.

93. *Major Poems*, p. 492; *Theology*, IV, 124-25. Note that Dwight made the father the family disciplinarian, either because he did not think the mother would be sufficiently stern, or because he did not want to compromise her role as the chief dispenser of affection.

94. *Theology*, IV, 122, 124, 371; *Major Poems*, 491.

95. *Major Poems*, 492; *Theology*, IV, 124. Compare the words of Judge Benjamin Barr Lindsey, one of the pioneers of the juvenile court movement in the early twentieth century: "No boy is told he is bad. He did something that was bad. . . . We despise the evil he did; but we love him." See "The Boy and the Court," *Charities*, XIII (Jan., 1905), 353.

96. *Theology*, IV, 118. According to Catharine Beecher, her father's establishment of an early and total authority "secured such habits of prompt, unquestioning, uncomplaining obedience as made few occasions for discipline. I can remember but one in my own case, and but few in that of the younger ones at East Hampton." See *The Autobiography of Lyman Beecher*, I, 104.

97. Benjamin Dwight, "Biographical Hints & Facts."

98. *Sermons*, I, 440.

99. William B. Sprague, "Life of Timothy Dwight," in *The Library of American Biography*, ed. Jared Sparks, 2nd Series, IV (Boston, 1864), p. 358; [Sereno Dwight], "Memoir," I, lxxiii.

100. *Theology*, IV, 104.

101. *A Discourse, on the Genuineness and Authenticity of the New Testament* (New York, 1794); H[arris] E[lwood] S[tarr], "Dwight, Timothy" *Dictionary of American Biography*, V (New York, 1946), 575-76.

102. *Theology*, IV, 104-5; [Sereno Dwight], "Memoir," I, v.

103. *Theology*, IV, 105-6; *A Discourse on Some Events of the Last Century* (New Haven, 1801), p. 44.

104. *Theology*, V, 134-38; *President Dwight's Decisions*, pp. 242-43.

105. *Theology*, IV, 114.

106. *Major Poems*, p. 494; *Theology*, IV, 121.

107. *Theology*, IV, 112-13, 369, V, 115.

108. Ibid., V, 127, 130.

109. *Sermons*, II, 490; *Theology*, IV, 114, V, 131; *The True Means of Establishing Public Happiness*, p. 8. Not until the 1830s did the clumsy division of the psyche between the understanding and the heart (which included the will along with the affections and the conscience) give way to a more useful classification of three faculties: heart (now synonymous with the affections); will; and intellect. See Foster, *Genetic History of the New England Theology*, pp. 214, 232-33, 243-44; Herbert W. Schneider, *A History of American Philosophy* (New York, 1946), pp. 232-34; and D. H. Meyer, *The Instructed Conscience* (Philadelphia, 1972), pp. 54-55.

110. [Sereno Dwight], "Memoir," I, lx.

111. *Virtuous Rulers*, pp. 14-15; *Theology*, V, 131. Leon Howard suggests that for a time Dwight held a tentative belief in an innate moral sense, but by 1791 had repudiated it. See *The Connecticut Wits*, pp. 226-27, 234-35.

112. Some Calvinists did take a view similar to Dwight's. See Linsley, *Lectures on the Relations and Duties of the Middle Aged*, pp. 60, 94-95. Others regarded conscience as an intuitive agency in the manner of the Scottish moral philosophy. See Emmons, *Sermons*, pp. 181-84, 190-92; and [Huntington], *Hints on Early Religious Education*, p. 4.

113. Fraiberg, *The Magic Years*, p. 147; Dodson, *How to Parent*, p. 119.

114. *The True Means of Establishing Public Happiness*, p. 37; *Theology*, IV, 308.

115. *Theology*, IV, 348-49, V, 139.

116. Ibid., IV, 234-35.

117. Ibid., II, 9, IV, 110-11, 115, 349.

118. *Virtuous Rulers*, p. 19.

119. *Theology*, IV, 236, V, 117-18, 130, 143-44.

120. David Riesman with Reuel Denney and Nathan Glazer, *The Lonely Crowd; A Study of the Changing American Character* (New Haven, 1950), pp. 15-16.

121. *Theology*, III, 405, IV, 98; *Nature and Danger of Infidel Philosophy*, p. 85; *The True Means of Establishing Public Happiness*, p. 20.

122. *The Nature and Danger of Infidel Philosophy*, p. 71; *Theology*, V, 138.

123. *Theology*, III, 440-44, 451-52.

124. Ibid., III, 452.

125. Ibid., IV, 104, V, 131.

126. "A Dissertation on the Nature of Virtue," *Works,* II, 412-13, 465-66.

127. *A Sermon, Preached at Northampton, on the Twenty-Eighth of November, 1781: Occasioned by the Capture of the British Army* (Hartford, [1781]), p. 30; *President Dwight's Decisions,* pp. 38-39; Sprague, "Life of Timothy Dwight," pp. 316-17. Dwight's approach is a good example of what Conrad Wright has termed "super-natural rationalism": reason alone could not have discovered the truths of revelation, but all true religion is reasonable. See *The Beginnings of Unitarianism,* pp. 3-4.

128. *Theology,* IV, 90, 104, 308; *Major Poems,* p. 474.

129. *Theology,* III, 306.

130. Joseph Haroutunian, *Piety versus Moralism* (New York, 1932), pp. 95-96. For other examples of the hedonist theme in early nineteenth-century Calvinism, see Nancy Sproat, *Family Lectures* (Boston, 1819), pp. 112-13; and Thomas Hopkins Gallaudet, *The Child's Book on the Soul* (Hartford, 1831, 2nd ed.), II, 105-6.

131. *Virtuous Rulers,* p. 15; *The True Means of Establishing Public Happiness,* pp. 20-21; *Travels,* IV, 403-4.

132. *Theology,* III, 147; *The Charitable Blessed,* p. 15; *Major Poems,* pp. 494, 498.

133. *Theology,* III, 147, IV, 236, V, 132.

134. *Sermons,* I, 447, 500.

135. *Theology,* V, 118, 132; *Major Poems,* p. 537, n. 447.

136. Locke, *Some Thoughts Concerning Education,* sections 10, 54, 56, 64, 66; Enos Hitchcock, *Memoirs of the Bloomsgrove Family* (Boston, 1790), I, 56-57, 271; Maria and Richard Edgeworth, *Practical Education* (New York, 1801), I, 152, 190, 195-96; Hoare, *Hints for the Improvement of Early Education and Nursery Discipline,* pp. 13-14, 80-81; Edgar Castle, *Educating the Good Man; Moral Education in Christian Times* (New York: Collier paperback, 1962), pp. 62-63, 319-21.

137. For a contemporary discussion of this issue from a pronounced behaviorist standpoint, see B. F. Skinner, *Beyond Freedom and Dignity* (New York, 1971): "There are, of course, valid reasons for thinking less of a person who is only automatically good, for he is a lesser person. In a world in which he does not need to work hard, he will not learn to sustain hard work. . . . In a world which promotes automatic goodness, he will not learn to take the punishments associated with behaving badly. . . . The problem is to induce people not to be good but to behave well" (pp. 66-67).

138. *Theology,* IV, 105-6.

139. Ibid., IV, 106-7, 307-8.

140. Ibid., IV, 236; *An Address to the Emigrants from Connecticut, and From New-England Generally, in the New Settlements in the United States* (Hartford, 1817), p. 16; *Travels,* I, 291; Kenneth A. Lockridge, *A New England Town: The First Hundred Years* (New York: Norton paperback, 1970), pp. 168-69.

141. *Sermons,* I, 295; *Theology,* IV, 108; Cunningham, *Timothy Dwight,* pp. 49-50.

142. *Theology,* IV, 129, 289-90; *Sermons,* II, 172-73; Cunningham, *Timothy Dwight,* p. 103.

143. *Theology*, IV, 107-8.

144. Ibid., 110-11, 235; *An Address to the Emigrants*, p. 7; *The True Means of Establishing Public Happiness*, p. 8; *Major Poems*, p. 523.

145. [Sereno Dwight], "Memoir," I, lxx-lxxi. See also Calvin Chapin, *A Sermon, Delivered, 14th January, 1817, at the Funeral of the Rev. Timothy Dwight* (New Haven, 1817), p. 19; and Sprague, "Life of Timothy Dwight," pp. 260, 269, 272.

146. *Theology*, IV, 129, 444, 447-49; *Sermons*, I, 388-90, 500-1, II, 173-74.

147. [Sereno Dwight], "Memoir," I, xliii.

148. For example, Curti, "The Great Mr. Locke," 113, 119.

149. *Theology*, I, 264-65; "Thanksgiving Sermon, Nov. 26, 1801," Dwight Family Papers, Yale University Library.

150. Fraiberg, *The Magic Years*, p. 286. According to Fitzhugh Dodson, "By the time a child is six years old, his basic personality structure has been formed. This basic personality he will carry with him for the rest of his life. It will determine, to a large extent, how successful he will be throughout school and in later life. His basic personality structure will largely determine how he will get along with other people, how he will feel about sex, what kind of adolescence he will have, what type of person he will marry, and how successful that marriage will be" (*How to Parent*, p. 28).

IV. The Structure of Child-Rearing Theory

1. "An Essay on Education," 349-52.

2. Quoted in Perry Miller, "Jonathan Edwards to Emerson," *New England Quarterly*, XIII (Dec., 1940), 613, see also 614-15, n. 33.

3. Antipas, "The Comparative Importance of Moral and Intellectual Culture," *Spirit of the Pilgrims*, III (Nov., 1830), 575; Senex, "On Christian Education," *Spirit of the Pilgrims*, I (Nov., 1828), 563. Consistent Calvinists like Samuel Hopkins, who deemphasized the means of grace in order to heighten the sovereignty of God, did not rigorously uphold this point of view for child rearing. Stephen E. Berk claims, in *Calvinism vs. Democracy*, that the Hopkinsians "obliterated all agencies of religious nurture" (p. 63). But Samuel Hopkins wrote: "The covenant, as it respects the children of believing parents, and includes them, promises spiritual blessings and salvation to them, on condition of the parents [sic] faithfulness in devoting them to God, and bringing them up for him, persevering in the exercises and duties, which are implied in this." See *The System of Doctrines*, II, 346, also 312, 358, 370-71.

4. Dwight, *Theology*, V, 114, 124.

5. Ibid., V, 127. See also Ezekiel L. Bascom, *Parental Duties Enjoined* (New-Ipswich, N.H., 1828), p. 5.

6. Dwight, *Theology*, IV, 236-37; Emmons, *Works*, II, 473; Comstock, *Essays on the Duty of Parents and Children*, pp. 145, 149.

7. "Religious Education of Children," *American Baptist Magazine*, N.S. I (Nov., 1817), 288; Dwight, *Theology*, IV, 528-31; Emmons, *Works*, II, 473.

8. Bernard Bailyn, *The Ideological Origins of the American Revolution* (Cambridge, Mass., 1967), p. ix.

9. For the most extreme instance, the McCarthy-like *Illuminati* scare, see Vernon Stauffer, *New England and the Bavarian Illuminati* (New York, 1918).

10. *Theology*, IV, 530; Beecher, *Sermons Delivered on Various Occasions*, p. 85.

11. Perry Miller, "'Preparation for Salvation' in Seventeenth-Century New England," *Journal of the History of Ideas*, IV (June, 1943), 255; Williston Walker, *The Creeds and Platforms of Congregationalism* (New York, 1893), 429. See also Bremner, ed., *Children and Youth in America*, I, 36-37.

12. Emmons, *Works*, II, 384-85, 485. See also Samuel Hopkins, *Twenty-One Sermons* (Salem, 1803), pp. 364-65, 381-82.

13. Beecher, *Works* (Boston, 1852), II, 91, 110.

14. [The Monadnock Association and the Rev. John H. Church], *Parental Faithfulness*, American Tract Society General and Occasional Series, VI, No. 171 (New York, [c. 1830]), pp. 1-2; Abbott, *The Mother at Home*, pp. 159-61; Hall, *Practical Lectures on Parental Responsibility*, p. vii.

15. Seth Williston, "An Address to Parents upon the Importance of Religiously Educating their Children," *New-York Missionary Magazine*, III (1802), 55. Williston, a native New Englander and a follower of Samuel Hopkins, was doing missionary work in New York on behalf of the Connecticut Missionary Society. See also Antipas, "The Comparative Importance of Moral and Intellectual Culture," 575.

16. Dwight, *Theology*, IV, 512; Abbott, *The Mother at Home*, pp. 111-12.

17. Linsley, *Lectures on the Relations and Duties of the Middle Aged*, pp. 33, 93.

18. *Family Lectures*, pp. 49-50, 126.

19. *Theology*, II, 520; "An Essay on Education," 350. See also Linsley, *Lectures*, p. 33.

20. Crispus, "On the Education of Children," 394; See also Dwight, *Theology*, I, 532, II, 8.

21. B. N., "On Early Religious Education," 397.

22. Senex, "On Christian Education," 563; [Jacob Abbott], *The Way for a Child to be Saved* (New York, 1835, 2nd ed.), p. 12; Samuel Spring, *Three Sermons to Little Children* (New York, 1790), pp. 25, 65, 71.

23. B. N., "On Early Religious Education," 397.

24. Comstock, *Essays*, pp. 9, 48, 210; [Huntington], *Hints on Early Religious Education*, p. 8.

25. Crispus, "On the Education of Children," 397 (emphasis added); Linsley, *Lectures*, p. 58 (emphasis added); Woods, *A Reply to Dr. Ware's*

Letters to Trinitarians and Calvinists, p. 59 (emphasis added). See also Comstock, *Essays,* pp. 32-33, 36. Contrast the conservative "Niagra Creed" of 1878: "Every child of Adam is born into the world with a nature which not only possesses no spark of divine life, but is essentially and unchangeably bad, being in enmity against God, and incapable by any education process whatever of subjection to His law." Quoted in Ernest Sandeen, *The Roots of Fundamentalism* (Chicago, 1970), p. 274.

26. Dwight, "An Essay on Education," 350; Dwight, *Theology,* I, 522, II, 15; Emmons, *Works,* IV, 519-25. For a rejection of the *tabula rasa* on the basis that it denies native depravity, see Mathetees Archaios [Samuel Mather], *A Serious Letter to the Young People of Boston* (Boston, 1783), p. 6.

27. A Mother, "Maternal Association," 279; Comstock, *Essays,* pp. 22, 25, 72. An early example of the Lockean influence is in John Mellen's *A Discourse Containing a Serious Address to Persons of Several Ages and Characters* (Boston, 1757): "The Heart of a Child is in some Respects like clean Paper, on which you may write what Characters you please" (p. 26). For this reference I am indebted to Daniel Calhoun, "Repression: The Lockean Tradition in Child-Rearing," MS of a paper delivered at the meeting of the American Historical Association, Toronto, Dec., 1967.

28. *Theology,* I, 532, V, 130-31. In Emmons, *Works,* cf. IV, 312, with III, 456.

29. Abbott, *The Mother at Home,* p. 82 (emphasis added); Dwight, *Theology,* V, 139-40; A Mother, "Maternal Association," 279. For a more providential formulation, see Williston, "An Address to Parents . . . ," 14: "Without [God's] special blessing, children will not profit, by the most pious instruction and admonitions."

30. Hopkins, *System of Doctrines,* II, 375; Senex, "On Christian Education," 564. See also Stephen West, *A Dissertation on Infant-Baptism* (Hartford, 1798), p. 104; "Religious Intelligence," *Christian Spectator,* IV (Sept., 1822), 492.

31. New England editions of Maria and Richard Edgeworth's two-volume *Practical Education* were Boston, 1815, and 1823. For examples of the Edgeworths' influence, see "Books for Children," *Christian Examiner,* V (Sept., 1828), 408, 415n, 418; and "Practical Education," *Ladies', Magazine,* III (Sept., 1830), 428.

32. According to Alice Morse Earle, Locke's work "found many readers and ardent followers in the new world. The book is in many old-time library lists in New England, and among the scant volumes of those who had but a single book-shelf or book-box. I have seen abstracts and transpositions of his precepts on the pages of almanacs, the most universally circulated and studied of all eighteenth-century books save the Bible. In contemporary letters evidence is found of the influence of Locke's principles." See *Child Life in Colonial Days,* p. 24. Curti, "The Great Mr., Locke," 110-14, corroborates the continuing influence of Locke on American ideas of child rearing. The appearance of Locke's book in American libraries is subjected to statistical analysis in David Lundberg and Henry F. May, "The Enlightened Reader in America," *American*

Quarterly, XXVIII (Summer, 1976), graphs. Mary Cable exaggerates in describing *Some Thoughts Concerning Education* as "the equivalent of Dr. Spock's *Baby and Child Care* wherever there were conscientious parents who knew how to read." See *The Little Darlings; A History of Child Rearing in America* (New York, 1975), p. 51. The 1830 New England edition of Locke was published in Boston.

33. "Locke certainly conceived himself to be, at least as far as beliefs were concerned, a devout and orthodox Christian." See Basil Willey, *The Seventeenth Century Background* (New York, 1962), p. 281. For the categorization of the Enlightenment into moderate, skeptical, revolutionary, and didactic phases, and the classification of Locke in those terms, I am indebted to Henry F. May, "The Problem of the American Enlightenment," *New Literary History*, I (Winter, 1970), 201-14; May, personal communication, Nov. 17, 1972; and May, *The Enlightenment in America* (New York, 1976), pp. xvi, 10, 337-38.

34. Cf. May, *The Enlightenment in America*, p. 178. For a typical comment about Rousseau, see Hall, *Practical Lectures on Parental Responsibility*, p. 159, which refers to "that excessive predominance of feeling and imagination for which the infidel Rosseau [sic] was noted." Rousseau can be said to have been of indirect influence through his effect on the Scottish philosopher Lord Kames and the Swiss educator Johann Pestalozzi, both of whom had followers in New England.

35. Cf. Gay, *The Science of Freedom*, pp. 511-12.

36. *Some Thoughts Concerning Education*, sections 1-2.

37. *Five Dissertations*, pp. 23, 131-32, 171, 175.

38. *Works*, VI, 161, VII, 333; Clarence H. Faust and Thomas H. Johnson, eds., *Jonathan Edwards: Representative Selections* (New York: Hill and Wang paperback, 1962, rev. ed.), p. xxv. Locke did believe in a form of predetermined inclinations: "Nature, I confess, has put into man a desire of happiness and an aversion to misery: these indeed are innate practical principles which . . . *do* continue constantly to operate and influence all our actions without ceasing." But he hardly regarded these inclinations as compelling men who had not received grace to do evil things or, at best, good things from evil motives. See *An Essay Concerning Human Understanding*, ed. Alexander Campbell Fraser (Oxford, 1894), I, bk. I, ii, 3 and n.

39. On a different issue, that of revivalism, Alan Heimert writes that Chauncy used Locke's *Essay Concerning Human Understanding* "not as Edwards did, but as Locke had intended his epistemology to be used: to counter religious 'enthusiasm.'" See *Religion and the American Mind: From the Great Awakening to the Revolution* (Cambridge, Mass., 1966), p. 44.

40. *Five Dissertations*, pp. 187-88, 191, 247-48, 275-76.

41. Ibid., pp. 177, 248.

42. Joseph S. Buckminster, *Sermons* (Boston, 1814), pp. 201-2; "Unitarian Belief," *The Unitarian*, I (Nov., 1827), 9-10; Briggs, "On Hereditary and Total Depravity," 95-97, 112.

43. "Unitarian Belief," 10; Buckminster, *Sermons*, p. 203; "On the

Importance of Christian Education," *Christian Disciple*, III (Feb., March, May, June, 1815), 145, 149; Daniel Howe, *The Unitarian Conscience* (Cambridge, Mass., 1970), pp. 116-18.

44. "On the Importance of Christian Education," 42, 45. According to Conrad Wright, *The Beginnings of Unitarianism in America*: "In the bare assertion that all power comes from God, Arminians did not differ from Calvinists. But by dropping the doctrine of election, the Arminians robbed salvation by grace of the significance it had for the orthodox theologian. . . . The doctrine lost its bite, and became a superfluous statement of the obvious fact that God sustains the universe" (pp. 124-25).

45. *Letters Addressed to Trinitarians and Calvinists*, pp. 20-21, 23, 24, passim.

46. Clifford K. Shipton, *Sibley's Harvard Graduates*, XVI: 1764-1767, 480.

47. "The Belknap Papers, Part II," *Collections of the Massachusetts Historical Society*, 5th Series, III (Boston, 1877), 228, 232, 238; Shipton, *Sibley's Harvard Graduates*, XVI, 483.

48. "The Belknap Papers, Part II," 232.

49. *Some Thoughts Concerning Education*, sections 2, 217.

50. Ibid., sections 66, 139. Paul Hazard writes of Voltaire: "Being a follower of Locke, he laid down that there was nothing innate in our minds, unless, of course, there were such things as innate dispositions; which put the whole thing back in the melting-pot again." See *European Thought in the Eighteenth Century*, p. 406.

51. Historical discussions of the moral sense hypotheses that help reveal the spectrum of positions include D[avid] Daiches Raphael, *The Moral Sense* (London, 1947); Basil Willey, *The English Moralists* (London, 1964); Basil Willey, *The Eighteenth Century Background* (New York, 1941); Leon Howard, "The Late Eighteenth Century," in *Transitions in American Literary History*, ed. Harry Hayden Clark (Durham, N.C., 1953), pp. 51-89; and L. A. Selby-Bigge, ed., *British Moralists* (Oxford, 1897), 2 vols.

52. This statement is one of Locke's marginalia. See *An Essay Concerning Human Understanding*, I, bk. I, ii, 3 n. Ernest Tuveson points out in "The Origins of the 'Moral Sense,'" *Huntington Library Quarterly*, XI (May, 1948), 245, that "Locke sees man as the product of experience, originally determined in no way whatever."

53. Hitchcock, *Memoirs of the Bloomsgrove Family*, I, 175, 207, 260, II, 195, 197; Kames, *Loose Hints Upon Education* (Edinburgh, 1782, 2nd ed.), pp. 74, 89, 104, 190-91, 208-9.

54. *Memoirs of the Bloomsgrove Family*, I, 103, 294; Kames, *Loose Hints Upon Education*, pp. 6, 188-89n. According to Henry May, "The primacy of sensation and the centrality of the moral sense could flourish at once, as long as each of these theories behaved itself and did not push too far." See "The Problem of the American Enlightenment," 207.

55. *Memoirs of the Bloomsgrove Family*, II, 193, 197; Kames, *Loose Hints Upon Education*, pp. 88-89.

56. Locke, *Some Thoughts Concerning Education*, section 70 (emphasis added); Kames, *Loose Hints Upon Education*, p. 26 (emphasis added);

Hitchcock, *Memoirs of the Bloomsgrove Family*, I, 258-59 (emphasis added). For other examples of Enlightenment sensationalism in child rearing, see "On the Influence of Education as a Source of Error," *Christian Disciple*, II (Sept., 1814), 264; and Edgeworth, *Practical Education*, II, 285.

57. Bronson Alcott, "PSYCHE" in *Emerson the Essayist*, ed. Kenneth Cameron (Raleigh, N.C., 1945), II, 106-7, 120.

58. *The Journals of Bronson Alcott*, ed. Odell Shepard (Boston, 1938), p. 28 (June 24, 1831); Odell Shepard, *Pedlar's Progress: The Life of Bronson Alcott* (Boston, 1937), pp. 138-45, 153-60.

59. "Maternal Instruction," 53-58.

60. Ibid., 56; Pestalozzi, *Letters*, pp. 6, 20, 49-50.

61. Emmons, *Works*, II, 480.

62. Charles Strickland, "A Transcendentalist Father: The Child-Rearing Practices of Bronson Alcott," *Perspectives in American History*, III (1969), 17. See also "PSYCHE," 124.

63. Strickland, op. cit., 16; *Journals*, p. 35. See also "PSYCHE," 102-3, 117-18. The influence of Wordsworth upon Alcott is discussed in Barbara Garlitz, "The Immortality Ode: Its Cultural Progeny," *Studies in English Literature, 1500-1900*, VI (Autumn, 1966), 645-46.

64. "Maternal Instruction," 55. See also Shepard, *Pedlar's Progress*, pp. 81-83, 167.

65. *Journals*, p. 85. Channing believed that man was *like* God, but not, as Alcott seemed to suggest, that in some respects man was directly a part of God.

66. *The Mother's Book*, p. 9.

67. Ibid., pp. 8-9.

68. Ibid., p. 3.

69. Ibid., p. 9.

70. For examples, see Anne L. Kuhn, *The Mother's Role in Childhood Education: New England Concepts, 1830-1860* (New Haven, 1947), pp. 151-59, passim.

71. For example, see Robert F. Winch and Robert McGinnis, eds., *Selected Studies in Marriage and the Family* (New York, 1953), pp. 207-8.

72. C[harles] A[llen] D[insmore] , "Bushnell, Horace," *Dictionary of American Biography*, III (1946), 353.

73. The publication of an earlier and briefer version, entitled *Discourses on Christian Nurture* (Boston, 1847), was suspended by the Massachusetts Sabbath School Society. A later and expanded version was entitled *Christian Nurture* (New York, 1861).

74. This relationship is suggested in Cassirer, *The Philosophy of the Enlightenment*, pp. 273-74.

75. *Views of Christian Nurture*, pp. 110-11, 200.

76. Ibid., pp. 8, 13, 15, 83, 185.

77. Ibid., pp. 8, 184.

78. Ibid., pp. 110, 212; Emerson, "Nature," 7.

79. *Views of Christian Nurture*, pp. 15, 25, 108; Emerson, "Nature," 44. In *Nature and the Supernatural, as Together Constituting the One*

System of God (New York, 1858), Bushnell moved away from *Views of Christian Nurture*'s quasi-Transcendentalist depiction of God as a force immanent in the world. The new motif emphasized the supernaturalism of God and His superiority to the world. See H. Shelton Smith, ed., *Horace Bushnell* (New York, 1965), pp. 129-31.

80. *Views of Christian Nurture*, pp. 15, 22, 195.

81. "Heaven Our Home," 51-52.

82. *Views of Christian Nurture*, p. 72. For the contemporary controversy over Bushnell's beliefs, see Mary Bushnell Cheney, *Life and Letters of Horace Bushnell* (New York, 1880), pp. 178-83; and Smith, *Horace Bushnell*, pp. 376-78.

83. *Views of Christian Nurture*, pp. 72-73.

84. Cf. Ibid., pp. 93-94.

85. Ibid., p. 18.

86. Samuel G. Goodrich ("Peter Parley") quoted in Roller, *Children in American Poetry*, p. 35.

87. Cf. H. Richard Niebuhr, *The Kingdom of God in America* (New York: Harper paperback, 1959): "Bushnell protested against the faith he had learned, but he had learned it nevertheless and his protest was significant in part because it arose out of an inner tension between the old and the new" (p. 195).

88. *Views of Christian Nurture*, pp. 17-18.

89. *Baby and Child Care*, p. 10. Michael Zuckerman argues that the deficiencies to which Spock refers are strikingly exemplified in his own approach to child rearing. See "Dr. Spock," pp. 205-7.

From The Puritans To Bushnell

1. *John Todd*, p. 192.

2. R. W. B. Lewis, *The American Adam* (Chicago, 1955), p. 28.

3. *Memoirs*, pp. 75-86, 144-45, 261. On the anxieties created in twentieth-century parents by a body of expert literature on child rearing, see Sarane Spence Boocock, "The Social Context of Childhood," *Proceedings of the American Philosophical Society*, 119, No. 6 (Dec. 5, 1975), 422-23; and Zuckerman, "Dr. Spock," p. 183.

4. For example, Jacob Abbott declared, *"Mothers have as powerful an influence over the welfare of future generations, as all other earthly causes combined."* See *The Mother at Home*, pp. 159-61. This new emphasis upon women's domestic duties is discussed in Kuhn, *The Mother's Role*, pp. 33-37, 72-75, 79, 152-53, 180-87; Barbara Welter, "The Cult of True Womanhood: 1820-1860," *American Quarterly*, XVIII (Summer, 1966), 162-74; and Kathryn Kish Sklar, *Catharine Beecher: A Study in American Domesticity* (New Haven, 1973), pp. 134-37, 155-63.

5. Parrington, *Main Currents in American Thought*, Vol. I, *The Colonial Mind* (New York, 1927), 360-63. For a positive evaluation of Dwight in different terms than I have used, see William Gribbin, "The Legacy of Timothy Dwight: A Reappraisal," *Connecticut Historical Society Bulletin*, XXXVII (April, 1972), 33-41. See also Wayne C. Tyner, "The Theology of Timothy Dwight in Historical Perspective," Diss. University of North Carolina, 1971.

6. The impact of Darwinism upon the New England approach is discussed in Wishy, *The Child and the Republic*, pp. 95-104.

7. Ginott, *Between Parent and Child*, p. 192.

8. Geoffrey H. Steere points out that American child-rearing literature "did not fully modernize until the 1920s." See "Child-Rearing Literature and Modernization Theory," *The Family in Historical Perspective: An International Newsletter*, No. 7 (Winter, 1974), 8-11. However, the professionalization and specialization of child study began at least a generation earlier. For examples of the attitudes of the new experts, see Oscar Chrisman, "Child-Study, A New Department of Education," *Forum*, XVI (Feb., 1894), 728-32, 736; and E. W. Scripture, "Aims and Status of Child-Study," *Educational Review*, VIII (Oct., 1894), 236-39. The new approaches are discussed in Wishy, *The Child and the Republic*, pp. 105-7.

Bibliography

Primary Sources

Manuscripts

Dwight Family Papers, Yale University Library

Published Primary Materials

Diaries, Autobiographies, Memoirs, Journals, Letters

Alcott, Bronson. *The Journals of Bronson Alcott*. Ed. Odell Shepard. Boston, 1938.

Ayer, Sarah Connell. *Diary of Sarah Connell Ayer*. Portland, Maine, 1910.

Beecher, Lyman. *The Autobiography of Lyman Beecher*. Ed. Barbara M. Cross. 2 vols. Cambridge, Mass., 1961.

"The Belknap Papers, Part II," *Collections of the Massachusetts Historical Society*. 5th Series, III (Boston, 1877), 1-371.

Cotton, John. "Letter of John Cotton to Mary Hinckley," in *Remarkable Providences, 1600-1760*, pp. 165-66. Ed. John Demos. New York, 1972.

Dexter, Samuel. "Diary of Rev. Samuel Dexter of Dedham," *New England Historical and Genealogical Register*, XIII (Oct., 1859), 305-10, XIV (Jan., April, July, 1860), 35-40, 107-12, 202-5.

Dow, George F., ed. *The Holyoke Diaries, 1709-1856*. Salem, Mass., 1911.

Eliot, John. "The Rev. John Eliot's Record of Church Members, Roxbury, Mass.," *New England Historical and Genealogical Register*, XXXV (July, 1881), 241-47.

Green, Joseph. "The Commonplace Book of Joseph Green." Ed. Samuel E. Morison. *Publications of the Colonial Society of Massachusetts: Transactions, 1937-1942*, XXXIV, 197-253.

Griffin, Edward D. *Memoir of the Rev. Edward D. Griffin, D.D.* Ed. William B. Sprague. New York, 1839.

Hallock, Jeremiah. *The Godly Pastor; Life of the Rev. Jeremiah Hallock, of Canton, Conn.* Ed. Cyrus Yale. New York, [1854].

Hammond, Lawrence. "Diary of Lawrence Hammond," *Proceedings of the Massachusetts Historical Society*. 2nd Series, VII (1891, 1892), 144-72.

Homes, William. "Diary of Rev. William Homes of Chalmark, Martha's Vineyard," *New England Historical and Genealogical Register*, XLVIII (Oct., 1894), 446-53.

Hull, John. "The Diaries of John Hull," *Transactions and Collections of the American Antiquarian Society*, III (1857), 109-316.

Huntington, Susan. *Memoirs of the Late Mrs. Susan Huntington, of Boston, Mass.* Ed. Benjamin B. Wisner. Boston, 1826.

Marshall, John. "Abstract of John Marshall's Diary." Ed. Charles F. Adams, Jr. *Proceedings of the Massachusetts Historical Society*. 2nd Series, I (1884-85), 148-64.

Mather, Cotton. "Diary of Cotton Mather," *Massachusetts Historical Society Collections*. 7th Series, VII (Boston, 1911), VIII (Boston, 1912).

———. *Selected Letters of Cotton Mather.* Ed. Kenneth Silverman. Baton Rouge, 1971.

Mather, Increase. "The Autobiography of Increase Mather." Ed. M. G. Hall. *Proceedings of the American Antiquarian Society*, 71 (1961), 270-360.

———. "Diary of Increase Mather," *Proceedings of the Massachusetts Historical Society*. 2nd Series, XIII (1899-1900), 337-74, 397-411.

Paine, John. "Deacon John Paine's Journal," *The Mayflower Descendant*, VIII (July, Oct., 1906), 180-84, 227-31, IX (Jan., April, July, 1907), 49-51, 97-99, 136-40.

Parkman, Ebenezer. "The Diary of Ebenezer Parkman." Ed. Francis G. Walett. *Proceedings of the American Antiquarian Society*, 71 (1961), 361-448.

Sewall, Samuel. "Diary of Samuel Sewall," *Collections of the Massachusetts Historical Society*. 5th Series, V (Boston, 1878), VI (Boston, 1879), VII (Boston, 1882).

———. "Letter-Book of Samuel Sewall," *Collections of the Massachusetts Historical Society*. 6th Series, I (Boston, 1886), II (Boston, 1888).

Shepard, Thomas. "The Autobiography of Thomas Shepard," *Publications of the Colonial Society of Massachusetts: Transactions, 1927-1930*, XXVII, 343-400.

———. *God's Plot; The Paradoxes of Puritan Piety, Being the Autobiography & Journal of Thomas Shepard*. Ed. Michael McGiffert. [Amherst, Mass.], 1972.

Thacher, Peter. "Rev. Peter Thacher's Journal," in *A History of Milton, Mass., 1640-1887*, Appendix B. Ed. A. K. Teele. N.p., [1887].

Todd, John. *John Todd, The Story of His Life*. Ed. John E. Todd. New York, 1876.

Watson, William. "Extracts from the Diary of William Watson of Hartford, Conn., 1819-1836," *The New England Historical and Genealogical Register*, LXXIX (July, Oct., 1925), 298-310, 401-9, LXXX (Jan., 1926), 54-72.

Wigglesworth, Michael. "The Diary of Michael Wigglesworth." Ed. Edmund S. Morgan. *Publications of the Colonial Society of Massachusetts: Transactions, 1942-1946*, XXXV, 311-444.

"The Winthrop Papers, Part IV," *Collections of the Massachusetts Historical Society*. 5th Series, VIII (Boston, 1882).

Works on Depravity, Death, the Covenants, the Afterlife

Adams, Nehemiah. *The Friends of Christ in the New Testament*. 5th ed., Boston, 1855.

Adams, Zabdiel. *Our Lapse in Adam, and Redemption by Christ Considered*. Boston, 1791.

Allen, James et al. *The Principles of the Protestant Religion Maintained, and Churches of New-England, in the Profession and Exercise Thereof Defended*. Boston, 1690.

Barnard, John. *Two Sermons: The Christians Behavior under*

*Severe and Repeated Bereavements and the Fatal Conse-
quences of a Peoples Persisting in Sin.* Boston, 1714.

Barrett, B. F. *Beauty for Ashes; Or, The Old and the New Doctrine,
Concerning the State of Infants after Death, Contrasted.*
New York, 1855.

———. *A Discourse on the State of Infants in the Spiritual World.*
New York, 1841.

"Beauties of Free Salvation," *Rhode-Island Baptist,* I (Aug., 1824),
243-52.

Beckwith, George. *The Infant Seed of Visible Believers, Their
Right to Church Membership and Baptism.* New London, 1770.

Beecher, Lyman. "Dr. Beecher's Reply to the *Christian Examiner,*" *Spirit of the Pilgrims,* III (Jan., Feb., April, 1830),
17-24, 72-86, 181-95.

———. "Future Punishment of Infants not a Doctrine of Calvinism," *Spirit of the Pilgrims,* I (Jan., Feb., March, 1828),
42-52, 78-95, 149-64.

———. "The Native Character of Man," *The National Preacher,*
II (June, 1827), 1-16.

[Bellamy, Joseph]. *A Letter to the Reverend Author of the Winter-
Evening Conversation on Original Sin.* Boston, 1758.

Bethune, George W. *Early Lost, Early Saved, An Argument for the
Salvation of Infants.* Philadelphia, 1846.

Bomberger, J. H. A. *Infant Salvation in its Relation to Infant
Depravity, Infant Regeneration, and Infant Baptism.*
Philadelphia, 1859.

Bridgman, Thomas, comp. *Inscriptions on the Grave Stones in
the Grave Yards of Northampton and of Other Towns in
the Valley of the Connecticut.* Northampton, Mass.,
1850.

———. *Memorials of the Dead in Boston.* Boston, 1853.

Briggs, Charles. "On Hereditary and Total Depravity," *The
Liberal Preacher,* II (Jan., 1829), 89-114.

Bulkeley, Peter. *The Gospel-Covenant; or The Covenant of Grace
Opened.* London, 1651.

Chauncy, Charles. *The Benevolence of the Deity, Fairly and
Impartially Considered.* Boston, 1784.

———. *Five Dissertations on the Scripture Account of the Fall;
and Its Consequences.* London, 1785.

[Chauncy, Charles]. *The Opinion of One that has Perused the Summer Morning's Conversation Concerning Original Sin.* Boston, 1758.

Clark, Peter. *A Defence of the Principles of the 'Summer-Morning's Conversation—Concerning the Doctrine of Original Sin.'* Boston, 1760.

[Clark, Peter]. *Remarks on a Late Pamphlet, Intitled 'The Opinion of One that has Perused the Summer Morning's Conversation,'* Boston, 1758.

————. *The Scripture-Doctrine of Original Sin, Stated and Defended. In a Summer-Morning's Conversation, Between a Minister and a Neighbour.* Boston, 1758.

Colman, Benjamin and Cooper, William. *Two Sermons Preached in Boston.* Boston, 1723.

Dexter, Franklin B., ed., "Inscriptions on Tombstones in New Haven Erected Prior to 1800," *Papers of the New Haven Colony Historical Society,* III (New Haven, 1882), 471-614.

"Dissertation on the Sinfulness of Infants," *Christian Disciple,* II (Aug., 1814), 245-50.

"Dr. Beecher's Letters," *Christian Examiner,* V (May, July, Nov., 1828), 229-63, 316-40, 506-42.

Dutch, Ebenezer. *A Discourse Delivered at Bradford, January 25th, 1795.* Haverhill, 1795.

Eliot, John. *A Brief Answer to a Small Book Written by John Norcot Against Infant-Baptisme.* Boston, 1679.

"An Epitaph on an Infant, Found Dead in a Field, Supposed to be Left by Vagrants, and which was Denied Christian Burial," *Boston Magazine,* I (Aug., 1784), 438.

"Examination of a Note by Dr. Beecher," *Christian Examiner,* (Sept. - Oct., 1827), 431-48.

Fitch, Eleazar. *An Inquiry into the Nature of Sin: in which the Views advanced in "Two Discourses on the Nature of Sin," are Pursued; and Vindicated from Objections Stated in the Christian Advocate.* New Haven, 1827.

————. *Two Discourses on the Nature of Sin; Delivered before the Students of Yale College, July 30th, 1826.* New Haven, 1826.

Flavel, John. *A Token for Mourners.* Boston, 1725.

Flynt, Henry. *The Doctrine of the Last Judgment, Asserted and Explained.* Boston, 1714.

Foster, Isaac. *The Holiness of Infants Explained and Improved.* Boston, 1766.

Gibbs, Henry. *Bethany: or, The House of Mourning.* Boston, 1714.

[Goodrich, Chauncey]. "Remarks on a Letter to the Editors, Respecting the Review of Dr. Taylor and Mr. Harvey," *Quarterly Christian Spectator*, N.S. I (Sept., 1829), 547-52.

[Goodrich, Chauncey]. "Review of Taylor and Harvey on Human Depravity," *Quarterly Christian Spectator*, N.S. I (June, 1829), 343-84.

[Green, Ashbel]. "Fitch's Discourses on the Nature of Sin," *Christian Advocate*, V (March, April, 1827), 136-41, 162-67.

[Harvey, Joseph]. *An Examination of A Review of Dr. Taylor's Sermon on Human Depravity, and Mr. Harvey's Strictures on that Sermon.* Hartford, 1829.

————. *A Review of a Sermon, Delivered in the Chapel of Yale College, September 10, 1828 by Nathaniel W. Taylor.* Hartford, 1829.

Haven, Joseph. "Sin, As Related to Human Nature and to the Divine Purpose," *Bibliotheca Sacra*, XX (July, 1863), 445-88.

Hayden, William B. *The History of the Dogma of Infant Damnation.* Portland, 1858.

Hewit, A. F. "Future Destiny of Infants," *Catholic World*, 51 (Aug., 1890), 576-83.

Hyde, Alvan. *Essay on the State of Infants.* New York, 1830.

"Infant Salvation," *American Church Review*, 26 (Oct., 1874), 519-25.

"Infants - How Affected by the Sin of Adam," *Congregational Journal*, XXXIX (Dec. 24, 1857), 206.

[Jenks, F.]. *Reply to Three Letters of the Rev. Lyman Beecher, D.D. Against the Calvinist Doctrine of Infant Damnation.* Boston, 1829.

Keith, George. *The Presbyterian and Independent Visible Churches in New-England and Else-Where Brought to the Test.* Philadelphia, 1689.

Kinnersley, Thomas, comp. *A Selection of Sepulchral Curiosities.* New York, 1823.

Krauth, C. P. *Infant Baptism and Infant Salvation in the Calvinistic System.* Philadelphia, 1874.

Lawry, Thomas. "Good News to All Parents of Such Children, As Die in the Infant State," in John Hepburn, *The American Defence of the Christian Golden Rule*, pp. 63-74. [New York?], 1715.

Loughlin, James F. "The Fate of Unbaptized Infants," *Catholic World*, 51 (July, 1890), 456-65.

Macclintock, Samuel. *The Justice of God in the Mortality of Mankind*. Portsmouth, N.H., 1759.

[March, Edmund]. *Fair Play! or, A Needful Word, to Temper the Tract, Entitled a Summer Morning's Conversation*. Portsmouth, N.H., 1758.

Mather, Cotton. *Baptismal Piety*. Boston, 1727.

———. *A Companion for Communicants; Discourses Upon the Nature, the Design, and the Subject of the Lord's Supper*. Boston, 1690.

———. *Golgotha; A Lively Description of Death*. Boston, 1713.

———. *Hades Look'd Into*. Boston, 1717.

———. *Meat out of the Eater; or Funeral-Discourses Occasioned by the Death of Several Relatives*. Boston, 1703.

———. *Perswasions from the Terror of the Lord; A Sermon Concerning the Day of Judgment*. Boston, 1711.

———. *Right Thoughts in Sad Hours: A Sermon Representing the Comforts and Duties of Good Men Under Afflictions, Particularly Under the Untimely Death of Children*. Dunstable, 1811. 1st ed., London, 1689.

———. *Seasonable Thoughts upon Mortality*. Boston, 1712.

———. *Silentarius*. Boston, 1721.

[Mather, Cotton]. *The Tribe of Asher*. Boston, 1717.

Mather, Cotton and Foxcroft, Thomas. *Two Funeral Sermons Preach'd upon Mournful Occasions*. Boston, 1722.

[Mather, Cotton]. *The Valley of Hinnan; The Terrours of Hell Demonstrated*. Boston, 1717.

[Mather, Cotton]. *Wholesome Words; A Visit of Advice Given unto Families that are Visited with Sickness*. Boston, 1713.

Mather, Increase. *The Believers Gain by Death*. Boston, 1713.

———. *The Divine Right of Infant-Baptisme Asserted and Proved from Scripture and Antiquity*. Boston, 1680.

———. *The Folly of Sinning Opened & Applyed*. Boston, 1699.

———. *Meditations on the Glory of the Heavenly World*. Boston, 1711.

————. *A Plain Discourse, Shewing Who Shall & Who Shall not Enter into the Kingdom of Heaven.* Boston, 1713.

————. *Pray for the Rising Generation.* Cambridge, Mass., 1678.

Mather, Moses. *The Visible Church in Covenant with God.* New York, 1769.

Morris, E. D. "The Salvation of Infants—Theologic Implications of the Doctrine," *Presbyterian and Reformed Review,* I (April, 1890), 294-301.

Murray, John. *The Original Sin Imputed.* Newburyport, 1791.

Norton, Andrews. "Views of Calvinism," *Christian Disciple,* IV (July - Aug., 1822), 244-80.

Paine, Thomas. *The Doctrine of Original Sin Proved and Applyed.* Boston, 1724.

Park, Edwards A. "Unity Amid Diversities of Belief, Even on Imputed and Involuntary Sin," *Bibliotheca Sacra,* VIII (July, 1851), 594-647.

[Parkman, F.] *An Offering of Sympathy to Parents Bereaved of their Children, and to Others under Affliction; Being a Collection from Manuscripts and Letters not before Published.* Boston, 1830.

Parsons, Jonathan. *Infant Baptism from Heaven.*Boston, 1765.

————. *Infant Baptism from Heaven.* 2nd. ed., Boston, 1767.

"Perdition of Infants," *Christian Register,* XXXVI (Dec. 26, 1857), 206.

Pond, Enoch. "The Character of Infants," *Bibliotheca Sacra,* IX (Oct., 1852), 746-61.

Powers, Peter. *A Humble Enquiry into the Nature of Convenanting with God.* Newburyport, 1796.

Rice, N. L. "Infant Damnation," *Presbyterian Expositor,* I (June 15, 1858), 357-61.

Rogers, John. *Death the Certain Wages of Sin to the Impenitent.* Boston, 1701.

Shields, Charles W. "The Doctrine of Calvin Concerning Infant Salvation," *Presbyterian and Reformed Review,* I (Oct., 1890), 634-51.

Smith, Samuel. *The Great Assize: or, Day of Jubilee.* Boston, 1727.

Smyth, Thomas. *Infants Die to Live: Solace for Bereaved Parents.* New York, 1848.

Spring, Gardiner. *A Dissertation on Native Depravity.* New York, 1833.

"State of the Calvinistic Controversy," *Christian Disciple*, V (May-June 1823), 212-35.

Strong, Cyprian. *An Inquiry; Wherein, the End and Design of Baptism . . .are Particularly Considered and Illustrated.* Hartford, 1793.

_____. *A Second Inquiry, into the Nature and Design of Christian Baptism.* Hartford, 1796.

Taylor, John. *The Scripture-Doctrine of Original Sin Proposed to Free and Candid Examination.* 3rd. ed., London, 1750.

Taylor, Nathaniel W. *Concio ad Clerum; Sermon Delivered in the Chapel of Yale College, September 10, 1828.* New Haven, 1828.

Taylor, Nathaniel W. and Hawes, Joel. *Correspondence between Rev. Dr. Taylor and Rev. Dr. Hawes.* N.p., [1832?].

[Taylor, Nathaniel W.] *An Inquiry into the Nature of Sin, as Exhibited in Dr. Dwight's Theology.* New Haven, 1829.

[Taylor, Nathaniel W.] "Review of Norton's Views of Calvinism," *Christian Spectator*, V (April, 1823), 196-224.

[Taylor, Nathaniel W.] "Review Reviewed," *Christian Spectator*, VI (June, July, 1824), 310-21, 360-74.

[Taylor, Nathaniel W.] "Spring on Native Depravity," *Quarterly Christian Spectator*, V (June, 1833), 314-32.

Tobey, Alvan. "The Salvation of Infants," *Bibliotheca Sacra*, XVIII (April, 1861), 383-409.

Tyler, Bennet. *Remarks on Rev. Dr. Taylor's Letter to Dr. Hawes.* Boston, 1832.

Wadsworth, Benjamin. *The Great and Last Day of Judgment.* Boston, 1709.

Ware, Henry. *Answer to Dr. Woods' Reply, In a Second Series of Letters Addressed to Trinitarians and Calvinists.* Cambridge, Mass., 1822.

_____. *Letters Addressed to Trinitarians and Calvinists, Occasioned by Dr. Woods' Letters to Unitarians.* Cambridge, Mass., 1820.

_____. *A Postscript to the Second Series of Letters Addressed to Trinitarians and Calvinists, in Reply to the Remarks of Dr. Woods on those Letters.* Cambridge, Mass., 1823.

Warfield, Benjamin. *The Development of the Doctrine of Infant Salvation.* New York, 1891.

Webb, John. *Practical Discourses on Death, Judgment, Heaven, and Hell.* Boston, 1726.

[Webster, Samuel.] *A Winter Evening's Conversation upon the Doctrine of Original Sin, Between a Minister and Three of His Neighbours Accidentally Met Together*. Boston, 1757.

[Webster, Samuel.] *The Winter Evening Conversation Vindicated; Against the Remarks of the Rev. Mr. Peter Clark of Danvers*. Boston, [1758].

West, Stephen. *A Dissertaton on Infant-Baptism; In Reply to the Rev. Cyprian Strong's Second Inquiry on that Subject*. Hartford, 1798.

Whiting, Samuel. *A Discourse of the Last Judgment*. Cambridge, Mass., 1664.

Willard, Samuel. *The Barren Fig Trees Doom*. Boston, 1691.

———. *The Child's Portion: or the Unseen Glory of the Children of God*. Boston, 1684.

———. *Impenitent Sinners Warned of their Misery and Summoned to Judgment*. Boston, 1698.

———. *The Mourners Cordial Against Excessive Sorrow*. Boston, 1691.

William, Williams. *An Essay to Prove the Interest of the Children of Believers in the Covenant*. Boston, 1727.

Woods, Leonard. *An Essay on Native Depravity*. Boston, 1835.

———. *Lectures on Infant Baptism*. Andover, 1828.

———. *Letters to Unitarians, Occasioned by the Sermon of the Reverend William E. Channing at the Ordination of the Rev. J. Sparks*. Andover, 1820.

———. *Remarks on Dr. Ware's Answer*. Andover, 1822.

———. *A Reply to Dr. Ware's Letters to Trinitarians and Calvinists*. Andover, 1821.

Worcester, Thomas. *Little Children of the Kingdom of Heaven, Only by the Blessing of Christ*. Concord, N.H., 1803.

Works on Child Rearing

Abbott, Jacob. "Early Piety," *The National Preacher*, VI (July, 1831), 210-24.

Abbott, John S. C. *The Mother at Home; or, The Principles of Maternal Duty Familiarly Illustrated*. 4th ed., Boston, 1834.

Alcott, Bronson. "Maternal Instruction. . . . In the Spirit of

Pestalozzi's Method," *American Journal of Education,* IV (Jan., 1829), 53-58.

Antipas. "The Comparative Importance of Moral and Intellectual Culture," *Spirit of the Pilgrims,* III (Nov., 1830), 572-75.

Barnard, John. *A Call to Parents, and Children.* Boston, 1737.

Bascom, Ezekiel. *Parental Duties Enjoined.* New Ipswich, N.H., 1828.

B.N. "On Early Religious Education," *Christian Spectator,* IV (Aug., 1822), 393-400.

"Books for Children," *Christian Examiner,* V (Sept., 1828), 402-20.

Bremner, Robert H., ed. *Children and Youth in America; A Documentary History.* 3 vols. Cambridge, Mass., 1970-71.

Bushnell, Horace. *Christian Nurture.* New York, 1861.

———. *Discourses on Christian Nurture.* Boston, 1847.

———. *Views of Christian Nurture, and of Subjects Adjacent Thereto.* 2nd ed., Hartford, 1848.

Child, Lydia M. *The Mother's Book.* Boston, 1831.

Chrisman, Oscar. "Child-Study, A New Department of Education," *Forum,* 16 (Feb., 1894), 728-36.

Comstock, Cyrus. *Essays on the Duty of Parents and Children.* Hartford, 1810.

[Cornelius, Mary H.] *Letters on Christian Education.* American Tract Society General and Occasional Series, VII, No. 197 (New York, [c.1830]).

Crispus. "On the Education of Children," *Panoplist,* X (Sept., 1814), 393-403.

Dewees, William P. *A Treatise on the Physical and Medical Treatment of Children.* 3rd ed., Philadelphia, 1829.

Dodson, Fitzhugh. *How to Parent.* New York: Signet paperback, 1971.

Dwight, Theodore, Jr. *The Father's Book.* Springfield, Mass., 1834.

Dwight, Timothy. "An Essay on Education," *Christian Spectator,* II (July, 1820), 349-52.

Edgeworth, Maria and Richard. *Practical Education.* 2 vols. 1st Amer. ed., New York, 1801.

Eumenes, "On the Evil of Neglecting Parental Restraint," *American Baptist Magazine,* N.S. III (May, 1821), 97-101.

Fraiberg, Selma H. *The Magic Years; Understanding and Handling the Problems of Early Childhood.* New York: Scribner paperback, 1959.

Freud, Anna. *Psycho-Analysis for Teachers and Parents, Intro-
    ductory Lectures.* New York, 1935.

Gallaudet, Thomas H. "Preliminary Essay," in Thomas
    Babington, *A Practical View of Christian Education,* pp.
    1-15. 4th Amer. ed., Hartford, 1831.

Gesell, Arnold, Ilg, Frances, and Ames, Louise Bates. *Infant and
    Child in the Culture of Today.* Rev. ed., New York, 1974.

Ginott, Haim G. *Between Parent and Child; New Solutions to Old
    Problems.* New York, 1965.

Greven, Philip J., Jr. *Child-Rearing Concepts, 1628-1861; Histor-
    ical Sources.* Itasca, Illinois: F. E. Peacock paperback,
    1973.

[Hadduck, Charles B.] *Christian Education.* American Tract
    Society General and Occasional Series, VI, No. 194 (New
    York, [c.1830]).

Hall, Samuel R. *Practical Lectures on Parental Responsibility,
    and the Religious Education of Children.* Boston, 1833.

Hamilton, Elizabeth. *Letters on the Elementary Principles of
    Education.* 2 vols. 3rd Amer. ed., Boston, 1825.

Hitchcock, Enos. *Memoirs of the Bloomsgrove Family. In a Series
    of Letters to a Respectable Citizen of Philadelphia.* 2
    vols. Boston, 1790.

[Hoare, Louisa.] *Hints for the Improvement of Early Education
    and Nursery Discipline.* Salem, 1827. 1st ed., London,
    1820.

[Huntington, Daniel.] *Hints on Early Religious Education.*
    American Tract Society General and Occasional Series,
    V, No. 143 (New York, [c.1830]).

James, John Angell. *The Family Monitor, or a Help to Domestic
    Happiness.* Boston, 1830. 1st ed., Birmingham, England,
    1828.

Kames, Henry Home, Lord. *Loose Hints upon Education, Chiefly
    Concerning the Culture of the Heart.* 2nd ed., enl.,
    Edinburgh, 1782.

Locke, John. *Some Thoughts Concerning Education.* Ed. R. H.
    Quick. Cambridge, England, 1884.

"Maternal Societies," *American Baptist Magazine,* IX (Aug.,
    1829), 284-86.

Mather, Cotton. *Cares About the Nurseries.* Boston, 1702.

Mather, Cotton et al. *A Course of Sermons on Early Piety.* Boston,
    1721.

Mather, Cotton. *A Family Well-Ordered*. Boston, 1699.

———. *Help for Distressed Parents; or, Counsels & Comforts for Godly Parents Afflicted with UnGodly Children: and Warnings unto Children, to Beware of all those Evil Courses, Which would be Affliction unto the Parents.* Boston, 1695.

[The Monadnock Association and the Rev. John H. Church.] *Parental Faithfulness*. American Tract Society General and Occasional Series, VI, No. 171 (New York, [c.1830]).

More, Hannah. *Strictures on the Modern System of Female Education; With View of the Principles and Conduct Prevalent Among Women of Rank and Fortune.* 3rd Amer. ed., Boston, 1802.

A Mother. "Maternal Association," *Panoplist*, XII (June, 1816), 278-80.

"On the Importance of Christian Education," *Christian Disciple*, III (Feb., March, May, June, 1815), 41-45, 72-77, 145-50, 167-71.

"On the Influence of Education as a Source of Error," *Christian Disciple*, II (Sept., 1814), 264-67.

Pestalozzi, Johann Heinrich. *Letters of Pestalozzi on the Education of Infancy*. Trans. James Greaves. 1st Amer. ed., Boston, 1830.

"Practical Education," *Ladies' Magazine*, III (Sept.,1830), 425-29.

Priestley, Joseph. *Miscellaneous Observations Relating to Education; More Especially as it Respects the Conduct of the Mind.* 1st Amer. ed., New London, 1796.

"Religious Intelligence," *Christian Spectator*, IV (Sept., 1822), 491-96.

Rev. of *A Practical View of Christian Education in its Earliest Stages*. By T. Babington, *Christian Disciple*, N.S. I (March-April, 1819), 144-51.

Rousseau, Jean Jacques. *Émile*. London, 1911.

Scripture, E. W. "Aims and Status of Child-Study," *Educational Review*, 8 (Oct., 1894), 236-39.

Senex. "On Christian Education," *Spirit of the Pilgrims*, I (Nov., 1828), 561-72.

Spock, Benjamin. *Baby and Child Care*. Rev. ed., New York: Pocket Books paperback, 1968.

Sproat, Nancy. *Family Lectures*. Boston, 1819.

Tabor. "Religious Education of Children," *American Baptist Magazine*, N.S. I (Nov., 1817, Jan., March, May, 1818), 209-13, 248-50, 287-88, 320-22.

Underwood, Michael. *A Treatise on the Diseases of Children and Management of Infants from the Birth.* 3 vols. in 1. 2nd Amer. ed., Boston, 1806.

Wadsworth, Benjamin. *The Well-Ordered Family.* 2nd ed., Boston, 1719.

Waterston, R[obert] C[aisse.] *Thoughts on Moral and Spiritual Culture.* Boston, 1842.

Williston, Seth. "An Address to Parents upon the Importance of Religiously Educating their Children," *New-York Missionary Magazine*, III (1802), 9-15, 47-58, 101-6, 139-47, 168-75, 210-15.

Witherspoon, John. *A Series of Letters on Education.* New York, 1797.

———. *A Sermon on the Religious Education of Children.* Elizabeth-Town, N.J., 1789.

Worcester, Thomas. *Two Sermons on the Government and Religious Education of Children.* Concord, N.H., 1804.

Works for Children

[Abbott, Jacob.] *The Way for a Child to be Saved.* 2nd ed., New York, 1835.

Abbott, John Stevens Cabot. *The Child at Home; Or the Principles of Filial Duty.* New York, 1833.

Archaios, Mathetees [Mather, Samuel]. *A Serious Letter to the Young People of Boston.* Boston, 1783.

Gallaudet, Thomas Hopkins. *The Child's Book on the Soul.* 2nd ed., Hartford, 1831.

Marshall, [Louisa] Mrs. *A Sketch of My Friend's Family, Intended to Suggest some Practical Hints on Religion and Domestic Manners.* Exeter, 1827. 1st ed., London, 1817.

Sigourney, Lydia, H. *Letters to Young Ladies.* 3rd ed., New York, 1837.

Spring, Samuel. *Three Sermons to Little Children: On the Nature and Beauty of the Dutiful Temper.* New York, 1790.

General Theological and Philosophical Works

Baxter, Richard. *The Practical Works.* Vol. I (London, 1707).

Beecher, Lyman. *Sermons Delivered on Various Occasions.* Boston, 1828.

———. *Works.* 3 vols. Boston, 1852-53.

Buckminster, Joseph S. *Sermons.* Boston, 1814.

Bushnell, Horace. *Horace Bushnell.* Ed. H[ilrie] Shelton Smith. New York, 1965.

———. *Nature and the Supernatural, as Together Constituting the One System of God.* New York, 1858.

Calvin, John. *Commentaries on the Book of Genesis.* Vol I (Edinburgh, 1847).

———. *Institutes of the Christian Religion.* 3 vols. Edinburgh, 1846.

———. *Tracts and Treatises in Defence of the Reformed Faith.* Vol. III (Edinburgh, 1958).

Channing, William E. *Works.* Boston, 1845.

Clarke, John. *Sermons.* Boston, 1799.

A Confession of Faith, Set Forth by Many of Those Baptists, Who own the Doctrine of Universal Redemption. Newport, R.I., [1730?].

The Confession of Faith, The Larger and Shorter Catechisms. Edinburgh, 1773.

Denzinger, Henry. *The Sources of Catholic Dogma.* Trans. Roy J. Deferrari. St. Louis, 1957.

Dewey, Orville. "Why I am a Unitarian," in *The Pitts-Street Chapel Lectures,* pp. 293-322. Boston, 1858.

Dwight, Timothy et al. *An Address to the Emigrants from Connecticut, and From New-England Generally, in the New Settlements in the United States.* Hartford, 1817.

Dwight, Timothy. *The Charitable Blessed.* New Haven, 1810.

———. *Discourse, Delivered at New-Haven, Feb. 22, 1800; On the Character of George Washington.* New Haven, 1800.

———. *A Discourse, In Two Parts, Delivered August 20, 1812, On the National Fast.* Utica, 1813.

———. *A Discourse on Some Events of the Last Century.* New Haven, 1801.

———. *A Discourse, on the Genuineness and Authenticity of the New Testament.* New York, 1794.

———. *The Duty of Americans, At the Present Crisis.* New Haven, 1798.

———. "The Friend," *American Museum,* V (Jan., March, May,

June, 1789), 69-71, 220-22, 445-47, 564-67, VI (Oct., 1789), 154-56.

———. *The Nature, and Danger, of Infidel Philosophy, Exhibited in Two Discourses.* New Haven, 1798.

———. *President Dwight's Decisions of Questions Discussed by the Senior Class in Yale College, In 1813 and 1814.* Comp. Theodore Dwight, Jr. New York, 1833.

———. *A Sermon, Delivered in Boston, Sept. 16, 1813, Before the American Board of Commissioners for Foreign Relations.* Boston, 1813.

[Dwight, Timothy.] *A Sermon, Preached at Northampton, on the Twenty-Eighth of November, 1781: Occasioned by the Capture of the British Army.* Hartford, [1781].

———. *Sermons.* 2 vols. New Haven, 1828.

———. *The True Means of Establishing Public Happiness.* New Haven, [1795].

———. *A Valedictory Address to the Young Gentlemen, Who Commenced Bachelor of Arts, at Yale-College, July 25th, 1776.* New Haven, 1776.

[Dwight, Timothy.] *Virtuous Rulers a National Blessing.* Hartford, 1791.

———. *Theology; Explained and Defended, in a Series of Sermons.* 5 vols. Middletown, Conn., 1818-19.

Edwards, Jonathan. *The Works of President Edwards.* 8 vols. Worcester, 1808-9.

Emerson, Ralph Waldo. *Collected Works.* Vol. I (Cambridge, Mass., 1971).

Emmons, Nathaniel. *Sermons on Some of the First Principles and Doctrines of True Religion.* Wrentham, Mass., 1800.

———. *Works.* Ed. Jacob Ide. 6 vols. Boston, 1842.

Gallaudet, Thomas Hopkins. *Discourses on Various Points of Christian Faith and Practice.* Hartford, 1818.

Griffin, Edward D. *A Series of Lectures, Delivered in Park Street Church, Boston, on Sabbath Evening.* Boston, 1813.

———. *Sermons.* 2 vols. New York, 1839.

Hodge, Charles. *Systematic Theology.* 3 vols. New York, 1877.

Hopkins, Samuel. *The System of Doctrines.* 2 vols. Boston, 1793.

———. *Twenty-One Sermons, on a Variety of Interesting Subjects, Sentimental and Practical.* Salem, 1803.

[Kames, Henry Home, Lord.] *Elements of Criticism.* 1st Amer. ed., Boston, 1796.

Lathrop, Joseph. *Sermons by the late Rev. Joseph Lathrop, New Series.* Springfield, Mass., 1821.

Lawson, Deodat. *The Duty and Property of a Religious Householder.* Boston, 1693.

Linsley, Joel Harvey. *Lectures on the Relations and Duties of the Middle Aged.* Hartford, 1828.

Locke, John. *An Essay Concerning Human Understanding.* Ed. Alexander Campbell Fraser. 2 vols. Oxford, 1894.

Mellen, John. *A Discourse Containing a Serious Address to Persons of Several Ages and Characters.* Boston, 1757.

Miller, Perry, ed. *The American Puritans; Their Prose and Poetry.* New York: Doubleday paperback, 1956.

Paterson, Isabel. "Introduction" in Richard Hughes, *A High Wind in Jamaica,* pp. v-xxii. New York, 1932.

Selby-Bigge, L. A., ed. *British Moralists, Being Selections from Writers Principally of the Eighteenth Century.* 2 vols. Oxford, 1897.

Skinner, B. F. *Beyond Freedom and Dignity.* New York, 1971.

Smalley, John. *Sermons, on Various Subjects, Doctrinal and Practical.* Middletown, Conn., 1814.

Tyler, Bennet. *Lectures on Theology.* Boston, 1859.

[Tyler, Bennet.] *Letters on the Origin and Progress of the New Haven Theology.* New York, 1837.

"Unitarian Belief," *The Unitarian,* I (Nov., 1827), 3-28.

Walker, Williston. *The Creeds and Platforms of Congregationalism.* New York, 1893.

Webster, Noah. *A Collection of Essays and Fugitiv Writings.* Boston, 1790.

Willard, Samuel. *A Compleat Body of Divinity.* Boston, 1726.

Woods, Leonard. *Works.* 5 vols. New York, Andover, 1849-50.

Poetry and Fiction

"An Address to a Fond Mother," *Merrimack Magazine and Ladies' Literary Cabinet,* I (Dec. 28, 1805), 80.

Bradstreet, Anne. *Works.* Ed. Jeannine Hensley. Cambridge, Mass., 1967.

Bryant, William Cullen. *The Poetical Works.* Ed. Parke Godwin. 2 vols. New York, 1883.

Cheever, George B., ed. *The American Common-Place Book of Poetry.* Boston, 1831.

Dwight, Timothy. *The Major Poems of Timothy Dwight.* Eds.
    William J. McTaggart and William K. Bottorff. Gaines-
    ville, Florida, 1969.

"The Dying Child," *Christian Examiner,* V (Jan., 1828), 13-14.

Griswold, Rufus Wilmot, ed. *The Female Poets of America.*
    Philadelphia, 1849.

_____. *The Poets and Poetry of America.* Philadelphia, 1842.

Heller, Joseph. *Something Happened.* New York: Ballantine
    paperback, 1975.

Hough, Mr. "On the Birth of an Infant," *American Baptist
    Magazine,* N.S. I (Sept., 1817), 209.

J. N. M. "A Visit to the Grave of a Child," *Ladies' Magazine,* II
    (Sept., 1829), 418-19.

Kettell, Samuel, ed. *Specimens of American Poetry.* 3 vols. Boston,
    1829.

"Lines Addressed to a Lovely Infant, Expiring in its Father's
    Arms," *Christian Disciple,* N.S. III (July - Aug., 1821),
    280.

"Lines, Addressed to a Mother, on the Death of Two Infants,"
    Christian Examiner, II (Jan., 1825), 33-34.

Longfellow, Henry Wadsworth. *The Complete Poetical Works.*
    Boston, 1893.

Lowell, James R. *The Poetical Works.* 2 vols. Boston, 1871.

May, Caroline, ed. *The American Female Poets.* Philadelphia,
    1848.

"The Mother," *Merrimack Magazine and Ladies' Literary Cabi-
    net,* I (Oct. 12, 1805), 36.

Read, Thomas Buchanan, ed. *The Female Poets of America.*
    Philadelphia, 1849.

S[igourney], L[ydia] H. "The Dead Twins," *Ladies' Magazine
    and Literary Gazette,* III (Feb., 1830), 71.

Stowe, Harriet Beecher. *Oldtown Folks.* Ed. Henry F. May.
    Cambridge, Mass., 1966.

Taylor, Edward. *Poems.* Ed. Donald E. Stanford. New Haven,
    1960.

Trent, William P. and Wells, Benjamin W., eds. *Colonial Prose
    and Poetry.* 3 vols. New York, 1901.

"The Voices of the Dead," *Christian Examiner,* IV (Nov. - Dec.,
    1827), 462-64.

Wheatley, Phillis. *Poems.* Ed. Julian D. Mason, Jr. Chapel Hill,
    1966.

Wigglesworth, Michael. *The Day of Doom, or a Poetical Description of the Great and Last Judgment.* Ed. Kenneth Murdock. New York, 1929.

Miscellaneous

Dwight, Timothy. *Travels; In New-England and New-York.* 4 vols. New Haven, 1821-22.

Furness, Clifton Joseph, ed. *The Genteel Female; An Anthology.* New York, 1931.

Lindsey, Benjamin Barr. "The Boy and the Court," *Charities,* XIII (Jan., 1905), 350-57.

"Reviews and Literary Notices," *Atlantic Monthly,* XV (May, 1865), 631-35.

"Sketch of the Origin and Character of the Principal Series of Tracts of the American Tract Society," *American Tract Magazine,* VI (Nov., 1831), 133-51.

Secondary Sources

Biographies and Reminiscences

Chapin, Calvin. *A Sermon, Delivered, 14th January, 1817, at the Funeral of the Rev. Timothy Dwight.* New Haven, 1817.

Cheney, Mary Bushnell. *Life and Letters of Horace Bushnell.* New York, 1880.

Crowder, Richard. *No Featherbed to Heaven; A Biography of Michael Wigglesworth, 1631-1705.* [East Lansing, Michigan], 1962.

Cunningham, Charles E. *Timothy Dwight, 1752-1817.* New York, 1942.

D[insmore], C[harles] A[llen]. "Bushnell, Horace," *Dictionary of American Biography,* III (New York, 1946), 350-54.

Incidents in the Life of President Dwight, Illustrative of His Moral and Religious Character. New Haven, 1831.

Mather, Cotton. *Ecclesiastes; The Life of the Reverend & Excellent Jonathan Mitchel.* Boston, 1697.

Mead, Sidney Earl. *Nathaniel William Taylor, 1786-1858, a Connecticut Liberal.* Chicago, 1942, Hamden, Conn., 1967.

Middlekauff, Robert. *The Mathers; Three Generations of Puritan Intellectuals, 1596-1728.* New York, 1971.

Miller, Perry. *Jonathan Edwards.* [New York], 1949.

Murdock, Kenneth. *Increase Mather, the Foremost American Puritan.* Cambridge, Mass., 1925.

Patten, William. *Reminiscences of the Late Rev. Samuel Hopkins, D.D., of Newport, R.I.* Providence, 1843.

Shepard, Odell. *Pedlar's Progress; The Life of Bronson Alcott.* Boston, 1937.

Shipton, Clifford K. "Enos Hitchcock," *Sibley's Harvard Graduates,* XVI: 1764-1767, 475-84.

Silliman, Benjamin. *A Sketch of the Life and Character of President Dwight.* New Haven, 1817.

Sklar, Kathryn Kish. *Catharine Beecher; A Study in American Domesticity.* New Haven, 1973.

Sprague, William B. "Life of Timothy Dwight," in *The Library of American Biography.* Ed. Jared Sparks. 2nd series, IV (Boston, 1864), 225-364.

S[tarr], H[arris] E[lwood]. "Dwight, Timothy," *Dictionary of American Biography,* V (New York, 1946), 573-77.

Works on Death and Bereavement

Ariès, Philippe. *Western Attitudes Toward Death: From the Middle Ages to the Present.* Baltimore, 1974.

Bermann, Eric. *Scapegoat; The Impact of Death-Fear on an American Family.* Ann Arbor, 1973.

Bowlby, John. "Processes of Mourning," *International Journal of Psycho-Analysis,* XLII (July - Oct, 1961), 317-49.

Bozeman, Mary F., Orbach, Charles E., and Sutherland, Arthur M. "Psychological Impact of Cancer and Its Treatment; III. The Adaptation of Mothers to the Threatened Loss of their Children Through Leukemia: Part I," *Cancer,* 8 (Jan. - Feb., 1955), 1-19.

Caulfield, Ernest. "Some Common Diseases of Colonial Children," *Publications of the Colonial Society of Massachusetts: Transactions, 1942-1946,* XXXV, 4-65.

————. *A True History of the Terrible Epidemic Vulgarly Called the Throat Distemper Which Occurred in His Majesty's New England Colonies Between the Years 1735 and 1740.* New Haven, 1939.

Chodoff, Paul, Friedman, Stanford, and Hamburg, David. "Stress, Defenses and Coping Behavior: Observations in Parents of Children with Malignant Disease," *American Journal of Psychiatry*, 120 (Feb., 1964), 743-49.

Deutsch, Helene. "Absence of Grief," *Psychoanalytic Quarterly*, VI (1937), 12-22.

Douglas, Ann. "Heaven Our Home: Consolation Literature in the Northern United States, 1830-1880," in *Death in America*, pp. 49-68. Ed. David E. Stannard. Philadelphia: University of Pennsylvania Press paperback, 1975.

DuCasse, C[arl] J[ohn]. *A Critical Examination of the Belief in a Life after Death*. Springfield, Illinois, 1961.

Duffy, John. *Epidemics in Colonial America*. Baton Rouge, 1953.

Dumont, Richard G. and Fox, Dennis C. *The American View of Death: Acceptance or Denial?* Cambridge, Mass., 1972.

Eliot, Thomas D. "The Adjustive Behavior of Bereaved Families: A New Field for Research," *Social Forces*, 8 (June, 1930), 543-49.

_____. "The Bereaved Family," *Annals of the American Academy of Political and Social Science*, 160 (March, 1932), 184-90.

Feifel, Herman, ed. *The Meaning of Death*. New York, 1959.

Friedman, Stanford B., Chodoff, Paul, Mason, John W., and Hamburg, David A. "Behavioral Observations on Parents Anticipating the Death of a Child," *Pediatrics*, 32 (Oct., 1963), 610-25.

Gorer, Geoffrey. *Death, Grief, and Mourning in Contemporary Britain*. London, 1965.

Green, Morris and Solnit, Albert J. "Reactions to the Threatened Loss of a Child: A Vulnerable Child Syndrome. Pediatric Management of the Dying Child, Part III," *Pediatrics*, 34 (July, 1964), 58-66.

Grinberg, Léon. "Two Kinds of Guilt—Their Relations with Normal and Pathological Aspects of Mourning," *International Journal of Psycho-Analysis*, 45 (April - July, 1964), 366-71.

Jackson, Edgar N. *Understanding Grief; Its Roots, Dynamics, and Treatment*. Nashville, 1957.

Kamm, Henry. "Israel Sees to War's Hidden Wounds," *New York Times*, Nov. 2, 1973, p. 19.

Kastenbaum, Robert and Aisenberg, Ruth. *The Psychology of Death.* New York, 1972.

Lehrman, Samuel R. "Reactions to Untimely Death," *Psychiatric Quarterly,* 30 (Oct., 1956), 564-78.

Lindemann, Erich. "Symptomatology and Management of Acute Grief," *American Journal of Psychiatry,* 101 (Sept., 1944), 141-48.

Lourie, Reginald S. "The Pediatrician and the Handling of Terminal Illness," *Pediatrics,* 32 (Oct., 1963), 477-79.

Ludwig, Allan I. *Graven Images; New England Stonecarving and its Symbols, 1650-1815.* Middletown, Conn., 1966.

Mann, Thomas C. and Greene, Janet. *Over Their Dead Bodies; Yankee Epitaphs & History.* Brattleboro, Vermont, 1962.

Moriarty, David. *The Loss of Loved Ones; The Effects of a Death in the Family on Personality Development.* Springfield, Illinois, 1967.

Naglack, James J. "Death in Colonial New England," *Historical Journal of Western Massachusetts,* 4 (Fall, 1975), 21-32.

Natterson, Joseph M. and Knudson, Alfred G. "Observations Concerning Fear of Death in Fatally Ill Children and their Mothers," *Psychomatic Medicine,* XXII (Nov. - Dec., 1960), 456-65.

Neale, A. V. "The Changing Pattern of Death in Childhood: Then and Now," *Medicine, Science, and Law,* 4 (Jan., 1964), 35-39.

Oraison, Marc. *Death—And then What?* Paramus, N. J., 1969.

Orbach, Charles E. "The Multiple Meanings of the Loss of a Child," *American Journal of Psychotherapy,* 13 (Oct., 1959), 906-15.

Orbach, Charles E., Sutherland, Arthur M., and Bozeman, Mary F., "Psychological Impact of Cancer and Its Treatment. III. The Adaptation of Mothers to the Threatened Loss of Their Children through Leukemia: Part II," *Cancer,* 8 (Jan. - Feb., 1955), 20-33.

Pike, Robert E. *Granite Laughter and Marble Tears; Epitaphs of Old New England.* [Brattleboro, Vermont], 1938.

Pollock, George H. "Mourning and Adaptation," *International Journal of Psycho-Analysis,* XLII (July - Oct., 1961), 341-61.

Rheingold, Joseph C. *The Mother, Anxiety, and Death: The Catastrophic Death Complex.* Boston, 1967.

Solnit, Albert, and Green, Morris. "Psychologic Considerations in
    the Management of Deaths on Pediatric Hospital Ser-
    vice. 1. The Doctor and the Child's Family," *Pediatrics,*
    24 (July, 1959), 106-12.
Stannard, David E. "Death and Dying in Puritan New England,"
    American Historical Review, 78 (Dec., 1973), 1305-30.
———. "Death and the Puritan Child," in *Death in America,* pp.
    9-29. Ed. David E. Stannard. Philadelphia: University of
    Pennsylvania Press paperback, 1975.
Steinmann, Marion. "Crib Death: Too Many Clues?" *New York
    Times Magazine,* May 16, 1976, pp. 40-43.
Switzer, David K. *The Dynamics of Grief.* Nashville, 1970.
Tashjian, Dickran and Ann. *Memorials for Children of Change;
    The Art of Early New England Stonecarving.* Middle-
    town, Conn., 1974.
Vernick, Joel J. *Selected Bibliography on Death and Dying.*
    Washington, D.C., n.d.
Vernon, Glenn M. *Sociology of Death; An Analysis of Death-
    Related Behavior.* New York, 1970.
Vinovskis, Maris A. "Angels' Heads and Weeping Willows: Death
    in Early America." MS of a forthcoming article in *The
    Proceedings of the American Antiquarian Society.*
———. "Mortality Rates and Trends in Massachusetts Before
    1860," *Journal of Economic History,* XXXII (March,
    1972), 184-213.

Works on Children and the Family

Ariès, Philippe. *Centuries of Childhood; A Social History of
    Family Life.* New York, 1962.
Axtell, James. *The School Upon A Hill: Education and Society in
    Colonial New England.* New Haven, 1974.
Beales, Ross W., Jr. "In Search of the Historical Child: Miniature
    Adulthood and Youth in Colonial New England,"
    American Quarterly, XXVII (Oct., 1975), 379-98.
Boas, George. *The Cult of Childhood.* London, 1966.
Boocock, Sarane Spence. "The Social Context of Childhood,"
    Proceedings of the American Philosophical Society, 119,
    Number 6 (Dec. 5, 1975), 419-29.

Bronfenbrenner, Urie. "Reality and Research in the Ecology of Human Development," *Proceedings of the American Philosophical Society*, 119, Number 6 (Dec. 5, 1975), 439-69.

Cable, Mary. *The Little Darlings; A History of Child Rearing in America.* New York, 1975.

Calhoun, Arthur W. *A Social History of the American Family from Colonial Times to the Present.* 3 vols. Rev. ed., New York, 1945.

Calhoun, Daniel. "Repression: The Lockean Tradition in American Child-Rearing." MS of a paper delivered at the meeting of the American Historical Association, Toronto, Dec., 1967.

Castle, Edgar B. *Educating the Good Man; Moral Education in Christian Times.* New York: Collier paperback, 1962.

deMause, Lloyd. "The Evolution of Childhood," in *The History of Childhood*, pp. 1-73. Ed. Lloyd deMause. New York, 1974.

Demos, John. "Demography and Psychology in the Historical Study of Family-Life: a Personal Report," in *Household and Family in Past Time*, pp. 561-69. Ed. Peter Laslett. Cambridge, England, 1972.

————. "Developmental Perspectives on the History of Childhood," in *The Family in History; Interdisciplinary Essays*, pp. 127-39. Eds. Theodore K. Rabb and Robert I. Rotberg. New York: Harper paperback, 1973.

————. "Families in Colonial Bristol, Rhode Island: An Exercise in Historical Demography," *William and Mary Quarterly*, XXV (Jan., 1968), 40-57.

————. *A Little Commonwealth; Family Life in Plymouth Colony.* New York, 1970.

————. "Notes on Life in Plymouth Colony," *William and Mary Quarterly*, XXII (April, 1965), 264-86.

Earle, Alice Morse. *Child Life in Colonial Days.* New York, 1899.

Erikson, Eric. *Childhood and Society.* 2nd ed., rev. and enl., New York, 1963.

Farber, Bernard. *Guardians of Virtue; Salem Families in 1800.* New York, 1972.

Fleming, Sandford. *Children and Puritanism; The Place of Children in the Life and Thought of the New England Churches, 1620-1847.* New Haven, 1933.

Forster, Colin and Tucker, G. S. L. *Economic Opportunity and White American Fertility Ratios, 1800-1860*. New Haven, 1972.

Frost, J. William. *The Quaker Family in Colonial America; A Portrait of the Society of Friends*. New York, 1973.

Furstenberg, Frank F., Jr. "Industrialization and the American Family; A Look Backward," *American Sociological Review*, 31 (June, 1966), 326-37.

Goode, William J. *World Revolution and Family Patterns*. New York, 1963.

Greven, Philip J., Jr. *Four Generations; Population, Land, and Family in Colonial Andover, Massachusetts*. Ithaca, 1970.

Higgs, Robert and Stettler, H. Louis, III. "Colonial New England Demography: A Sampling Approach," *William and Mary Quarterly*, XXVII (April, 1970), 281-94.

Hunt, David. *Parents and Children in History; The Psychology of Family Life in Early Modern France*. New York, 1970.

Illick, Joseph E. "Child-Rearing in Seventeenth-Century England and America," in *The History of Childhood*, pp. 303-50. Ed. Lloyd deMause. New York, 1974.

Kiefer, Monica M. *American Children Through Their Books, 1790-1835*. Philadelphia, 1948.

Kuhn, Anne L. *The Mother's Role in Childhood Education: New England Concepts, 1830-1860*. New Haven, 1947.

Lasch, Christopher. "What the Doctor Ordered," review of Edward Shorter's *The Making of the Modern Family*, in *New York Review of Books*, XXII (Dec. 11, 1975), 50-54.

MacLeod, Anne Scott. *A Moral Tale: Children's Fiction and American Culture, 1820-1860*. Hamden, Conn., 1975.

McLoughlin, William G. "Evangelical Childrearing in the Age of Jackson: Francis Wayland's Views on When and How to Subdue the Willfulness of Children," *Journal of Social History*, 9 (Fall, 1975), 20-43.

Mechling, Jay. "Advice to Historians on Advice to Mothers," *Journal of Social History*, 9 (Fall, 1975), 44-63.

Morgan, Edmund S. *The Puritan Family; Religion & Domestic Relations in Seventeenth-Century New England*. Rev. ed., New York: Harper paperback, 1966.

Norton, Susan L. "Population Growth in Colonial America: A Study of Ipswich, Massachusetts," *Population Studies*, 25 (Nov., 1971), 433-52.

O'Neill, William L. *Divorce in the Progressive Era*. New Haven, 1967.

Paul, Sherman. "Alcott's Search for the Child," *Boston Public Library Quarterly*, 4 (Jan., 1952), 87-96.

Rich, Adrienne. *Of Woman Born: Motherhood as Experience and Institution*. New York, 1976.

Roller, Bert. *Children in American Poetry, 1610-1900*. Nashville, 1930.

Ryerson, Alice Judson. "Medical Advice on Child Rearing, 1550-1900," *Harvard Educational Review*, XXXI (Summer, 1961), 302-23.

Sangster, Paul. *Pity My Simplicity; The Evangelical Revival and the Religious Education of Children, 1738-1800*. London, 1963.

Schenck, Lewis Bevan. *The Presbyterian Doctrine of Children in the Covenant; A Historical Study of the Significance of Infant Baptism in the Presbyterian Church in America*. New Haven, 1940.

Schücking, Levin L. *The Puritan Family; A Social Study from the Literary Sources*. New York, 1970.

Shorter, Edward. *The Making of the Modern Family*. New York, 1975.

Slater, Peter Gregg. "Views of Children and of Child Rearing During the Early National Period: A Study in the New England Intellect." Diss. University of California, Berkeley, 1970.

Smith, Daniel Scott. "The Demographic History of Colonial New England," *Journal of Economic History*, XXXII (March, 1972), 165-83.

Sommerville, C. John. "Bibliographic Note: Toward a History of Childhood and Youth," in *The Family in History: Interdisciplinary Essays*, pp. 229-35. Eds. Theodore K. Rabb and Robert I. Rotberg. New York: Harper paperback, 1973.

————. "The English Puritans and Children: Psychohistory or Cultural History?" MS of a paper delivered at the meeting of the American Historical Association, Atlanta, Dec., 1975.

Steere, Geoffrey H. "Child-Rearing Literature and Modernization Theory," *The Family in Historical Perspective; An International Newsletter*, No. 7 (Winter, 1974), 8-11.

Stettler, H. Louis, III. "The New England Throat Distemper and Family Size," in *Empirical Studies in Health Economics; Proceedings of the Second Conference on the Economics of Health*, pp. 17-27. Ed. Herbert E. Larman. Baltimore, 1970.

Stone, Lawrence. "The Rise of the Nuclear Family in Early Modern England," in *The Family in History*, pp. 13-57. Ed. Charles E. Rosenberg. Philadelphia, 1975.

Strickland, Charles. "A Transcendentalist Father: The Child-Rearing Practices of Bronson Alcott," *History of Childhood Quarterly*, I (Summer, 1973), 4-51.

_____. "A Transcendentalist Father: The Child-Rearing Practices of Bronson Alcott," *Perspectives in American History*, III (1969), 5-77.

Sunley, Robert. "Early Nineteenth-Century American Literature on Child Rearing," in *Childhood in Contemporary Cultures*, pp. 150-67. Eds. Margaret Mead and Martha Wolfenstein. Chicago, 1955.

Vinovskis, Maris A. "The Field of Early American Family History: A Methodological Critique," *The Family in Historical Perspective: An International Newsletter*, No. 7 (Winter, 1974), 2-8.

Walzer, John. "Comment by John Walzer," *History of Childhood Quarterly*, I (Summer, 1973), 57-61.

_____. "A Period of Ambivalence: Eighteenth-Century American Childhood," in *The History of Childhood*, pp. 351-82. Ed. Lloyd deMause. New York, 1974.

Wells, Robert. "Family History and Demographic Transition," *Journal of Social History*, 9 (Fall, 1975), 1-19.

Welter, Barbara. "The Cult of True Womanhood: 1820-1860," *American Quarterly*, XVIII (Summer, 1966), 151-74.

Winch, Robert F. and McGinnis, Robert, eds. *Selected Studies in Marriage and the Family*. New York, 1953.

Wishy, Bernard. *The Child and the Republic; The Dawn of Modern American Child Nurture*. Philadelphia, 1968.

Yasuba, Yasukichi. *Birth Rates of the White Population of the United States, 1800-1860; An Economic Study*. The Johns

Hopkins Studies in Historical and Political Science, Series LXXIX (Baltimore, 1962).

Zuckerman, Michael. "Dr. Spock: The Confidence Man," in *The Family in History*, pp. 179-207. Ed. Charles E. Rosenberg. Philadelphia, 1975.

Works on Religion and Theology

Alexis, Gerhard T. "Wigglesworth's 'Easiest Room,'" *New England Quarterly*, 42 (Dec., 1969), 573-83.

Alger, William Rounseville. *A Critical History of the Doctrine of a Future Life*. Philadelphia, 1864.

Baird, Samuel J. *A History of the New School*, Philadelphia, 1868.

Bellamy J. "Baptême (Sort des enfants morts sans)," in *Dictionnaire de Théologie Catholique*, pp. 364-78. Vol. II, Part I (Paris, 1910).

Berk, Stephen. *Calvinism vs. Democracy; Timothy Dwight and the Origins of American Evangelical Orthodoxy*. Hamden, Conn., 1974.

Dearmer, Percy. *The Legend of Hell: An Examination of the Doctrine of Everlasting Punishment in the Light of Modern Scholarship*. London, 1929.

Edwards, Charles Eugene. "Calvin on Infant Salvation," *Bibliotheca Sacra*, 88 (1931), 316-28.

Elliott, Emory. *Power and the Pulpit in Puritan New England*. Princeton, 1975.

Faust, Clarence H. and Johnson, Thomas H. "Introduction" in *Jonathan Edwards: Representative Selections*, pp. xi-cxv. Eds. Clarence H. Faust and Thomas H. Johnson. Rev. ed., New York: Hill and Wang paperback, 1962.

Fisher, George. "The Augustinian and the Federal Theories of Original Sin Compared," *New Englander*, 27 (July, 1868), 458-516.

Foster, Charles I. *An Errand of Mercy: The Evangelical United Front, 1790-1837*. Chapel Hill, 1960.

Foster, Frank Hugh. *A Genetic History of the New England Theology*. Chicago, 1907.

Gabriel, Ralph Henry. *Religion and Learning at Yale; The Church of Christ in the College and University, 1757-1957*. New Haven, 1958.

Gaustad, Edwin Scott. *The Great Awakening in New England*. Gloucester, Mass., 1965.

Gribbin, William. "The Legacy of Timothy Dwight: A Reappraisal," *Connecticut Historical Society Bulletin*, XXXVII (April, 1972), 33-41.

Haroutunian, Joseph. *Piety versus Moralism: The Passing of the New England Theology*. New York, 1932.

Heimert, Alan. *Religion and the American Mind; From the Great Awakening to the Revolution*. Cambridge, Mass., 1966.

Holbrook, Clyde A. "Original Sin and the Enlightenment," in *The Heritage of Christian Thought; Essays in Honor of Robert Lowry Calhoun*, pp. 142-65. Eds. Robert E. Cushman and Egil Grislis. New York, 1965.

Holifield, E. Brooks. *The Covenant Sealed: The Development of Puritan Sacramental Theology in Old and New England, 1570-1720*. New Haven, 1974.

Howe, Daniel Walker. *The Unitarian Conscience; Harvard Moral Philosophy, 1805-1861*. Cambridge, Mass., 1970.

McLoughlin, William G. *Isaac Backus and the American Pietistic Tradition*. Boston, 1967.

Meyer, Donald. "The Dissolution of Calvinism," in *Paths of American Thought*, pp. 71-85. Eds. Arthur M. Schlesinger, Jr. and Morton White. Boston, 1963.

Miller, Perry. "Jonathan Edwards to Emerson," *New England Quarterly*, XIII (Dec., 1940), 589-617.

———. "The Marrow of Puritan Divinity," *Publications of the Colonial Society of Massachusetts: Transactions, 1933-1937*, XXXII, 247-300.

———. *The New England Mind: From Colony to Province*. Cambridge, Mass., 1953.

———. *The New England Mind; The Seventeenth Century*. New York, 1939.

———. "'Preparation for Salvation' in Seventeenth-Century New England," *Journal of the History of Ideas*, IV (June, 1943), 253-86.

Morgan, Edmund S. "The Puritans and Sex," *New England Quarterly*, XV (Dec., 1942), 591-607.

———. *Visible Saints; The History of a Puritan Idea*. New York, 1963.

Murdock, Kenneth B. *Literature and Theology in Colonial New England*. Cambridge, Mass., 1949.

Nash, Gary B. "The American Clergy and the French Revolution," *William and Mary Quarterly*, XXII (July, 1965), 392-412.

Niebuhr, H. Richard. *The Kingdom of God in America*. New York: Harper paperback, 1959.

Pope, Robert G. "New England Versus The New England Mind: The Myth of Declension," *Journal of Social History*, III (Winter, 1969-70), 95-108.

Sandeen, Ernest. *The Roots of Fundamentalism; British and American Millenarianism, 1800-1930*. Chicago, 1970.

Smith, H[ilrie] Shelton. *Changing Conceptions of Original Sin: A Study in American Theology since 1750*. New York, 1955.

Tuveson, Ernest Lee. *Redeemer Nation; The Idea of America's Millennial Role*. Chicago, 1968.

Tyner, Wayne C. "The Theology of Timothy Dwight in Historical Perspective." Diss. University of North Carolina, 1971.

Walker, D[aniel] P. *The Decline of Hell; Seventeenth-Century Discussions of Eternal Torment*. London, 1964.

Wright, Conrad. *The Beginnings of Unitarianism in America*. Boston, 1955, Hamden, Conn., 1976.

General Secondary Works

Adams, Henry. *History of the United States of America during the Administrations of Thomas Jefferson and James Madison*. Vol. I (New York, 1921).

Bailyn, Bernard. *The Ideological Origins of the American Revolution*. Cambridge., Mass., 1967.

Barnes, Gilbert H. *The Anti-Slavery Impulse, 1830-1844*. New York, 1933.

Branch, E[dward] Douglas. *The Sentimental Years, 1836-1860*. New York, 1934.

Burrows, Edwin G. and Wallace, Michael. "The American Revolution: The Ideology and Psychology of National Liberation," *Perspectives in American History*, VI (1972), 167-306.

Calhoun, Daniel. *The Intelligence of a People*. Princeton, 1973.

Cameron, Kenneth. *Emerson the Essayist*. 2 vols. Raleigh, N.C., 1945.

Cassirer, Ernst. *The Philosophy of the Enlightenment.* Boston, 1955.

Crane, Ronald S. "Suggestions Toward a Genealogy of the 'Man of Feeling,'" *Journal of English Literary History,* I (Dec., 1934), 205-30.

Crawford, Mary Caroline. *Social Life in Old New England.* Boston, 1915.

Curti, Merle. "The Great Mr. Locke, America's Philosopher, 1783-1861," *Huntington Library Bulletin,* Number 11 (April, 1937), 107-51.

———. "Human Nature in American Thought: The Age of Reason and Morality, 1750-1860," *Political Science Quarterly,* LXVIII (Sept., 1953), 354-75.

Eggleston, Edward. *The Transit of Civilization from England to America in the Seventeenth Century.* New York, 1901.

Fay, Jay W. *American Psychology Before William James.* New Brunswick, N.J., 1939.

Freud, Sigmund. *Totem and Taboo; Resemblances between the Psychic Lives of Savages and Neurotics.* London, n.d.

Garlitz, Barbara. "The Immortality Ode: Its Cultural Progeny," *Studies in English Literature, 1500-1900,* VI (Autumn, 1966), 639-49.

Gay, Peter. *The Enlightenment: An Interpretation.* 2 vols. New York, 1966, 1969.

Hazard, Paul. *European Thought in the Eighteenth Century, from Montesquieu to Lessing.* Cleveland, 1963.

Henretta, James A. *The Evolution of American Society, 1700-1815.* Lexington, Mass.: Heath paperback, 1973.

———. "The Morphology of New England Society in the Colonial Period," in *The Family in History; Interdisciplinary Essays,* pp. 191-210. Eds. Theodore K. Rabb and Robert I. Rotberg. New York: Harper paperback, 1973.

Higham, John. "American Intellectual History: A Critical Appraisal," *American Quarterly,* XIII (Summer, 1961), 219-34.

Howard, Leon. *The Connecticut Wits.* Chicago, 1943.

———. "The Late Eighteenth Century: An Age of Contradictions," in *Transitions in American Literary History,* pp. 51-89. Ed. Harry Hayden Clark. Durham, N.C., 1953.

Lewis, R. W. B. *The American Adam; Innocence, Tragedy, and Tradition in the Nineteenth Century.* Chicago, 1955.

Lockridge, Kenneth A. *A New England Town: The First Hundred Years*. New York: Norton paperback, 1970.

Lovejoy, Arthur O. "On the Discrimination of Romanticisms," *Publications of the Modern Language Association of America*, XXXIX (June, 1924), 229-53.

Lundberg, David and May, Henry F. "The Enlightened Reader in America," *American Quarterly*, XXVIII (Summer, 1976), 262-71, and graphs.

May, Henry F. *The Enlightenment in America*. New York, 1976.

———. "The Problem of the American Enlightenment," *New Literary History*, I (Winter, 1970), 201-14.

Meyer, D. H. *The Instructed Conscience; The Shaping of the American National Ethic*. Philadelphia, 1972.

Miller, Perry. *The Life of the Mind in America: From the Revolution to the Civil War*. New York, 1965.

Morgan, Edmund S. "Ezra Stiles and Timothy Dwight," *Proceedings of the Massachusetts Historical Society*, LXXII (Oct., 1957 - Dec., 1960), 101-17.

Murrin, John M. "Review Essay," *History and Theory*, XI (1972), 226-75.

Nason, Elias. *A History of the Town of Dunstable, Massachusetts*. Boston, 1877.

Orians, G. Harrison. "The Rise of Romanticism, 1805-1855," in *Transitions in American Literary History*, pp. 163-244. Ed. Harry Hayden Clark. Durham, N.C., 1953.

Parrington, Vernon L. *Main Currents in American Thought*. Vol. I: *The Colonial Mind*. New York, 1927.

Raphael, D[avid] Daiches. *The Moral Sense*. London, 1947.

Riesman, David, with Denney, Reuel, and Glazer, Nathan. *The Lonely Crowd; A Study of the Changing American Character*. New Haven, 1950.

Schneider, Herbert W. *A History of American Philosophy*. New York, 1946.

Shryock, Richard Harrison. *Medicine and Society in America: 1660-1860*. New York, 1960.

Silverman, Kenneth. *Timothy Dwight*. New York, 1969.

Smith, Wilson. *Professors & Public Ethics; Studies of Northern Moral Philosophers before the Civil War*. Ithaca, 1956.

Stauffer, Vernon. *New England and the Bavarian Illuminati*. New York, 1918.

Tuveson, Ernest. "The Origins of the 'Moral Sense,'" *Huntington Library Quarterly*, XI (May, 1948), 241-59.

Tyler, Moses Coit. *A History of American Literature*. 2 vols. New York, 1878.

Weinstein, Fred, and Platt, Gerald. *The Wish to be Free; Society, Psyche, and Value Change*. Berkeley and Los Angeles, 1969.

Willey, Basil. *The Eighteenth Century Background; Studies in the Idea of Nature in the Thought of the Period*. New York, 1941.

———. *The English Moralists*. London, 1964.

———. *The Seventeenth Century Background; Studies in the Thought of the Age in Relation to Poetry and Religion*. New York, 1962.

Zuckerman, Michael. *Peaceable Kingdoms; New England Towns in the Eighteenth Century*. New York, 1970.

Index

Abbott, John S.C., 94, 156
Adams, Henry, 72
Afterlife. *See* Infant damnation, doctrine of; Infants: damnation of; Infants: salvation of; Heaven; Hell.
Alcott, Bronson, 20, 23, 111, 149-51, 204n.
American Revolution, 62, 106, 132
American Tract Society, 93
Appetites. *See* Emotions, psychology of.
Aquinas, St. Thomas, 25
Ariès, Philippe, 72, 98
Arminianism, 51, 135, 140, 144, 154. *See also* Liberals.
Associationalists, 120, 140
Atlantic Monthly, 90
Augustine, St., 20, 25, 52, 56, 59, 60
Authority, parental, 105-11, 114, 144, 193n., 194n., 195n., 196n.
Autobiography of Lyman Beecher, The, 90
Ayer, Sarah Connell, 69

Bailyn, Bernard, 132
Baptism, 25, 29-30, 32, 51-52, 89, 172n.
Baptists, 51, 82, 129
Baxter, Richard, 26
Beecher, Lyman

Calvinist leader, 58, 77-79, 81-84, 86, 90, 133
parent, 96, 193n., 196n.
Behaviorism, 119, 123-24, 198n.
Belknap, Jeremy, 145
Bellamy, Joseph, 57-58, 67, 83
Bentham, Jeremy, 120
Bereavement, state of, 17-18
infant fate in, 11, 17, 23-24, 38 ff., 51, 54 ff., 68-70, 161 ff.
mourning process, 18, 32 ff., 54-55, 68-70, 161-62, 171n., 176n., 178n., 179n.
Beza, Theodore, 83
Bible, 108-9, 110, 116, 120, 131, 144, 178n., 194n.
Birth rates, 16, 48, 73, 162, 185n.
Boehme, Jakob, 149
Boston Temple School, 149
Bradstreet, Anne, 15, 22, 34, 71
Bushnell, Horace, 8, 161, 204-5n., 205n.
on child rearing, 11, 129, 148, 152-57, 164
on infant damnation, 87-88, 162
Butler, Joseph, 118

Calvin, John, 25-26, 56, 60, 83, 116, 139, 170n., 182n.

241